T0377548

DEAR INCOMPREHENSION

DEAR INCOMPREHENSION

On American Speculative Fiction

STÉPHANE VANDERHAEGHE

THE UNIVERSITY OF ALABAMA PRESS   TUSCALOOSA

The University of Alabama Press
Tuscaloosa, Alabama 35487–0380
uapress.ua.edu

Copyright © 2024 by the University of Alabama Press
All rights reserved.

Inquiries about reproducing material from this work should
be addressed to the University of Alabama Press.

Typeface: Arno Pro

Cover image: Rob Potter (@robpotter)/Unsplash
Cover design: Michele Myatt Quinn

Published with the support of the University of Paris 8 (TransCrit Laboratory).

Cataloging-in-Publication data is available from the Library of Congress.
ISBN: 978-0-8173-2187-1 (cloth)
ISBN: 978-0-8173-6137-2 (paper)
E-ISBN: 978-0-8173-9489-9

To Brigitte Félix—
fellow text-surveyor, traveler, mapper, swimmer . . .

Observing, of course, is the wrong word for the patient cultivation of blind spots, for trying to understand, by the ways in which, yes, I do *not* understand . . .

Shelley Jackson, *The Melancholy of Anatomy*

CONTENTS

List of Illustrations   ix

Acknowledgments   xi

List of abbreviations   xiii

Author's Note: Dear Incomprehension   xv

APPROACH   1

Speculative Fiction

A Definition   3

Critique Speculative   9

Speculative Fiction: Its Resistance   13

Speculative Tools   16

Mapping Speculation   21

SIGHTINGS   31

Speculative Endings, Or "Rate This Apocalypse"   35

Speculative Topologies, Or "This Is Not for You"   73

Speculative Sublime, Or "_____"   109

Speculative Language, Or "Understanding Is Overrated"   141

Speculative Interface, Or "cr!tical fa1lure/r3port loX0red"   173

WITHDRAWAL   205

Notes   211

Works Cited   227

Index   233

ILLUSTRATIONS

Figure 1. Blake Butler, *Ever*   6

Figure 2. Double-page spread from Blake Butler's *Scorch Atlas*   37

Figure 3. Table of contents ("A Belated Primer") from Blake Butler's *Scorch Atlas*   56

Figure 4. Blank page from Shelley Jackson's *Half Life*   94

Figure 5. Screenshot from Shelley Jackson's *my body*   122

Figure 6. Shelley Jackson, *Riddance*   174

Figure 7. Two pages from Mark Doten's *The Infernal*   195

Figure 8. Double-page spread from Mark Doten's *The Infernal*   201

Figure 9. Mark Doten's *The Infernal*   204

ACKNOWLEDGMENTS

This book was written, for the most part, between September 2019 and March 2021, at a time when the world as we knew it suddenly stopped. News kept coming from China, and like many others I must have believed that China was another world entirely and that the news would remain just that—news, soon to be replaced with other news in what is the endless cycle of our constantly updated newsfeeds.

Writing these lines now, in early 2022, I remember that when the COVID-19 pandemic ceased to be some noise in the background and became instead *real*, word was that the disease was mainly spread by children who somehow remained immune to it. This, unfortunately, sounded all too familiar, as I was in the midst of rereading Ben Marcus's *The Flame Alphabet*—a novel concerned with the outbreak of a pandemic spread by children. What, in the course of my previous readings of the novel, had seemed overly fictional suddenly found new resonance in the world at large, the one lying in all its precariousness beyond my books' covers. What was fiction? What was the real? What if *speculation*, in other words, and the *speculative fiction* I was trying to grapple with were but other names for reality and realism in this post-everything world of ours? Benefiting at the time from a research leave, I was—or felt—hard-pressed to keep writing as best I could in these new, worrisome circumstances, and the question remained one that I never actually or consciously raised. Not as such, it seems. But I realize now, too late somehow, that this may have been one of the questions this book was perhaps trying to articulate.

What became *Dear Incomprehension* had been floating somewhere at the back of my mind for several years before my friend and colleague Vincent Broqua suggested I solicit a leave from teaching at Université Paris 8-Vincennes-Saint-Denis and apply for a *délégation* from the French National

Centre for Scientific Research (CNRS). Which I did. For that, I am grateful not only to Vincent but also to Rémy Bethmont, who at the time headed the research unit I was affiliated with and approved my application. So did the heads of my department, Audrey Fogels and Anne Chalard-Fillaudeau, thus granting me time off teaching, and I would like to express my gratitude for their support. Thanks to all four of them, I momentarily left my research unit at Université Paris 8, TransCrit (Transferts critiques anglophones), to join LARCA (Laboratoire de Recherche sur les Cultures Anglophones), an interdisciplinary research unit of Université Paris Cité and CNRS, which afforded me the necessary time and support to plan, start, and eventually complete this book. Without LARCA, to which I am thus hugely indebted, I am not sure I would ever have set aside some time to launch the research that went into this book. My thanks go to Cécile Roudeau and all at LARCA—and chief among the colleagues, the late François Brunet, who was so kind as to back my application with a detailed, generous cover letter—who welcomed me into their research unit for two years that proved to be strange and scary and uncertain and yet rich, yet passionate, yet life-saving in many ways.

To the writers I've had the chance to communicate with in the course of this project or before, writers who sometimes generously answered the few questions I may have thrown their way, I'd like to express my thanks. I would also like to offer my apologies for whatever misconceptions, mistakes, or misrepresentations I might have given of their work.

But this, somehow, and for what it's worth, is the critic's prerogative. As the saying goes, what follows is a work of criticism; the views, ideas, concepts, and interpretations found in this book are but products of the author's speculations.

ABBREVIATIONS

3HM	*300,000,000*
AK	*Alice Knott*
AWS	*The Age of Wire and String*
BX	*The Book of X*
BN	*Book of Numbers*
FA	*The Flame Alphabet*
FK	*Fra Keeler*
GP	*A German Picturesque*
HL	*Half Life*
HO	*Hyperobjects*
HOL	*House of Leaves*
I	*The Infernal*
JP	*John the Posthumous*
LH	*Love Hotel*
LS	*Leaving the Sea*
MA	*The Melancholy of Anatomy*
NAW	*Notable American Women*
OHA	*One Hundred Apocalypses and Other Apocalypses*
R	*Riddance*
RM	*Realist Magic*
SA	*Scorch Atlas*
SS	*Sky Saw*
TINY	*There Is No Year*
TSA	*Trump Sky Alpha*
WM	*Wittgenstein's Mistress*
YTCH	*You Too Can Have a Body Like Mine*

Dear Incomprehension,

This book, I'm afraid, is a contradiction. Or so I tell myself, partly perhaps to give me if not confidence, then at least a starting point, something to take my cue from, some possible grounds to tread on. Something to pit my ideas against as I advance to meet you, as though there were in these lines a mistake to fix, an incoherence to correct, a wrong to right maybe. Or maybe not. Maybe this is but the mere recognition that something is amiss and that the critical discourse I've been struggling to elaborate as you faced me cannot start here but only over there, if at all:

at a critical remove. Only in the acknowledgment of its, my, failure. A critical failure, yes. To come to terms with you. Well, will I at least be myself in the end? Who knows. I'm afraid I've been cultivating too many blind spots to say.

DEAR INCOMPREHENSION

APPROACH

SPECULATE (verb)

spec·u·late | \ ˈ spe-kyə-ˌlāt \

speculated; speculating

intransitive verb

1a: to meditate on or ponder a subject: **REFLECT**

1b: to review something idly or casually and often inconclusively

2: to assume a business risk in hope of gain *especially*: to buy or sell in expectation of profiting from market fluctuations

transitive verb

1: to take to be true on the basis of insufficient evidence: THEORIZE

2: to be curious or doubtful about: **WONDER**

From Latin *speculatus*, past participle of *speculari* to spy out, examine, from *specula* lookout post, from *specere* to look, look at—more at SPY

Speculative Fiction

A Definition

Of course I ought to define it first, explain what it might consist in, list the elements that constitute it, say who its partisans or actors are, give names, titles, and dates. I should probably strive to delimit it, circumscribe it, draft its contours, test its seams, try its resilience, assay its impact, maybe appraise its value—in a word, I should somehow start proving that it exists and that its existence vouches for me, in turn, to make it an object of study and analysis, if only to ensure that beneath the label "speculative fiction," there is matter enough. Matter for what or to what effect would be a secondary question, if not a superfluous one. Indeed, I should begin by positing it, if not patenting it, for authentication's sake; I should begin by placing it within safe, clearly delineated bounds. Such an initial gesture appears to be the indispensable premise to the elaboration of any critical discourse—a discourse that is derivative by nature, that is transitive by definition, and whose very existence can be validated only by the link it establishes with the object it appropriates, the raw material from which it takes its cue.

Then, and only then, could I raise this other question like a veil: Can I approach speculative fiction? Does it let itself be approached? Read? Commented upon? If so, from what vantage?

•

What I propose to do, however, as I am now tentatively approaching it, or trying to, is not to presume the existence of "speculative fiction" per se but, rather, to *speculate* it. For the rapport I am trying to establish may not be a mimetic one; not one, that is, through which my critical gesture would be aiming to

4   Approach

represent the texts it purports to grasp, would be aiming to seize their image as reflected in my own discourse, no matter how fragmentary or distorted this image might be—and my discourse consequently. In fact, the very issues of reference and referentiality seem to be at stake here, questioned by what, in such fiction, pertains to the properly speculative. As defined in these pages, then, all discourse is or becomes speculative as soon as it ceases to refer to anything known or knowable, to anything given, fixed, and stable, as soon as it relinquishes all claims to certainty, to any form of authority that it challenges and undermines in the process of its own utterance. The speculative thus strives to come into being while paradoxically aiming at self-erasure in the same gesture, avoiding all closure. This would be language that, speculating, journeys along all too short a circuit, turns back upon itself not so much to grasp as to eradicate its own reflection—to obliterate it, to abstract it, to absolve it.

And yet.

Can discourse as such, and literary fiction in particular, whatever its shape and genre, thus easily short-circuit all reference, given that its very material, language, is by essence defined by referentiality? No matter its object, its contents and theme, a text is *text* insofar as it refers, mirrors, symbolizes, reflects, or distorts, insofar as it somehow connects, coheres, and engages with a world. The latter may be assembled from scratch, entirely made up, wholly illusory, yet for all that, it isn't free-floating nor *unrelated* altogether; it remains inseparable from, or tied to, the constructedness of its language, some referents lying behind or beyond the words that give birth to the text upon the page and make it happen there. It *means* something. *Has* to.

However, as I view it—from afar then, by necessity—or rather as I *speculate* it, "speculative fiction" would impossibly endeavor to break free from and bypass the mimetic or referential hold. The writing that shapes such fiction would thus in one way or another turn against the language mechanisms that bring it into putative existence. Eventually such speculative texts might be traversed by a counterforce or current, a contrary or antagonistic flow that brushes up against them and folds them back upon themselves, rewinding them as it were, discontinuing them—unanchoring them.

•

"Speculative fiction," as defined in this book, has very little to do with the fictions of anticipation that the phrase is often associated with as a subgenre or branch of science fiction.[1] The point may not be to project or question the possibility of a (future, distant, utopian, or dystopian) world, or hypothesize about the ramifications and offshoots of the present, so much as to muddle, confuse, fade out the contours of the known world—to abstract it from the very heart of representation.[2]

Hence, sometimes, those texts may try to discard the narrative modalities I as reader am accustomed to in favor of abstraction, for lack of a better word. Is this a novel? one may ask. No—*This Is Not a Novel* claims David Markson. Generic labels might indeed waver as the fictional contents of such works themselves become an object of speculation: "story," "frame," "characters," "timeline," "plot," "linearity," "consecution," "causality," "verisimilitude," and all such elements constitutive of a fictional, narrative world, one that would mimic and question the real one in some way, may tend to dissolve into a specific regime of writing that would no longer strive to connect the dots, order events, or round up psychologies, that would no longer try to explicate or embody them into a larger coherent unit—a "story," a "world"—but would instead list them, file them, space them out, or story them up or down, spatially, in the course of the text's unfolding and enfolding along the page. As such, narrative proper, being now and again disrupted, would yield to other modalities more akin to forms of iteration; as though, as I am immersing in it, the text were to retreat, pull back, withdraw and distance itself in ways reminiscent of what Graham Harman says of objects in general. The better perhaps to start anew. And again. Thus at times the page's layout comes undone, is shattered, visually fragmented and spaced out, rendered somewhat loose—the paragraph no longer offering a visual, consistent unit.[3] As though what mattered were not what the text had to say so much as what it achieved on the page, the process of its own coming unbound, its own retraction, its slow withdrawal along a simple column or backbone of text that makes all its blanks visible, all its disruptions, all its disjunctions. Narrative thus becomes a virtual presence, a mere possibility, to be found in its gaps, absences, spacings—in its flowings out once the story-as-story's plug has been pulled (see Fig. 1).

Such speculative texts might thus run on leakages, drainages, outpourings beyond the felt limits of language. Yet these texts, or these fictional attempts, should not be seen as tentative sallies outside language itself in search of different representational tools; for the point may not be to bore holes at the outskirts of language, to deflate language and escape from it as one would relinquish a lover to look elsewhere and try to flirt with new and different (whether visual, computational, performative, or hypermedia) modes. Quite the opposite perhaps; the point might indeed be to try to go deeper to the very heart of language, not so much in the hope of finding a way out of it as an attempt to rediscover it, or its *languageness*, for what it is rather than what it does, to unbury, from under a reified, functional, debased language, a poetic infra-language

6 Approach

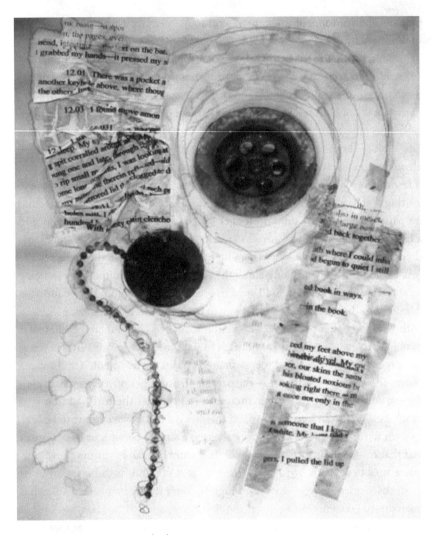

Figure 1. Blake Butler, *Ever* (50)

maybe; or maybe not, maybe something else—a language within language, like a garment's lining, an excavated, gouged, topsy-turvy language. What would its consistence be? Does this even make sense? I actually don't know nor do I pretend to vouchsafe for the existence of that which I am describing in these lines apart from a purely theoretical and rhetorical standpoint. Unless, precisely, this is all that matters: rhetoric pure and simple, freewheeling and emptied-out language that grasps at nothing but itself, its own texture and experience—an *experimentum linguae* of sorts, as defined by Italian philosopher Giorgio Agamben in the preface to his *Infancy and History: The Destruction of Experience*; an experience "in which what is experienced is language itself" (4) and "in which the limits of language are to be found not outside language, in the direction of its referent, but in an experience of language as such, in its pure self-reference" (5).

•

The question recurs: Does speculative fiction let itself be approached? Does it offer itself up for reads? In other words, can I properly speaking read those texts that run along and according to such short(-)circuits? Whose sole image, whose only reflection, would immediately fold back upon itself and shortly be distorted in the process of a language rendered unto some form of self-referentiality or autotelism? If such books, as suggested by Blake Butler's *Ever*, "read themselves aloud" (67) in what can only be a frantic and unyielding feedback loop, what befalls the reader whom, so doing, they somehow bypass or pass by? What happens to the link, to the relationship in which reading consists, formerly materialized by a so-called reading contract?

Could it be that in place of said reading contract—according to which terms of agreement between reader and text were tacitly set—the grounds for disagreement have been paved? For division and dissonance? Is something like an "objective witness," as called forth by Ben Marcus at the outset of *The Age of Wire and String*, anything but a contradiction in terms? Could one imagine something along the lines of dissent as a possible way of approaching those texts? For "what if," asked Lyotard about the equivocalness of the most ordinary language, "what if the stakes of thought (?) concerned differend rather than consensus?" (*The Differend: Phrases in Dispute*, 84).

•

In short: "speculative fiction" resists, tries my patience, persists beyond my grasp. Unable to read the putative texts that make up its bulk, I watch them act as screening devices while remaining at an unbridgeable distance from them, a stranger of sorts; a questing, questioning shadow hovering over them, probing them for meaning, waging an interpretive war against them so as to wring something out of them at least, some profit, some gain, some victory, whether pleasure, knowledge, or understanding. *Something*. So I read them, after all, and read at all costs—in a word, I *speculate*. Count on them to yield at last. Yet in that sense, "how can a commentary not be a persecution of what is commented upon? . . . a prescription provided with a content, a sense, to which the work is held, as a hostage is held for the observance of a promise?" (Lyotard, 114).

•

8　Approach

As I view it, as I read it by *not* reading it, in short as I speculate it, "speculative fiction" might pertain to a form of misunderstanding or miscalculation; the improbable encounter of a reader who no longer exists and a text that as yet, and as such, cannot be. It might be there, in this hiatus, that speculation truly takes place; at the heart of this hesitancy, this radical suspension of meaning— as both possibility and dissolution.

Something along the lines of a paradox could thus be pervading it. It could be that "speculative fiction" offers itself up as an interdiction, turning the act of reading into some transgression, some kind of voyeurism that irrevocably destroys the object of its gaze if, as per Marcus, "The outer gaze alters the inner thing . . . By looking at an object we destroy it with our desire . . . For accurate vision to occur the thing must be trained to see itself, or otherwise perish in blindness, flawed" (*AWS*, 3–4).

•

"Speculative fiction" dodges, it withstands critical assaults. If anything, it turns down my every move, it counters each of my gambits. It's fiction with a vengeance, all the way down to the language that makes it up and that it in turn fashions, undermining its grounds, mimicking its mechanisms, its arbitrariness, its contingency too, sometimes pushing as far as absurdity, sometimes as far as illegibility.

It's not just a question of contents, then, but of language, too. In some cases, syntax unfolds along problematic lines that make the narrative stutter. It has to start again, reiterate a number of instances or sequences riddled with errors, glitches, repetitions, punctures that appear as so many markers of textual contingency. The writing wavers on the page. Unless narrative itself, supposedly weaving the continuity that gives it shape and momentum from one page to the next, is the very thing that dissolves in my hands—into new configurations, quasi random textual layouts that appear tabular rather than linear, spatial rather than temporal. The text may thus appear to have been "storied" along diverse planes that relay it into multiple shifting networks, rendering all grasp untenable, fleeting at best.

If meaning is not absent altogether—for can it truly be?—it crops up on the page in all its contingency and arbitrariness. At stake here might be what, in a different context, Brian Massumi in his *Parables for the Virtual* refers to as the text's "quotient of openness," which he conceives of as the actualizing of the text's virtualities in the act of reading comprised as circulation or navigation through the text. It's quite relevant, albeit misleading, that in order to theorize this "quotient of openness," Massumi evokes literary hypertexts, that is, a literature that promotes an aesthetic of linkage. However, what befalls all those (hyper)links when the writing gets rid of them in order to couch itself back on the page, to enclose itself back into the book, without, though, reneging on the aesthetic of the literary hypertext but pursuing its undermining of linearity and narrative straightforwardness? This "quotient of openness," it seems, has not been compromised by this return to print—quite the contrary.

Perhaps.

At its most radical, "speculative fiction" would link up words, placing them alongside the syntagmatic axis of the sentence without, though, directing it toward a more and more predictable end. Albeit "infinitely catalyzable" (Barthes 1975, 50), the unfolding sentence would remain indefinitely open onto its paradigmatic axis as each new word is added; no longer oriented toward an end that would make it susceptible to yielding meaning or closure, the speculative sentence would participate instead in a regime of mutation, of transformation, generation, iteration, even perhaps simulation. The speculative sentence is thus one that simulates, or speculates, itself. Yet there would be no guarantee, ever, of any profit whatsoever or return on investment. The sentence moves on, links up words—or unlinks them rather the more it opens itself up. Meaning might still be there somewhere, though in bad shape sometimes. Words themselves become somewhat speculative, no longer or not only indexes to some signified meaning lying beyond or outside them in the direction of a world, no matter how fictive and artificial it might be, whose stability would be warranted by the very mechanisms of language. A rose is a rose and a heart is a heart. Until they're not.

What happens, then, in such circumstances, to the act of reading? What does reading amount to if such texts freewheel and slip through my fingers? What can still be the purpose of venturing a critique, assumedly defined by the grasping of some sense or an attempt at interpretation, if sense is battered?

Critique Speculative

Like the narrator of Butler's novella, no doubt I too, then, should endeavor to "read without reading" (*Ever*, 37), to resist the urge to make all those texts converge toward some meaning, some sense, that would act as their unifying core. One possibility in that respect might be—pure speculation on my part—to look for modes of reading that would no longer be *optic* but *haptic* instead; that is to say, modes of reading focused on sensation or senses rather than signification or meaning. Says Lev Manovich in *The Language of New Media*: "Haptic perception isolates the object in the field as a discrete entity, whereas optic perception unifies objects in a spatial continuum" (253–54). Haptic reading

10   Approach

would thus target the text for what and as it is—to wit, fully detached, quite un-related to anything but itself. A *text-in-itself* as it were, on condition that such a thing exists, independent of any relation whatsoever I or anyone else might establish with it while reading, or of any account I may give of it in my attempt at critical rendition.

Eventually, what is taking shape here may be the *absolute* character of such fiction in the etymological sense of the word, as recalled by French philosopher Quentin Meillassoux in his book *After Finitude*—"a being whose severance (the original meaning of *absolutus*) and whose separateness from thought is such that it presents itself to us as non-relative to us, and hence as capable of existing whether we exist or not" (Meillassoux 2008, 28).

Maybe that is how speculative fiction thwarts all tentative approaches in the end; unless it does just that, merely let itself be approached from afar, all the while frustrating my efforts to grab, grasp, appropriate it, to cross over and take hold of it, to ever lay claim to it. The very act of reading, from then on, thus given over to its own contingency, the hypothetical—maybe hypocritical[4]—outcome of an encounter that may not take place at the heart of a language rendered alien unto itself, opaque and toxic, moving along multiple, brittle, unsteady lines. Always on the verge of collapse—on the edge of severance.

•

Despite all its inherent contradiction, this book purports to be a work of criticism. That is, it aims to provide a critical investigation into specific works of experimental fiction—works that at the risk of an initial misunderstanding I'd wish to label "speculative." For if in the critical literature there exists such a genre as *speculative fiction* already, often defined in relation, or in opposition, to science fiction,[5] the works I in turn target as bearing on the speculative in these pages have not much in common with the staples of the genre, or else, only incidentally so, when they happen to meddle with genre fiction. Some of them indeed overtly flirt with so-called science-fictional or speculative scenarios about possible futures and alternate realities, dystopias and uchronias, apocalyptic ends-of-the-world and what might come next.

As I define it, however, "speculative fiction" goes beyond mere generic issues and considerations of content. More often than not, the works that interest me are experimental ones, maybe conceptual ones in some cases. They may not have specific, distinctive features beyond that. They certainly do not form a genre of their own. They're sometimes radically different from one another, both in content and shape. Some are published by mainstream venues, others by small, independent presses. Yet what they do have in common, at least as I read them, what thus makes them properly *speculative* in my understanding of the word, is their conspicuous challenge to readerly expectations, their blatant questioning of their relation to reading—what I view as a potential attempt at thwarting critical interpretation, at willy-nilly eluding the reader's grasp.

•

By nature or definition, the discourse that is taking shape in these pages ought to be, in its critical dimension, endowed with a certain amount of authoritativeness, the latter required or implied by the very notion of critique. Critical discourse,[6] in other words, is a *knowing* discourse, an analytical discourse that sheds light upon, clarifies, and explicates other texts whose complexity it has formerly and/or formally mastered. Yet as this book's title suggests, the discourse that permeates it eschews such initial mastery or comprehension. This book, I suggested, may as such be a contradiction, the sign or product of my own bafflement, the testimony to the abstruseness of its object—what I doggedly call "speculative fiction."

Forced by the impenetrability of its subject to forgo its own intrinsic expertise or mastery, my discourse in turn cannot help but tilt toward the speculative, then. Speculation, as the Latin origin of the word suggests, indeed appears as a form of observation and examination whose truth value or result is problematic: among the various definitions found in the dictionary by Merriam-Webster are words like "inconclusively," "insufficient evidence," or "doubtful." If one takes into account the economic or monetary connotations of the word, along with the reflexivity also inscribed in its etymology, "speculation" seems an apt enough concept to refer to criticism itself as a specific form of reflexive discourse in search of its own validation.

Therefore the "speculative fiction" of the subtitle is inevitably both object and subject of these pages; what they wonder about, what they discuss, as well as what they are, what they do. To put it differently, this book in turn is bound to remain speculative—"inconclusive" at best, if not downright "doubtful."

To some degree, this book too is bound to remain a fiction of sorts—a book that cannot do otherwise than somehow speculate and fictionalize in its own turn and terms. Yes, speculating fiction.

•

Perhaps another way of addressing speculative fiction would be to emphasize its absoluteness. It is not uncommon to come across disparaging declarations about anything "experimental," that is, about anything that resists immediate apprehension whether in literature or in art more generally. One may recall,

12   Approach

for instance, how postmodernist fiction and self-reflexive works were at times viewed negatively as narcissistic or self-centered. I submit this tentatively for now, but this may be not unlike the concept of "self-enjoyment" that Steven Shaviro derives from his reading of Alfred North Whitehead: "Self-enjoyment is 'absolute' in that it unfolds entirely in itself and for itself, without conditions" (Shaviro, 14). It may well be the case with speculative fiction; for it too seems to withdraw from my grasp. It's in that sense that it could be said to be somehow "absolute"—"unbound, set free, released from all relation" (Shaviro, 14).

However, spurred by the project's inherent contradiction, these pages unavoidably belie the fact that in the end I do engage these works; that between me and them something does happen, albeit in the recognition that what happens does not happen as it should, that is, as I thought it would; that while what I get is not what I bargained for perhaps, an exchange or interaction may have taken place all the same, along lines that from the start were biased against me and my ingrained postulates.

Reading such texts, then, letting them baffle me or letting myself be puzzled somehow forces the realization that the usual paradigms may be shifting, that something is changing the way one apprehends fictional works or is modifying the way fictional works approach the world at large. That what such works might have to tell about this world no longer passes through their mimetic rendition of it; that, in short, their very inoperability is itself trenchant. And that what it tells is precisely this: there is no such thing as *knowledge* of the text. The text's "truth"—a dubious concept if there is one—remains intractable. All I can do, then, and again, is *speculate*.

•

Maybe that's what these texts make me do, indeed—speculate—as they somehow keep me at bay (*specula*), condemning me for better or worse to merely look at them (*specere*), examine them, perhaps, but at a distance, from beyond a problematic divide (*speculari*).

The texts I have in mind are those that, try as I might, leave me in the lurch; I read, or try to, reread, or try to, but to not much avail. As one eloquent reviewer puts it about one of them: "I gotta say, it's a complicated and fractured read. I had a couple of '*what-the-fuck-am-I-reading?*' moments."[7]

Often referred to as experimental, these texts indeed often venture off the beaten narrative tracks, sometimes throw the dice, take the bet, dare their readers and graze the limits of readability. Sometimes they do offer themselves up for reads. They tell stories, albeit bizarre ones; ones that do not abide by the usual, if stale, conventions of mimetic realism; ones that leave things unexplained, open to indecisive, inconclusive interpretation—to speculation. In that sense, "speculative fiction" is not so much a question of genre or of kind as it is of degree or of manner. I repeat myself, but *as such* "speculative fiction" may not even exist or might well be just a way for me to save up critical appearances.

•

"I always find myself deployed amidst a specific geography of objects, each of them withdrawing from view into a dark primal integrity that neither our theories nor our practices can ever fully exhaust," writes Graham Harman as he reframes, in what he calls "tool-analysis," Heidegger's *Vorhandenheit* and *Zuhandenheit* concepts (Harman 2010, 51). As Heidegger famously put it, it is only when a thing becomes unusable or broken that one notices it in all its conspicuous objective presence. Expanding on this, Harman chooses to refer to objects in general as "tool-beings," explaining that

> to refer to an object as a "tool-being" is not to say that it is brutally exploited as means to an end, but only that it is torn apart by the universal duel between the silent execution of an object's reality and the glistening aura of its tangible surface. In short, the tool isn't "used"; it is. (Harman 2010, 97–98)

I wonder myself if, by frustrating reading expectations, speculative fiction might not similarly be challenging my basic assumptions of what fiction is and what it does, and if, concomitantly, it may not also be questioning and undermining the way I as reader and critic relate to it. Does the text have to mean anything, to be *used* in relation to something or someone? Or is it just that it just *is*? Might this not be the only possible understanding to be derived from speculative fiction? That it *is*? So that, in the end, issues of what, when, how, or why could very well be irrelevant.

Speculative Fiction: Its Resistance

What these pages posit, in short, what lies at the heart of this book, is indeed the problematic nature of the relationship that unites this text to the texts it strives and in part fails to comment upon; those various American works of fiction that I claim not to understand.

If I were to sum up the book's argument, then, it could be this: speculative fiction, as defined in these pages, is a specific regime of fictional discourse that eludes understanding; it is experimental fiction at times aggressively directed against readerly expectations—of plot, character consistency, realism or verisimilitude, logic, sense, and readability. Such fiction baffles reason, foils interpretation, thwarts the meaning-making process, tears it apart, opacifies language, resists or frustrates conventional narrative moves—and, in the process, may challenge what fiction is and what it does.

Hence, the failure that I am now trying to articulate is not only or necessarily mine as I read those texts: failure may be scripted at their core. It could be part of their (un)operating mode, of their (dys)functional strategies. Their peculiar way of withdrawing behind the screen of their very own fiction. The fiction of themselves.

•

Speculative fiction besets and resists readerly intervention, it frustrates every customary move I seem to make in order to grasp it. It exists, if it does, only negatively—or in absentia. In the lacunae of the discourse that attempts to seize and gauge it.

•

As broadly defined here, speculative fiction may somehow be seen as "flawed" texts; texts that do not abide by the usual standards of conventional fiction. They may well seem "broken," and much like Heidegger's equipment or tools, they as such suddenly appear in all their obtuse conspicuousness—they're *there*, but I no longer know what to do with them, how to *use* them. As Robbe-Grillet pointed out, "A new form will always seem more or less an absence of any form at all, since it is unconsciously judged by reference to the consecrated forms" (Robbe-Grillet, 17). That might be part of the problem actually—this impossibility of viewing the work independently of all reference, the ingrained incapacity to read it for what it *is*, rather than for what it could possibly mean or be likened to. Yet, as Robbe-Grillet argued back in the late 1950s, in words that somehow anticipated or, if not, at least echo with Harman's "object-oriented ontology," "the world is neither significant nor absurd. It is, quite simply" (Robbe-Grillet, 19). Despite its refusal to make sense, despite its rebuff of interpretation, despite its apparent disengagement from conventional mimeticism, speculative fiction may be yet another name for *realism*—a realism no longer and not so much defined in mimetic terms, or by its putative correspondence or correlation to the world outside, but rather a form of realism more in line with that elaborated by Anna Kornbluh in *The Order of Forms*, as "a mode of production instead of a mode of reflection," as formal constructivism, texts that "build fiercely, soundly, cohesively, firmly—but without correlate" (Kornbluh, 41). This absence of correlate paves the way for the speculative, which may not be understood in opposition to the real.

Insofar as what I identify as speculative texts appear to, if not make impossible, at least disrupt narrative, speculative fiction could be seen as an intensification of what Quentin Meillassoux calls "extro-science fiction" (*fiction des mondes hors-science*).

> By extro-science worlds we mean worlds where, *in principle, experimental science is impossible* and not unknown *in fact*. Extro-science fiction thus defines a particular regime of the imaginary in which structured— or rather destructured—worlds are conceived in such a way that experimental science cannot deploy its theories or constitute its objects within them. The guiding question of extro-science fiction is: what should a world be, what should a world resemble, so that it is in principle inaccessible to a scientific knowledge, so that it cannot be established as the object of a natural science? (Meillassoux 2015, 5–6)

This, for Meillassoux—who aims to solve Hume's famous metaphysical problem about the so-called necessity of the laws of nature—concerns a properly ontological problem rather than a merely epistemological one. Hume's problem indeed bears on the stability of physical laws—why do they appear stable and immutable when "neither experience nor logic can give us such an assurance" (Meillassoux 2015, 9)?—and not on the limitations or "nature of scientific knowledge" per se (Meillassoux 2015, 15). Meillassoux thus imagines "extro-science fiction" as a genre of fiction that would be apt to represent worlds in which, in principle, it is impossible to vouch for—calculate, predict, deduce, infer, or, in a word, *comprehend*—anything but the necessity of pure, absolute contingency.

Because, as I view it, speculative fiction does just that, namely, elude understanding and rationalization, it could be seen as a theoretical variant of extro-science fiction. What is at stake, though, is not so much an epistemological or hermeneutic problem, one that pertains to my own incapacity as of yet to meet them on their own grounds, as an ontological one, one that is inseparable from the very materiality of those texts *as such*.

However, Meillassoux acknowledges the paucity of extro-science-fictional texts, whose sole representative he can think of would be René Barjavel's novel *Ravage*. Meillassoux accounts for this scarcity by explaining that contrary to science fiction, which "appears to permit the construction of a storyline, of a narration that is certainly fanciful but coherent . . . in extro-science fiction, on the other hand, it seems that no order of any sort can be constituted and, therefore, no story can be told" (Meillassoux 2015, 23). Meillassoux however contests this view, for according to him it doesn't follow that such a world would necessarily be incoherent and detrimental to narrative.

Extro-science fiction, as defined by the philosopher, may be part of what I choose to refer to as speculative fiction instead. The difference, if there is one, is that speculative fiction is not limited to mere questions of content and narrative. It doesn't have to *represent* "extro-science worlds" or their equivalents, worlds in which science is impossible, in which laws are unstable and contingent, in order to *be* speculative. True, speculative fiction does at times venture into extro-science worlds or possible versions thereof, but its speculative aspect does not rely on representation only but is, more often than not, woven directly into its very fabric, into its language and materiality; it instantiates or embodies a radical shift or break away from habitual ways of ordering, approaching, understanding "the world"—a world that appears to be more and more estranged from itself, an obtuse, *alien* world, "an exotic world of utterly incomprehensible objects" (Bogost, 34). Objects that speculative fiction somehow addresses for what they are.

•

Speculative fiction, in a way, would be fiction that resists the reader; fiction that does not *work*, or at least not according to preconceived notions of how fiction used to work. One of the best definitions one could possibly give would be this, perhaps: speculative fiction is fiction that recedes from the reader's grasp, is fiction that shies away from reading, that won't be read or understood. Fiction, maybe, that has an obtrusive will of its own, refusing all interpretations, or explanations, or justifications, or rationalizations. That withdraws behind diverse forms of opacification. Something I cannot read, not addressed to me, that does away with me.

Somehow (?).

Speculative Tools

Yet how does one read fiction that supposedly can't be read? Fiction that won't be approached? How can anyone navigate those speculative, contrary currents running through a stream of contemporary American fiction? Thanks to what tools?

In the course of my previous attempts throughout the years, when I first started grappling with some contemporary experimental fiction, my attention was drawn to a recent trend in continental philosophy that emerged in 2007 and that goes by the name or brand of "speculative realism." Under the label are to be found philosophers and philosophies that follow different orientations but whose starting point is roughly the same: the desire to step out of what Quentin Meillassoux termed "the correlationist circle" and thus go beyond its diverse implications for understanding reality without falling prey to a form of "naïve realism" or "a commonsense middle-aged realism of objective atoms and billiard balls located outside the human mind."[8] Because "speculative realism" is far from presenting a unified front, it's virtually impossible to summarize its tenets and nuances.[9] Plus, I'm no philosopher myself and do not intend to take sides in current debates, nor do I aim to judge the philosophical validity of the diverse theses propounded by the speculative realists or materialists or neovitalists or object-oriented ontologists or alien phenomenologists or whatever-other-isms "speculative realism" has since 2007 divided into. What I propose to do, however, is to use it as a possible navigational tool to try to come to terms with what, following "speculative realism," I chose to call "speculative fiction." So doing, my intention was not to suggest that all works potentially matching the appellation "speculative fiction" would or could serve as illustrations of the ideas diversely put forward by speculative realists. Some might, others wouldn't. Speculative realism—at any rate some of its main arguments—simply helped me understand why it seemed that all these works I was striving to read and comment on somehow foiled each of my endeavors, or at least left me with the impression that such was the case.

Summarily stated, "speculative realism"—I stick to that label for convenience's sake but could indifferently use "ooo" (object-oriented ontology) or any other designation, for that matter—aims to contest Kant's supposedly unsurpassable idealism, which posited that it was impossible to have access to any object *in itself*. This impasse is what Quentin Meillassoux describes as "correlationism":

> Correlationism consists in disqualifying the claim that it is possible to consider the realms of subjectivity and objectivity independently of one another. Not only does it become necessary to insist that we never grasp an object "in itself," in isolation from its relation to the subject, but it also becomes necessary to maintain that we can never grasp a subject that would not always-already be related to an object. (Meillassoux 2008, 5)

I've often felt, contemplating the works I'm dealing with, that they eventually demanded that as a reader I considered them for themselves, *in themselves*—as objects, pure objects, or "tool-beings" in Graham Harman's terminology. That, somehow, they were forcing me to read them or, minimally, to

18   Approach

view them from outside a version of the "correlationist circle" that Meillassoux describes. Is this even possible, though, one may wonder. To read the text independently of the "correlation" that unites it to the reader, me to it? To read the text as though I *was not*.[10] Put differently, can a text exist without there being a reader (real or constructed) to voice it or give it some sort of presence or actuality? Can a text achieve an independent, autonomous life of its own? Can a novel, then, as one such text proclaims, *read itself*? Can it thus radically expel any form of (reading) subjectivity out of itself? Or are all such questions utterly devoid of meaning? That might possibly be the case. Yet a text is an object just like any other, after all, and as such has a share in the object's withdrawn ontology—a point made by Harman in his essay "The Well-Wrought Broken Hammer" when he rejects the new critics' tendency, embodied in Cleanth Brooks's conception of the poem, to view literature "as a special case." This, for Harman, amounts to "taxonomic fallacy, which consists in the assumption that any ontological distinction must be embodied in specific *kinds* of entities" (Harman, 189). A poem may well be autonomous and resist all attempts at literalization, yet for all that, it is no different than any other type of discourse, or any real object. The poem is thus *no* special case. What could be true of a tree, the sun, or a speck of dust could, for that very reason, also be true of any text, and vice versa. In theory.

So this, in the end, is the fiction that I propose to read and/or write—a speculative fiction that posits the existence of texts that *withdraw* (Harman's concept) from all relations. Texts that, perhaps, tell the story of their own unreadability; that make, as I read them, their own "tale[s] [themselves] progressively impossible" (Meillassoux 2015, 57).

•

Speculative realism comes in handy for diverse reasons, one of them being that it challenges all forms of anthropocentrism. One orientation taken by speculative realism precisely consists of thinking a world of "objects" or "things"—even *hyperobjects* in Timothy Morton's case; that is, a world rid of all human bias, in which everyday objects, concrete as well as abstract, infinitesimal or massive, occupy no less privileged a position in the universe at large than do human beings: "my being is not everything it's cracked up to be," says Morton—"or rather . . . the being of a paper cup is as profound as mine" (*HO*, 17).[11]

As such, speculative realism is finely attuned to fictional scenarios that would envisage the disappearance of humanity or that would rigorously displace the narrative viewpoint in trying to render it as "objective" as possible by removing, as much as can be done, any subjective slant. Now, whether or not such story lines belong to fiction exclusively or already inform reality in part or as a whole remains debatable in the face of ecological catastrophe, global terror, a worldwide pandemic, and/or nuclear apocalypse. However, as defined in these pages, speculative fiction relishes these types of scenario insofar as they force us to adopt a non-correlationist perspective on the world, concomitantly placing the reader in the uncomfortable position that consists in thinking (of) something that radically does away with the very possibility of thinking it. Thinking the end of the world in any literal sense, for instance, can be achieved only if one thinks the end of their thinking in the same breath and process, given that the end of the world, if complete, implies the end of all thought.[12] This is perhaps as radical as it gets, but such is, at least theoretically, what the "absolute" placed at the heart of speculation entails—the very possibility of "access[ing] *an absolute*, i.e. a being whose *severance* (the original meaning of *absolutus*) and whose separateness from thought is such that it presents itself to us as non-relative to us, and hence as capable of existing whether we exist or not" (Meillassoux 2008, 28). Hence my contention here that a truly apocalyptic novel, say, is one that demands to be read in and for its absolute separateness from the act of reading as such.

•

Beyond mere theoretical or philosophical concerns, speculative realism is also interested in the question of aesthetics, which in itself allows for a tentative dialogue between philosophical speculation and experimental fiction. Harman, Shaviro, and Morton, for instance, all place aesthetics at the heart of both philosophy and the real. For Harman, "metaphysics may be a branch of aesthetics, and causation merely a form of beauty" (Harman 2010, 139). A claim seconded by Steven Shaviro whose reading of Whitehead as a possible counterpoint to speculative realism makes him reach the conclusion that "speculative philosophy has an irreducibly aesthetic dimension; it requires new, bold inventions rather than pacifying resolutions" (Shaviro, 43). Morton agrees, who similarly views causality in terms of aesthetics since "if things are intrinsically withdrawn, irreducible to their perception or relations or uses,[13] they can only affect each other in a strange region out in front of them, a region of traces and footprints: the aesthetic dimension" (*RM*, 17–18).

For those reasons, like other philosophers before them, speculative realists often resort to literary works if not to prove their points, then at least to articulate them. Meillassoux's interest in science fiction and the way it can be twisted or "decomposed" so as to offer the speculative experience of pure contingency and thus "explore the truth of a worldless existence" (Meillassoux 2015, 57)

20 Approach

finds other developments in *The Number and the Siren,* his book on Mallarmé, which can be read as a performative demonstration of "the necessity of contingency," as first expounded in *After Finitude.* Further, as Harman himself points out, if the views diversely propounded by speculative realists may at times appear discordant, "all of [them] turned out independently to have been admirers of Lovecraft," whose "weird fiction sets the stage for an entire philosophical genre" (Harman 2018). If Harman notably devotes a book to Lovecraft,[14] Eugene Thacker similarly gathers, in his *Horror of Philosophy* series,[15] all sorts of literary examples from romantic, gothic, horror, or "weird" literature.[16]

Such focus on aesthetic issues renders speculative realism, in its broad spectrum, a potentially useful tool for approaching works of speculative fiction as defined in these pages, that is, works that somehow "withdraw" as one tries to approach them, that resist interpretation, whose connections more often than not dissolve beyond conventional categories, and whose intrinsic logic appears flimsy, in some cases even challenging narrativity as it depicts strange and uncanny worlds.

•

I realize that I've chosen to refer to speculative realism—broadly defined and in deliberate ignorance of possible objections, as well as of its inner conflicts—as a "tool" that would help me navigate speculative waters. However, my point in doing so is not to use its main arguments or concepts instrumentally in order to translate them to the study of contemporary American fiction. If I've elected speculative realism as a prospective "method" for approaching speculative fiction, for reasons in part exposed above, it's also because it appeared that at the heart of speculative realism there existed specific modalities that were notably open to *fiction* itself.

Of course, fiction is not philosophy any more than philosophy is fiction. Yet the very concept of *speculation* might appear as a fruitful site where both philosophy and fiction meet. Fiction, especially when it waxes *experimental,* may indeed thrust toward philosophy by offering singular, speculative thought experiments that undermine both my sense of what fiction or narrative is and does and my understanding of, or difficulty with, what goes by the name of reality.[17]

For despite its apparent predilection for absurdism or irrationality or ontological improbabilities, speculative fiction may not be that abstractly removed from reality, after all. Not only does reality have a notorious tendency of outdoing fiction, but it is also increasingly harder and harder to fathom now that "the end of the world has already occurred" according to Timothy Morton— an end brought about by what he calls "hyperobjects," that is, "things that are massively distributed in time and space relative to humans" (*HO*, 7/1).[18] It results from this that "the hyperobject is not a function of our knowledge" (*HO*, 2). As Morton specifies in *Realist Magic*, there is an uneradicable part of mystery lodged at the core of reality; the word "mystery" itself, says Morton, "suggests a rich and ambiguous range of terms: secret, enclosed, withdrawn, unspeakable." Thus "the realness of things [is] bound up with a certain mystery, in these multiple senses: unspeakability, enclosure, withdrawal, secrecy. . . . Things are *encrypted*. But the difference between standard encryption and the encryption of objects is that this is an unbreakable encryption. 'Nature loves to hide' (Heraclitus)" (*RM*, 17).

Speculative fiction may be just that, in the end: fiction about which there could be nothing to say, after all, whose secret code cannot be broken—or broken only to the extent that it immediately reciphers itself and thus remains undecidable, a point Meillassoux addresses in *The Number and the Siren* when concluding about "the undecidable nature of [the count's] procedure" (208) that is supposed to reveal the secret Number or Meter of Mallarmé's *Un coup de dés*.

And it might be this undecidability, perhaps another name for speculation eventually, that undoes the critical act.

Mapping Speculation

Having said all that, or tried to, I can now venture to draw up an exploratory map of speculative fiction. Of course, given its volatile nature, speculative fiction as such is hard to locate or put down; the map itself remains tentative and in no way exhaustive. On it, a text can appear then disappear to relocate elsewhere, contesting margins, ignoring edges. Others should probably figure on the map but were left out, as yet undiscovered or unexplored. Once placed on the map, though, a text's position can never truly be ascertained. The map itself is a fiction. The map itself speculates—it calls up texts, assesses them; some comply while others resist, erasing the contours of the map, forcing it to fold out differently, to reconsider its outline. For as already explained, speculative fiction as such may not exist, or exists only as a theoretical construct—some texts may not *be* speculative (for the question remains whether or not any one text can *truly* be speculative and as such elude all forms of "correlation") yet appear here or there tinged with the speculative hypothesis, traversed in some of their regions by a speculative current.

•

The texts that first sent me down the speculative track were Ben Marcus's early collection *The Age of Wire and String* (1995) and his novel *Notable American*

Women (2002). Marcus's next novel, *The Flame Alphabet* (2012), seemed to break with the peculiar aesthetics of his previous works in favor of a more straightforward narrative, although its premise—a world in which language turns poisonous and where it becomes virtually impossible to ever *relate* (to) anything—is in itself adamantly speculative. Throughout Marcus's fiction, a dystopian streak is clearly perceptible that alienates the world as we know or think we know it, a world turned strange, creepy, uncanny, "weird," in which the relationships between characters appear often contrived and tinged with obtuse technology in which communication and understanding are never granted.

Ben Marcus's work, including his latest collections of stories, *Leaving the Sea* (2014) and *Notes from the Fog* (2018), could thus serve to chart one region of speculative fiction. In its vicinity would be found such texts as Gary Lutz's (now Garielle Lutz) or Jason Schwartz's. In both instances, the worlds described are ones that appear coldly objectified, in which interaction—social, personal, familial, marital—is never a given. The syntactic constructions defamiliarize the environments in which characters are supposed to play their part; paragraphs follow up on one another without any manifest connection, resulting in strange non sequiturs that constantly jam the narrative impetus; words aggregate yet obfuscate meaning. Stories as such appear "in the worst way" (Lutz)—they never really *tell* anything, connect dots, or give access to any information that would add up toward some possible resolution or understanding. They often leave off or disconnect in abrupt, baffling fashion after characters have been acting erratically, if at all, remaining at best bizarre, often undecipherable, unnamed and hard to identify, let alone relate to, when not altogether discarded from the text. In the words of Ben Marcus in his introduction to Jason Schwartz's *A German Picturesque* (1998), words that could easily apply to Gary (now Garielle) Lutz's fiction too, these stories remain "beneath reason and understanding" (*GP*, viii).

The radical strangeness inherent in such fiction can at some point seem to devolve into some form of absurdism or surrealism. Of course, these as such may not be intrinsically speculative; the logic behind surrealism, for instance, appears different, obeys other patterns and rules but is not altogether absent. It's just *other(ed)*. Meaning in itself is not contested so much as displaced or translated. Bona fide surrealistic fiction is thus not truly speculative in the sense the word is used in these pages. However, some speculative works may flirt with surrealism, and the boundary between the two can be thin and not easily located. *Wild Milk* (2018), by Sabrina Orah Mark, might be one such work in which the partition between what could appear as surrealism and as speculation gets blurred. So are Sarah Rose Etter's *The Book of X* (2019) or Alexandra

Kleeman's *You Too Can Have a Body Like Mine* (2015) or Lucy Corin's collection *One Hundred Apocalypses and Other Apocalypses* (2013), texts that float about the map not far from the Marcus-Lutz-Schwartz province, along perhaps with Renee Gladman's Ravicka series of short novels, consisting in the invention of what could at first sight appear as a uchronia, a radically alien city with its own rules and language.[19]

The positioning of those texts on the map by and by leads to another region that may be charted by Shelley Jackson's body of works, from her collection *The Melancholy of Anatomy* (2002) to her latest novel, *Riddance* (2018). Jackson's work mixes and blurs diverse narrative genres to treat the text as an organic, mysterious body of its own, the grappling of which is never evident.

Materiality is indeed a key feature of Jackson's writing, her texts being inseparable from the media they are couched in/on, whether a book (*Half Life* or *Riddance*), a hypertext (*Patchwork Girl*), the weather ("Snow"), or the human body (the "Skin" project). Because Jackson's work openly questions its materiality, it demands to be read in specific ways, ways that possibly remain to be invented as each text also plots its own withdrawal—either via technological obsolescence (which is the case of the Storyspace hypertext *Patchwork Girl*, for instance) or through the calculated disappearance of its "media" (whether human flesh or snow—or paper too, for that matter). The text that I as reader have open access to thus never truly is what it seems nor coincides with itself—an idea that the novel *Half Life* (2006) toys with—but remains a trompe l'oeil duplicate, an imperfect rendition of another text left or positioned elsewhere, possibly distributed through space and time, at any rate unreachable, elusive, and deceitful.

This region on the map of speculative fiction opens out onto what Katherine Hayles has termed "technotexts"—that is, "literary works that strengthen, foreground, and thematize the connections between themselves as material artifacts and the imaginative realm of verbal/semiotic signifiers they instantiate" (Hayles 2002, 25)—of which Jackson's works can be seen as avatars. In this area of the map would be found works by Mark Doten, Michael Joyce, Joshua Cohen, and Mark Z. Danielewski, different though they are in scope, contents, or style. As Hayles argues, such artifacts demand to be read along the lines of "media-specific analysis" and as such invalidate the usual hermeneutic props. Meaning is not to be discovered *in* the text but rather lies somewhere in the interaction I have (or fail to have) with the objects qua objects I am manipulating. This, of course, is not enough to turn them into speculative artifacts. Speculation registers, however, as soon as the object ceases to function or operate. Which might be said to be the case with Doten's *The Infernal* (2015), for example, or with Michael Joyce's *Was* (2007), riddled with interferences and constant dis- or re-locations. It may not be a coincidence if, further, Danielewski's *House of Leaves* (2000) or Mark Doten's *The Infernal* both build upon what appears to be an insoluble enigma that cannot fully be rationalized, whether in the form of the unfathomable hallway at the heart of the Navidsons' house in Danielewski's book, or the presence of the "Akkad Boy" at the onset of Doten's novel. In both instances, there would be something akin to what Meillassoux theorizes as "extro-science fiction."

If Meillassoux acknowledges that true extro-science works are almost impossible to locate, their narratives as narratives impossible to tell, extro-science may however be made manifest by degrees. This leads me to another possible corner on the map where texts revolving around apparently insolvable mysteries are to be found, like Azareen Van der Vliet Oloomi's *Fra Keeler* (2012) or Jane Unrue's *Love Hotel* (2015), a novel that somehow takes the form of the titular hotel, asking readers to move up and down along diverse fringed story lines that come apart on the page in hypertextual fashion. What such formal strategies eventually develop can no longer be patterned on the traditional narrative arc, stretching more or less linearly from beginning to end. Both Van der Vliet Oloomi's and Unrue's novels, despite their obvious differences in shapes, build upon a series of iterations or duplications that challenge sequentiality and, eventually, chronology—that is, the ordering of events without which a story-as-story comes loose or undone, falls apart, and does not and cannot cohere. What novels like *Fra Keeler* or *Love Hotel* might as such be doing is indeed isolate fictional lives (Fra Keeler's in Van der Vliet Oloomi's story; the narrator's in Unrue's novel) and "[tighten them] around their own flow in the midst of gaps" (Meillassoux 2015, 57), gaps made all the more apparent by the iterations or doublings surrounding them.

Such iterations gain formal visibility in the work of Blake Butler, whether in *Ever* (2009), *There Is No Year* (2011), or *Sky Saw* (2012). Even when the text appears to play along more conventional narrative lines, as in *Scorch Atlas* (2009), which models itself upon postapocalyptic fiction, or *300,000,000* (2014), which initially feigns to borrow from detective fiction, the stories end up iterating rather than telling proper, indulging in lists and endless rehashings that run counter to the idea one usually has of what literature—and fiction—is and does. "Perhaps," ventures Ian Bogost in *Alien Phenomenology*, "the problem is not with lists but with literature, whose preference for traditional narrative acts as a correlationist amplifier" (40). But beyond that, iteration also implies a purely mechanical operation tending toward the algorithm or the computational, an operation that can leave traces—errors, glitches—on the surface of texts, pointing to their underlying illegible nature as a reminder that such fictions, eventually, are "not for you," to quote the epigraph of Danielewski's *House of Leaves*.

•

This map, so far, works by association and possible family traits, ascribing likenesses between this or that text, whether in "spirit" or "letter." But if speculative fiction were a family of texts, it would almost, by necessity and definition, have to be a dysfunctional one. There is very little in common between, say, Danielewski's maximalist strategy in *House of Leaves* and Jason Schwartz's minimalist fiction; or between Mark Doten's stylized, technological future and Renee Gladman's neat, stripped-down Ravicka. Other works, like David Ohle's or David Markson's, remain definitely apart, bearing virtually no or very little organic resemblance with texts that may form specific neighborhoods on the map.

Another possibility would thus be to rearrange or draw another version of the map, along more thematic and/or generic lines. Because speculation, in the philosophical sense used in these pages, is concerned with ways of bypassing what Quentin Meillassoux has defined as "correlationism," genres or themes that undermine ways of relating may serve as catalysts for speculative scenarios. Among them would be genres whose precepts are intrinsically speculative, that is, genres that depict situations to which it is impossible to relate, that appear in themselves unthinkable insofar as they, as such, presuppose either the nonexistence of thought (this is the "ancestrality" thesis expounded by Meillassoux in *After Finitude*) or its abolition.

One such genre is postapocalyptic fiction—fictions of the end or end-time fictions that compel thought to think through or beyond its own annihilation. Stories about the end of the world abound, and some of them are sometimes referred to as "speculative" in the usual, literary, "what-if?" sense of the word. But to be speculative in the sense I wish to convey in this study, so-called (post) apocalyptic stories somehow have to radicalize the genre, unsettle it so as to include and embody the catastrophe or disaster in their formal layouts or narrative strategies, thus pushing narrative as such over the abyss—exploding it or ending it altogether.

In that regard, though far less sensational than any other stories in the genre,[20] David Markson's *Wittgenstein's Mistress* (1988)—in its fragmented, iterative layout, as well as in its narrative paucity—strikes me as overtly speculative in its premises. Along with Markson's novel, Mark Doten's *The Infernal* and *Trump Sky Alpha* (2019), David Ohle's work, comprised of *Motorman* (1972), *In the Age of Sinatra* (2004), *The Pisstown Chaos* (2008), and *The Old Reactor*

(2013), or Blake Butler's *Scorch Atlas* all share similar speculative concerns and fit within the postapocalyptic framework. Others, though less literally postapocalyptic, can be seen as implementing another take on the end-time story: Ben Marcus's *The Flame Alphabet* is one; and so might be, in their own terms, Shelley Jackson's *Half Life*, exploring the consequences of the nuclear age, or Joshua Cohen's *Witz* (2010), telling the story of the mysterious, simultaneous death of all Jews on the planet at the turn of the twenty-first century, with the exception of one.

In some, not to say most, texts revolving around catastrophism and postapocalyptics, the distinction between science fiction and extro-science fiction can often appear blurry. Shelley Jackson's *Half Life*, to quote but one, remains on the surface a science-fictional text to the extent that none of its oddities challenge the very concepts of science and reason. On a purely thematic level then, *Half Life* is *not* speculative. Yet one reason why Meillassoux finds locating extro-science works difficult could be that his vantage remains fixated on the diegetic, mimetic level and never really includes the formal dimension nor the narrative strategies set up by the text. Yet if one focuses on the formal games played by Shelley Jackson in *Half Life*, it becomes possible to pick up a speculative whiff flowing through the text itself, in the way the writing destabilizes reading and interpretation.

To some degree—though that might very well be the point I've been trying to make all along, namely, that speculative fiction *is* a question of degrees—the same applies to David Ohle's work, from *Motorman* on. For on the surface of it, for all its quirkiness, David Ohle's universe can be put away on the sci-fi shelves. Replete with all sorts of strange inventions, creatures, and life-forms, Ohle's texts read in part like dystopian science fiction gone berserk through parody and absurdism. As such, they may not be truly speculative, yet they often resist interpretation through abrupt and grotesque narrative shifts highlighting sheer arbitrariness—whether thematically or formally. This, in turn, makes of Ohle's texts a loose concatenation of anecdotes or episodes rather than a consistent story with beginning, middle, and end. The very fact that each novel by Ohle can be seen as the (discontinuous) sequel to the previous one further reflects this: Ohle's oeuvre is not one, does not constitute a whole so much as a series, an aggregate of parts that never truly cohere, an aspect concordant with the way object-oriented ontology views "objects" as "uncanny," according to Timothy Morton, "compos[ing] an untotalizable nonwhole set that defies holism and reductionism" (*HO*, 116).

Postapocalyptics, in a broad sense, can thus occupy a whole region on the map of speculative fiction as one genre predicated upon a speculative hypothesis, namely, what Meillassoux called "dia-chronicity" to refer to statements hinging on "a *temporal discrepancy* between thinking and being—thus, not only statements about events occurring prior to the emergence of humans, but also statements about possible events that are *ulterior* to the extinction of the human species" (Meillassoux 2008, 112).

•

Along with (post)apocalyptic fiction, in ways not quite unrelated to it, another genre that could almost naturally lead to some form of speculation is dystopian fiction. Because they depict situations that are not the case, though they could be, because they distort social and political realities, dystopias posit a connection to, a resemblance with, the world as we know it and, as such, beg to be related to. But because they often take the form of nightmarish scenarios, or at least bizarre states of affairs, they also question the very relation they want me to establish with them, leading me to view them as untenable, undesirable, not to say *unthinkable.*

In that corner of the map could thus be found early works by Ben Marcus, for instance, *The Age of Wire and String, Notable American Women,* and early stories like "The Father Costume" (*Leaving the Sea*). Marcus's first novel, *The Age of Wire and String,* is set in an unspecified "age" and purports to depict, rather than *tell* about, the ways and rules of a mysterious community. Dates and places, when mentioned, tend to obfuscate rather than pin down this enigmatic age, which could quite indifferently be set in the distant past or the distant future. Instead of stories in any due sense, the book is indeed comprised of a series of short, definitional vignettes placed under such headings as "Sleep," "God," "Food," "The House," "Animal," "Weather," "Persons," "The Society." Yet the texts often appear to be cryptically unrelated to the topic they're supposed to exemplify. Their pseudo authoritative, encyclopedic tone, devoid of subjective investment, further estranges their content, making it difficult to relate— which, as exposed in the book's "Argument," might precisely be the point: "Let this rather be the first of many forays into the mysteries, as here disclosed but not destroyed. For it is in these things that we are most lost, as it is in these things alone that we must better be hidden" (*AWS*, 4). Jason Schwartz's *A German Picturesque* and *John the Posthumous* (2013) function in ways similar to Ben Marcus's *The Age of Wire and String.* Overly, although paradoxically descriptive, not to say ekphrastic in the case of *John the Posthumous,* these texts favor indecision and address their reader in ambivalent ways.

Notable American Women follows a more openly dystopian line, as it posits the takeover of a group of radical women dedicated to silence and stillness under the leadership of one Jane Dark. However, the dystopian streak of the text is counterbalanced, or perhaps strengthened, by the sheer grotesqueness of the situations it gives birth to. Differing in tone, more straightforward in its telling, Alexandra Kleeman's *You Too Can Have a Body Like Mine* follows in a similar dystopian vein, sketching an inscrutable world almost entirely given over to conformism, advertisement, and mass consumerism. Verging on surrealism, Sarah Rose Etter's *The Book of X*, with its "meat quarries" and bodily aberrations, is another novel that could find its place nearby on the map, along with Shelley Jackson's *The Melancholy of Anatomy*, or, in a different mode, Renee Gladman's series of novels devoted to Ravicka, an imaginary city-state with a shifting geography, a history, and a language all its own.

However, as for postapocalyptic fiction—as well as for any other genre for that matter—dystopian fiction may not be de facto speculative. Speculative fiction, as this book endeavors to define it, remains a borderline construct, an evanescent presence on the (experimental) fringes of literary American fiction. If it speculates, it also has to be speculated in return. Hence, speculative fiction cannot be codified as a genre per se—obeying fixed rules, following preordained patterns. If it can work itself into a specific genre, speculative fiction becomes so only insofar as it unsettles it in the process, opening it up onto some indetermination or, perhaps, some contingent orientations. In short, the genre—though at first recognizable—happens to be alienated from itself as the fiction takes its speculative turn. The genre as such ceases to operate somehow, veers off in unexpected directions. Or is radicalized in fortuitous ways, overlaid with foreign elements that interfere with its smooth, conventional rendition.[21]

•

Another region on the map could then be settled by works akin to investigative (rather than detective) fiction. If the link between postapocalyptics and speculative fiction can more or less appear self-evident due to the "dia-chronic" hiatus end-time stories instantiate, the association between mysteries to be investigated and speculation might seem more problematic, if only because as a genre such stories muster up what Barthes, in *S/Z*, defined as "the hermeneutic code" (17), and they thus call upon the reader, solicit, and ask for her interpretation as well as collaboration in the meaning-making process. In other words, this type of fiction does not openly aim to sever the relationship with and withdraw from the reading act. Rather, it eschews the absolutization of the text—in the etymological sense of the absolute recalled by Meillassoux in *After Finitude* (i.e., "severance" or "separateness from thought" [28])—that speculative fiction may strive to propound.

A novel like Blake Butler's *300,000,000* quite explicitly starts as an investigation into the mind, words, and deeds of mass murderer Gretch Nathaniel Gravey. Similarly, Azareen Van der Vliet Oloomi's *Fra Keeler* opens on the narrator's firm intention to investigate Fra Keeler's death—a death that, though apparently caused by lung cancer, "need[s] to be thoroughly investigated" (*FK*, 7). But instead of moving toward their resolution, both enigmas—very different though they are in nature and scope—tend to quite literally thicken around the narrator/investigator, in whose baffled image I as reader/critic have no real choice but to recognize myself: "Of course this is me searching for meaning. Likely there is no meaning but it is my job to persist in the identification of tragedy nailed to nothing, and so I will" (*3HM*, 85).

Such works lean on the speculative precisely to the extent that the mystery lodged at their hearts never really dissipates or *opens* up. As evoked by Morton in his introduction to *Realist Magic*, "*Mysteria* is a neuter plural noun derived from *muein*, to close or shut" (17). To various degrees, such works as Butler's, Van der Vliet Oloomi's, or even Danielewski's *House of Leaves* and Jane Unrue's *Love Hotel*, for that matter, all revolving around an insoluble "mystery," remain impenetrably shut; I can never truly find my way into them. Faced with the task of explaining them, I realize that this is virtually impossible, as the solution to such enigmas keeps receding farther and farther away from my grasp as I read. The mystery withdraws, deepens, leaves me with the paradoxical understanding that, in the words of *Fra Keeler*'s narrator, "to attempt to make sense in regards to all of this is senseless. Rather one must attempt to make senselessness" (*FK*, 70)—an agenda already stated quite explicitly at the outset of Shelley Jackson's *Melancholy of Anatomy*, whose opening story, "Heart"—thus irradiating the whole body of following texts—stages a narrator "trying to understand, by the ways in which, yes, I do *not* understand" (*MA*, 4).

Other texts to be found in this region of the map—which could include Michael Joyce's *Disappearance* or Shelley Jackson's *Riddance*—would thus develop similar frustrating strategies, simultaneously articulating and evaporating a mystery, shaping it while hiding it from view, positing and translating it in the same breath. All such texts would somehow appeal to the hermeneutic code yet at the same time, in the same move, would immediately jam or invalidate it, making it all the harder for me to respond to them on their own terms, since their own terms, it seems, perforce elude me.

●

The maps I have been elaborating, if only to give "speculative fiction" some substance, are what they are in the end—maps, representations held at an unbridgeable distance from the reality they aim to depict, sketches subject to a particular viewpoint. Though they strive to be faithful to their model, they may err here or there, or lose sight of their model's elusive nature. The scale might not be accurate, or some crucial details may have been overlooked, replaced by others utterly foreign to the topography in question. Perhaps such maps are misguiding more than they are helpful. They may lose me and belie their own inadequacy. Faced with the muteness and inscrutability of their model, they make, after all, their own reality. They have to.

For speculative fiction, as here defined and tentatively approached, eventually sighted in the pages that follow through thematic and conceptual lenses, remains hard to locate, difficult to pin down, impossible to grasp. As I've had occasion to say already, it may not even exist *as such*—pure invention on my part. Maybe. A daunting contradiction to get me started. A rhetorical, theoretical, heretical fiction. For can a text, any text, ever pretend to remain that radically inscrutable? That far withdrawn into itself as to bypass meaning and pursue sheer senselessness instead? Perhaps not. Or these lines I'm writing would not, could not be penned down. For they do make sense, after all. Or so I think, or hope. Some discourse has taken shape, arguments have been put forward, concepts forged, examples given, names named and quotes quoted; ideas have started circulating and extending their sway. Of course all of that could be downplayed, contradicted, disproved. For whether I like it or not, I'm still playing by the rules of critical writing. The so-called incomprehension I've been hinting at from the start is not, nor can it be, complete. Behind my various attempts, choosing my own "tools" and drafting my own "maps," I insist on trying to probe and open up these texts' mysteries, to lift their secrets—even if to say at the end of the day that they don't conceal any.

This, then, might be my failure eventually. Not having failed the way I claimed. Meaning is resilient. The telltale sign of my own critical prejudices.

Speculative fiction, in that sense, that is, in yet *another* sense, *is* a fiction; indeed it is.

The fiction of its own impossibility. The fiction of its own contradictions. A bet, a dare. A challenge. Posed. Suspended.

An end. In itself.

For itself.

That is, not for me.

But with me, yet.

Yes. This book *is* a contradiction.

SIGHTINGS

What follows is a list of possible sightings—what I've observed, now and then, in the course of my journeys through contemporary American fiction, at least through a specific region of it that is often deemed "experimental," or "innovative," or "difficult," or "avant-garde," or "anti-mimetic," or whatnot. What follows are my recollections of the times spent in strange speculative territories, along with the speculations my observations fed. Needless to say, these may be as much the offshoots of the textual objects I've stumbled upon as the suggestive signs of my own inadequacies to meet them on their own grounds—that is, as objects, obtuse artifacts devoid of meaning as such, granted that "meaning" is a construct, always meaning-for, or the product of correlation. Instead, says Timothy Morton, objects are "strange strangers," "irreducibly uncanny" (HO, 185); they remain mysterious, silent, weird, alien, withdrawn. It follows, then, that much of what is recounted in the subsequent pages is unavoidably prone to omissions, shortcomings, inventions, errors in judgment or of interpretation. Of course. It is necessarily incomplete, probably dubious, open to question; inconclusive at best.

I'm merely speculating, after all.

For the reasons noted above, speculative fiction is indeed hard to pin down or map—the maps attempted above, mere projections of routes not taken. It exists, if at all, in degrees or momentarily only, from specific viewpoints. It comes loose more often than not, slips through fingers, withdraws, and relocates elsewhere. What it has to offer in the end are mere fleeting glimpses. From which it is hard to reconstruct the whole picture, provided there is such a thing. Instead, I'm left with different bits and pieces, parts, fragments, surface reflections, possible decoys, which crisscross, duplicate, mirror one another while each time belying their singularity, their ungraspable fluidity—or "viscosity," to adapt Morton's notion of what, among other things, characterizes hyperobjects.

If the following pages do tell a story, it is one that cannot properly be told, one punctured with holes, beset with repetition, perhaps at times con-tradictory, equivocal, distorted, or partisan. It is a story that, between its lines, somehow tells of its own impossibility; a story that takes its specula-tive cue from the end of story *as such, reviewing narratives of the end and other speculative endings, to move on to what might lie behind or beyond sto-ry's ends: its reification, its* becoming-object—*no doubt a contradiction in terms—enhancing its materiality, foregrounding the text as object, whether through its "interface," in Alexander Galloway's definition of the term, or what Katherine Hayles referred to as the "technotext," leaving me no other choice,* dear Incomprehension, *but to conclude on my own critical failure eventually, in the face of what may be new forms of unreadability.*

Speculative Endings, Or "Rate This Apocalypse"

The end can come in several guises—floods, nuclear warfare, poison through language, rare disease, global pandemic, divine decree, or sheer contingency; you name it . . . With such ends in sight, though, often comes the notion of apocalypse, crudely understood as annihilation or total destruction—the end of the world, the end of times, the end of (great) narratives, of everything. Etymologically, however, and from a religious standpoint, the apocalypse signifies the advent of a revelation; it is an "uncovering," an "unveiling," the "revelation" of universal, everlasting truth. If it is pitted against, and can only occur in the midst of calamities—floods, fires, the unleashing of the Armageddon—the end of the world is also posited as the unveiling of meaning. In that sense, at least, the apocalypse is nothing short of a literary concept aimed toward signification, acceptance, understanding, and justification. The apocalypse *explains*, accounts for, makes sense of everything that led to it. In that regard, the apocalypse may well be anti-speculative.

But end-time stories in any garb do exemplify what Quentin Meillassoux defines as "dia-chronicity," a concept forged to "provide a general characterization of all such statements about events that are anterior or ulterior to every terrestrial-relation-to-the-world" (Meillassoux 2008, 112). In short, diachronic events such as "the end of the world" by definition unhinge all possible relations to "the world," making it impossible to *think* or *reason* with the event, given that in itself the latter destroys the very conditions on which thinking is grounded. Not only is there no world to think about anymore, but there is no one to think that thought.

As a genre—and like others perhaps[1]—apocalyptic fiction always falls short of its promise, for it can never truly, fully deliver on the apocalypse it claims to depict. The same holds, of course, for so-called postapocalyptic fiction, which belies its own premises from the outset: the end never is an end in itself—somewhere, something or someone does survive in or through time to pen their own sequel to the (failed) apocalypse.

Following this line of thought, one has to acknowledge the hiatus between the concept (the apocalypse) and the form it takes (the story that tells it). Something is not quite right; some unbalance prevails that threatens to collapse the narrative enterprise. Most stories—whether novels or films—in the (post)apocalyptic genre usually pass over that paradox, disregard the narrative impossibility on which, theoretically, they rest. They form the bulk of what is sold as postapocalyptic fiction and as such respond to codified generic standards, which they may undermine in the process or depart from in other ways. But because they tend not to question or abstain from thwarting the relation that reading presupposes, such works in themselves *appear* not to be speculative. What they lack or fail to heed somehow is the *diachronicity* lodged at the heart of (post)apocalyptics, which alone may render the work speculative in the sense used here—that, and the radical absence of, or challenge to, meaning that it entails.

•

For various, albeit different, reasons, Blake Butler's *Scorch Atlas* (2009) and Mark Doten's *Trump Sky Alpha* (2019) could be seen as postapocalyptic novels that do not try to brush off their speculative, "dia-chronic" grounds.

Butler's *Scorch Atlas* stages its own apocalyptics in quite tangible fashion. The book indeed bears the very marks of the serial destructions it not only details but also embodies on its physical surface. Through its visual layout, with its pages blotted, stained, sullied, and worn, the book displaces the catastrophe from the narrative level to the material, thus showing that as an artifact the book is not exempt from the cataclysms and strange deregulations or ruinations it tells about (see Fig. 2).

The book, the object held between the reader's hands, presents itself as a vestige, a remainder, and as such forces the questions: Where is one reading this book *from*? And *when* in relation to what it tells? The comfortable reception of the texts that compose *Scorch Atlas* is unavoidably threatened by the visually deteriorated object I have in my hands. True, this remains make-believe in the end—the object only simulates its own damaged aspect through its visual, trompe l'oeil components; yet the materiality of the book *as* book is part and parcel of its own aesthetics and as such begs to be taken into consideration. Any analysis of *Scorch Atlas* that doesn't include its material dimension and focuses

Figure 2. Double-page spread from Blake Butler's *Scorch Atlas*

on its "contents" exclusively misses the point, which precisely resides in the gaps between what the stories as stories may have to tell and the materiality that instantiates them, both mirroring and simultaneously invalidating the texts by ushering them into a problematic beyond, both in space and time, that I, as reader, am made to inhabit.

The strategy might seem less conspicuous in Ben Marcus's *The Flame Alphabet*, but it rests on similar diachronic grounds. The novel tells of a mysterious language disease that affects adults only and quickly gains pandemic proportions to prevent characters from communicating and corresponding. *The Flame Alphabet* thus functions along paradoxical lines, and the whole narrative enterprise can result only in a blatant contradiction: its narrator Sam may pledge never to "want anything in writing ever again" (*FA*, 220), but he does end up *writing* his own narrative of survival, somehow eschewing the language toxicity that ought to have rendered the undertaking impossible.

38 Sightings

By the end of the novel, three full years into the epidemic with yet no sign of the disease abating, Sam's immunity can be gained only by violently extracting the "Child's Play serum" from kids whose own immunity to the language toxin that plagues the world wears thin as they grow up. The context now proves eminently speculative, since Sam, secluded in his forest cabin, happens to be the only character able to communicate in language after having hoarded his serum supplies. This turns him into a lone survivor addressing no one supposedly fit or immune enough to be able to read him. No one, that is, but the reader, who is forcefully placed in a questionable position by the novel's conceptual framework.

> When I picture you examining this account, dangling each decaying page aloft with a tweezers, I wonder if you are alone, barricaded from someone with whom you once spoke freely. Are you reading this with assistance, an inhibitor cutting into the folds of your mouth? Does some cold, salted tonic sluice through your blood to give you shield, if briefly? Or is your protection something more, shall we say, bitter and problematic, achieved at a greater cost? (*FA*, 260)

The reader cannot but feel radically estranged from the world depicted in the novel, then, by the very fact that she *is* holding Sam's narrative in her hands and consuming its language in ways shown to be impossible; or if not, the "cost" entailed in the feasibility is revealed to be monstrous and inhuman, which Sam finally insists upon: "You are monstrous and unreal to me now, it is important that you know that" (*FA*, 261). As with *Scorch Atlas*, a gap thus opens between the text and its reception, pointing to some form of "dia-chronic" situation, a radical discrepancy between the time frame of the novel—one that does away with or denies all access to language—and the time frame of its reception, when language turns out to be operative still: "Perhaps you live in a time when someone else's harm is not bound up with your pursuit of words and you traffic easily with the acoustical weapon, the clustered scripts. Congratulations, if so. I remember those days, too" (*FA*, 261). What the novel eventually forces one to think, then—both using and having one use language, if only to articulate such a thought and derive meaning from it—is the thought of a world paradoxically, and impossibly, deprived of language, given that, as Wittgenstein famously put it, "*the limits of [one's] language* mean the limits of [one's] world" (Wittgenstein, 5.6), a world that thus inevitably dissolves and ultimately ends as meaning, understanding, and knowledge can no longer be articulated, processed, or shared.

•

One Hundred Apocalypses and Other Apocalypses—the title of Lucy Corin's 2013 collection challenges at once the concept of the apocalypse and the genre of (post)apocalyptic fiction. How many "unveilings" can there be without the event turning into a grotesque rehearsal with no purpose other than its own gratuitous reiteration? How many ends can the world be gratified with? And which ones, then, to choose from?

Any reader approaching Corin's book with specific expectations modeled on the conventions of the genre is in for a treat. Very few elements in the stories collected are indeed in keeping with the staples of the apocalyptic scenario and its standard fictional handling. No pandemics, no nuclear explosions, no alien invasions, no natural disasters, no walking dead. Or if there are traces of something remotely resembling an apocalypse here or there along the book's pages, as in the story "Godzilla versus the Smog Monster," for instance—in which, on a snowy day in the life of teen Patrick, "There's footage of raging, raging fire" featured on the news broadcast live in Patrick's biology class—the supposed apocalypse cues no apparent reaction and is often immediately downplayed by its casual treatment:[2] "[The fire] is raging in a box in the upper-right of the screen. Patrick's seen commercials for a videotape of fire you can play to make your television more festive—" (*OHA*, 56). Elsewhere, reminiscing about her parents, a narrator suddenly interrupts, thus ending the conversation (and the story) she's been having with a putative "audience" that could be herself, someone on the phone, a relative sitting beside her in the back of a car, the reader, or no one: "Oh wow, do you see that, that thing? What is it, a tornado over the water? It's pretty" (*OHA*, 130). End of story.

If Corin's reader, prompted by the book's title and expertly trained through the recent proliferation of postapocalyptic novels, shows, or movies in Western culture, might be on the lookout for the usual signs of fictional doom, she's bound to admit with Shelley Jackson's narrator in the story "Cancer" that, contrary to her expectations, "there [is] no epochal shift, no grind of planets swerving in their spheres" (*MA*, 68). Apocalypses come, apocalypses go, a mere grammatical trick in the end: "Apocalypto. Apocalypteis. Apocalyptei. Apocalyptomen. Apocalyptete. Apocalyptousi" (*OHA*, 132). And a new story is immediately embarked upon. A different one, or perhaps the same, told time and again, whose end remains shifty; the setting changes, the tone, the voice, characters in the foreground while somehow, somewhere in the background, like "the raging, raging fire" in California, the apocalypse keeps playing like an old movie on videotape that doesn't scare anyone anymore, a movie that could or should have been another one: "That afternoon [Patrick]'d gone into his father's dresser for a sweatshirt and found the tape there, at the bottom of the

40   Sightings

drawer where porn ought to be" (*OHA*, 52–53). Instead, Patrick finds *Godzilla vs. the Smog Monster*—itself, ironically enough, but one element in a long movie franchise. Corin obviously plays with apocalyptics as a genre, rehearses it, parodies it, subverts it, displaces it, thwarts it, thus deliberately opening a gap between the texts as such and their (failed) reception, programmed along lines and rules by which the texts will blatantly not abide.

Composed of three medium-length stories ("Eyes of Dogs," "Madmen," "Godzilla versus the Smog Monster") and a catalogue of "A Hundred Apocalypses" made up of short vignettes collected in four equal parts, *One Hundred Apocalypses and Other Apocalypses* builds up readerly expectations the better to question and frustrate them. This is made quite explicit in what is the longest "story" in the "A Hundred Apocalypses" section: "Baby Alive (2012) 109 minutes"—which consists of a short synopsis of a "part thriller, part reality TV" movie featuring Sissy Spacek and "MTV *Teen Mom* and *16 and Pregnant* reality stars" (*OHA*, 107). The synopsis is immediately followed by online starred reviews, ranging from one—"You should have a way to rate it zero stars" (109), the reviewer complains—to five stars—"The movie, enjoyable as it was, left me with many lingering questions" (108). As such, the story is *not* a story in any proper sense: it doesn't *tell* anything but instead merely reviews, lists, catalogues, compiles comments on an object that isn't available. One reviewer says it all in words that could easily be put on the lips of any fervent reader of hardcore postapocalyptic fiction with regard to Corin's own collection:

> I had that [Baby Alive] doll as a kid and was expecting a movie inspired by it, but if that's the case for you, you will be surely disappointed in this travesty of a film production. What we really want is to be entertained, instead you get something totally unexpected. (110)

Whether in the case of the movie or the book, the title proves deceptive; it posits an object answering preconceived notions of what it is or should be, and it summons a backdrop of conventions against which it can be appraised. But something doesn't quite work out the way it should. Or not the way it was expected to. What Timothy Morton in *Realist Magic* calls a "rift" has opened between the book's essence and its appearance: "The 'Rift' is irreducibly part of a thing: a thing is both itself and not-itself. I call this double truth of a thing its *fragility*" (*RM*, 199). In that sense, Corin's book showcases its fragility by being both apocalyptic and non-apocalyptic at the same time, hovering somewhere in this in-betweenness or withdrawing within itself.

•

Trump Sky Alpha by Mark Doten proceeds differently. Situated after a cyber-attack that prompted Donald Trump to start World War III in retaliation, thus causing the world (as we know it) to end in a nuclear apocalypse, the novel tells of the slow, painstaking reconstruction of the American society and its communication networks a year after the events. *Trump Sky Alpha* is a postapocalyptic novel in a very literal, conventional sense, then. But beyond its sensational take on Trump's presidency and a one-dimensional, grotesque, Twitter/Reddit/Facebook understanding of our contemporary Zeitgeist, *Trump Sky Alpha* is also concerned with the impact of any catastrophe on the very concept of story—that is, as a continuous, chronological sequence of events governed by causal links, adding up to form a whole unified picture *in the end*. What the novel, on the contrary, is somehow showcasing is that, *in the end*, nothing adds up, and meaning, deprived of its protocological apparatus, evaporates as mere ephemeral construct prone to contingency.

More amenable to the conventions of the genre, Doten's *Trump Sky Alpha* is told from multiple perspectives but focuses on Rachel mainly, a former journalist working on a piece for the *New York Times* when the world ended "on 1/28," a year or so prior to the story's present. The main plot revolves around Rachel's quest for the bodies of her wife and their daughter, both reported dead after the catastrophe. Rachel, as any other survivor would, needs closure. But this can only be brought about through a narrative that she can handle. In other words, Rachel is searching for a valuable, meaningful story to tell herself, knowing that in such circumstances this story is impossible.

This narrative line is mirrored by the fact that her former boss, Galloway, resurfaces after the disaster to task her with a new piece, scheduled for publication in the first authorized issue of the *New York Times*, which has been dormant for a year. In what could be read as a parody of pragmatism à la William James, for whom "you must bring out of each word its practical cash-value, set it at work within the stream of your experience" (James, 28), Galloway eventually admits to Rachel, who has been complaining about the futility of the piece in question—"Internet humor at the end of the world"—that it is the government or whatever/whoever replaced it in the aftermath that decides what story is good to tell and what story is not. As one general has it: "What works, though, with the nation's image of itself? That's in a sense the truth—what is real, and what the people will accept. Where those meet" (*TSA*, 159).

In the age of the internet or, to quote Alexander Galloway (from whom Doten's character borrows his last name), in the age of "protocol"—that is, "the principle of organization native to computers in distributed networks" (Galloway 2004, 3)—the very concept of "story," understood as a closed,

42 Sightings

self-sufficient, manageable unit, is at stake. In a sense, *Trump Sky Alpha* could be read as a dirge lamenting the end of story and the radical absence of meaning or *relief* that appears in its wake. As Rachel realizes while immersing into what remains of the internet after the 1/28 attack—tweets, memes, racist and sexist jokes, hashtags, trolls—"it was this, it was the structure of the internet, that had amplified the stupid and the evil, and at the same time flattened them, made them impossible to distinguish. Or made distinguishing them somehow beside the point" (*TSA*, 100).

The "structure of the internet" might be responsible for everything, according to Rachel, as it transformed what for many held a promise of radical freedom into an inescapable apparatus of control. For despite the widespread view that, "since new communication technologies are based on the elimination of centralized command and hierarchical control, it follows that the world is witnessing a general disappearance of control as such," that is not the case: "Protocol is how technological control exists after decentralization" (Galloway 2004, 8). Hence the "flattening" of everything witnessed by Rachel and the impossibility of distinguishing and differentiating, of ascribing importance or relevance to things, of making some of them *matter* by giving them "either more or less value" (Garcia, 31), that is, by making them signify and thus separating them from a plane constitutive of some *flat ontology*[3]—"a flat world in which each thing is neither more nor less than a thing" (Garcia, 31).

Doten's novel imagines the end of the world by crashing its virtual double, the internet that supplanted it IRL, as the saying goes. This enables Doten to explore the history of the internet from its military origins to its present-day vacuity via its protocological setup. So doing, the novel's structure makes itself loose and wobbly, moving back and forth from Trump impersonation to Rachel's story, from inner debate to the obsessive ramblings of cyberterrorist Birdcrash, shifting genres from postapocalyptics to political satire to queer aesthetics to sci-fi. The novel thus formally mimics the decentralized, nonhierarchical feel of the internet; it comes in fragments, disseminated contents, and deliberately eschews closure, ending instead with images of a run "into the white" (*TSA*, 285)—the whiteness of the snow covering Prospect Park as much as the whiteness of the page that goes silent and blank, killing off the story. As such, *Trump Sky Alpha* could be said to embody the paradigmatic shift that Friedrich Kittler pointed out in *Discourse Networks 1800/1900*, a shift "from a discourse driven by meaning and sense, to our present milieu of pattern and code" (Galloway 2004, 18). For as Galloway makes clear, "protocol is *against interpretation*" and is alien to "the sciences of meaning (representation/interpretation/reading)" (Galloway 2004, 52), a move that is itself included in *Trump*

Sky Alpha, whose "story"—which perhaps consists in a metafictional quest for story—comes undone somehow, appearing frayed on its fringes, multilayered, and lacking a center to hold it together.

·

Perhaps on the surface less compliant with the conventions of the genre than Butler's *Scorch Atlas* and Doten's *Trump Sky Alpha*, David Markson's *Wittgenstein's Mistress* could be seen as another speculative take on postapocalyptic fiction for somewhat similar formal reasons. A mere glance at the novel makes one feel its disjointed aspect as lines visibly accumulate without ever consolidating into full-fledged paragraphs. Not quite as refined yet as what it would later become in such (anti-)novels as *Reader's Block, This Is Not a Novel,* or *Vanishing Point,* all consisting in clearly spaced-out textual chips, Markson's fragmentary technique points to the rarefaction of the novelistic. In lieu of plot and story line proper, the reader is offered a concatenation of loose historical anecdotes and coincidences that float through the text like remnants or ruins from a culture on the verge of extinction—if not extinct already.

Though rid of all the sensational parts, the premise to *Wittgenstein's Mistress* is in that sense almost unambiguously postapocalyptic—"almost," because exposed through the recollections and ramblings of an unreliable narrator who from the outset declares that "All of this [is] indisputably true" even if, of her own accord, she "may well have been mad" (*WM*, 9). Willy-nilly, the narrator thus presents us with a hardly reconcilable alternative between indisputable truth, on the one hand, and sheer madness, on the other. By and by, "Kate" (33)—unless her name is "Helen" (228)—lets it be known that she's the only survivor of some unnamed catastrophe, which makes of her the last human being on earth. However, the cause for this is never explicated. Coupled with the narrator's madness, such lack of narrative explanation hints at a radical absence of reason, which eventually locks the narrator up into her own memories, reconstructions, speculations, fallacies, assumptions, contradictions, all of which act up as a smoke screen behind which the story, *as* story—that is, as a sequence of events enmeshed in causes and consequences—evaporates or, to use Harman's term, withdraws.

As the mention of Wittgenstein's name in the novel's title suggests—a title that already signals its interferential aesthetics, incongruously crediting gay Wittgenstein with a straight mistress—what Markson stages is a philosophical problem revolving around the opposition between realism and idealism. The question raised by the narrator's predicament is whether or not reality, or whatever's left of it, exists independently of what she, or anyone else for that matter,

44   Sightings

may think of it. The narrator admits: "Meantime that question of things existing only in one's head may still be troubling me slightly, to tell the truth" (152). Hence, the novel's referential plane, although exacerbated through its intertextual frenzy, constantly wobbles: "What do any of us ever truly know, however?" asks Kate time and again (49/97/103/227), thus challenging her own painstaking, often dubious edifice of cultural references and quotes. Kate may frame her question—whose plainly rhetorical aspect is made manifest through her use of first-person plural at a time when the reality of "us" has supposedly ceased to exist—in purely epistemological terms, knowledge nonetheless remains indexed to the reality that it aims to match. In the end, what matters may not be whether Kate's telling the truth so much as *what* constitutes the very material grounds upon which that so-called truth could be made to rest. Of course, if Kate alone survived whatever event or catastrophe caused the world to end and all life-forms to be wiped off the surface of the earth, no one remains to *verify* what she claims to be or not to be the case. Yet if "the world is everything that is the case"—a sentence Kate somehow remembers from Wittgenstein, although she has "no idea what [she] mean[s] by the sentence [. . .] just typed" nor where it may come from (78)—then the abolition of what constitutes a world leaves one stranded in the midst of loose, untethered fragments made up of emptied-out language. *Wittgenstein's Mistress* may as such turn the premise of *The Flame Alphabet* around: where, in Marcus's novel, characters drift about with no language to speak, in Markson's text, language, with no one else to speak it anymore but Kate, appears autonomized. The sheer, almost automatic repetition and proliferation of such set phrases as "to tell the truth" or "as a matter of fact," "as it happened" or "incidentally," "doubtless" or "in any event," tend to suggest that once "everything that was the case" disappears, language runs idle on the page, disconnected from any reality.

It may be, then, that reality is only in Kate's head, after all; yet whether or not that is the case, it remains radically inaccessible, withdrawing further and further behind the language that might be desperately trying to evoke it. Indeed, Kate keeps reminding herself that she is typing everything and that, therefore, the reality of what she thinks is eclipsed by the language through which it is thought, occasioning some sort of infinite regress into the dismantling of the real:

> The cat I began to think about instead was the cat outside of the broken window in the room next to this one, at which the tape frequently scratches when there is a breeze.
>
> Which is to say that I was not actually thinking about a cat either,

there being no cat except insofar as the sound of the scratching reminds me of one.

As there were no coins on the floor of Rembrandt's studio, except insofar as the configuration of the pigment reminded Rembrandt of them.

As there was, or is, no person at the window in the painting of this house.

As for that matter there is not even a house in the painting of this house, should one wish to carry the matter that far.

Certain matters would appear to get carried certain distances whether one wishes them to or not, unfortunately. (*WM*, 62–63)

Kate's writing thus keeps withdrawing into itself, taking back whatever claims it may have staked at any time, and eventually bypasses what lies at the heart of Kate's aborted narrative: the cause of her traumatic solitude, the reason why the world ended, leaving her to curate for a world abandoned by history—a world composed of bits and pieces, of facts and "matter" impossible to unify and make sense of.

As a narrator, Kate hardly shares anything about herself. What personal item she does entrust her typewriter with is the death of her son—alternatively named Adam, Simon, and Lucien. Yet she never ventures beyond mere anecdotes, and whenever her account gets too personal she suddenly retracts and stops writing:

I have snapshots of Simon, of course. For some time one of them was in a frame on the table beside my bed.

But quite suddenly I do not feel like typing any more of this, for now.

I have not been typing, for perhaps three hours.

All I had anticipated doing, actually, was going to the spring for water. (*WM*, 69)

Despite its sutured, continuous aspect, Kate's text appears to be riddled with holes and gaps that prevent the narrative from ever taking shape and momentum.

As such, *Wittgenstein's Mistress* remains a motley assemblage of quotes, rumors, anecdotes, reminiscences out of which it is hard to make heads or tails. Although discreetly premised upon the postapocalyptic genre, the novel thoroughly resists it while eluding the reader's grasp; the reader is left with a puzzle of cultural references sometimes truncated, misquoted, erroneous,

46 Sightings

misplaced—references that only occlude the truly narrative dimension of Kate's personal story, drowned out in the midst of mere odds and ends that may echo but never really harmonize.

•

The apocalyptic underpinnings of all fiction were revealed, as it were, by Frank Kermode in his canonical essay *The Sense of an Ending*, inasmuch as the apocalypse, as narrative, answers a basic human "need in the moment of existence to belong, to be related to a beginning and to an end" (Kermode, 4). The teleological pattern of any (conventional) story, based on the linear understanding of time, is modeled on an apocalyptic motif whose aim is to make ends meet, so to speak; to harmonize between beginning and end, show how the one leads to the other and how, consequently, it all *makes sense*. "Apocalypse depends on a concord of imaginatively recorded past and imaginatively predicted future, achieved on behalf of us, who remain 'in the middest'" (Kermode, 8). Fiction, when conventionally conducted along Aristotelian lines, thus follows a narrative arc oriented toward an end that acts as revelation and epiphany: meaning is revealed, sense is made—the text can be related to, understood, seized, grasped, rationalized.

What end(s) does the text serve? That might be one of the questions raised by speculative fiction when it waxes postapocalyptic. Corin's agenda in that regard is stated as early as the opening story of her collection *One Hundred Apocalypses and Other Apocalypses*, "Eyes of Dogs," a rewriting of Hans Christian Andersen's tale "The Tinderbox." The fairy tale, as a genre, is quite adamantly directed toward an unambiguous, formulaic ending, and it is perhaps no wonder that Corin's collection, being assumedly about "apocalypses," opens with a story whose generic conventions channel the need for an ending. Yet at some point "Eyes of Dogs" splits into two different narrative threads, one appearing in the main text's margins in smaller font. Ironically enough, the variant of the text pursued in the margins—that is, literally dislodged, displaced, removed, appended, offset—is the one providing the traditional ending of Andersen's tale:

> there come the dogs who tear the king and queen to pieces and also much of the town and its people. Those who remain make the soldier king, and he marries the princess, who is said to enjoy being queen very much—all plausible enough, except the part about the flour. (*OHA*, 17)

True to Andersen's ending, this version is however undermined by the narrator's final critical remark that finds fault with a narrative detail—the use of "flour from a bag with a hole in it stashed under the girl's skirt" to track the princess's whereabouts (17). A sense of disappointment or frustration is perceptible, and is all the more ironical, as it fails to comment on the overall meaning—or *morality*—of such an ending, namely, what the other, alternative thread of the story, which makes up the main body of text, implicitly points to: "and what about the dogs, what about the dogs, saying nothing, so blue and enormous, with their eyes, with everything in the world, fierce and dopey and incomprehensible. Never coming to our rescue even when we don't deserve it" (18).

This variant substitutes for the traditional ending an alternate one in which the dogs do not come to the soldier's rescue, *even if he doesn't deserve it.* This new ending can be read not only as a comment on the tale's usual conclusion, ousted in the text's margins and thus highlighting the moral discrepancy or lack of harmony between the character's actions and their outcome, but also as a metafictional withdrawal exposing the end as such and the narrative ground it rests on, along with the purpose it supposedly serves. Both endings, in their own opposite ways, point to some frustration, a sense of dissatisfaction, an ending that is immediately remarked upon as inappropriate and that, as such, fails to conclude and freeze or reveal meaning in any convincing way.

So much for the promised apocalypse then. Or if there is one, it has to come with the realization that the end doesn't settle much but leaves a lot to be desired. Both endings, in their symmetrical renditions, hark back to, fold back upon, and eventually cancel one another. Somehow similar in spirit, they cannot be reconciled or taken together, thus ultimately stressing their mutual *incomprehensibility.*

•

Like Corin's *One Hundred Apocalypses and Other Apocalypses*—whose title points to the book's thematic unity around a unique concept—*Scorch Atlas* by Blake Butler is more than just a collection of stories. Formally and thematically, the book revolves around destruction, disaster, disease, catastrophe. Each story tells about the consequences of some untold cataclysm, real or imagined, lived through or merely felt, and depicts the remains of a world gone stale and meaningless, broken and unrecognizable. Unlike Corin's book, though, *Scorch Atlas* abounds in bona fide apocalyptic imagery. As its main title indicates, Butler's collection-slash-novel provides a series of textual maps charting catastrophe on diverse scales, from the disappearance of the sea or the flooding of a whole neighborhood to a family breakdown or strange birth of some unknown proportions, whose aftermath each time becomes the piece's focus. As such, *Scorch Atlas* is unambiguously postapocalyptic in its generic orientations. The book's visual layout—reproducing soiled, crumpled, damp, rotten, moldy, stained, blackened paper—from the start projects its reader again and again into a time frame posited *after* whatever catastrophe may have occurred, thus casting them in the role of sheer survivor. Whatever happened, you have been spared; if you're reading those texts, hearing those voices and their testimonies, it means you're still alive somehow. Somewhere, sometime. A ghost, a remnant, a leftover, a miracle. Count your blessings. The book you're holding in your hands is a vestige from other times, another barely remembered era; the book is blessed indeed. Reading is a gift. Enjoy it while you can.

•

"Eyes of Dogs" having complicated the notion of ending, there is not much else to do for *One Hundred Apocalypses and Other Apocalypses* but to enter into repeat mode. Cued from its initial cancellation, the collection is indeed bound to reiterate the same gesture over and over again. The story "Madmen," second in the collection and following in the wake of "Eyes of Dogs," ironically points to this iterative pattern by opening on the narrator's having her period for the first time: "The day I got my period, my mother and father took me to pick my madman" (*OHA*, 21). This day of all days in the narrator's life is thus bound to repeat, first in a cyclical series. The end—or *period*—sought for by the apocalyptic model is here replaced by the starting point of some cyclical, *periodic* event that needs to be marked through tradition and ritual: the selection of a madman from a local facility. This day is nonetheless full of apocalyptic implication for the narrator, who admits: "I know it sounds stupid, but this was a big day for me, and everything felt like it might be important at any second" (25).

The choice or selection of the madman is serious business indeed—"No one cares about this more than I do" (28). It underlines an "epochal shift," in Shelley Jackson's words, marks a *crisis* in the narrator's life;[4] it arrests time and forever changes its course by offering the possibility of a revelation: "This decision is going to make me who I am," she confesses (*OHA*, 36).

Yet after reviewing some of the madmen's histories, the story veers from this life-defining orientation when the narrator's mother suddenly objects to her daughter's choice, leading her to opt at the last minute for a madman she hasn't seen, picked almost at random: "I didn't throw a dart, but the way I chose my madman had very little magic in it, and what should I learn from that?" (41). What started then as a day full of promise has eventually led to frustration and disappointment: "If the world looked different so far, the difference was it didn't look so symbolic. That is not what a girl wants when she comes of age" (45).

The story draws to a conclusion as "the sun was starting to set" (48). With the close of day, the narrator—whose mother at this point may or may not have committed suicide—is still looking for some epiphany, framed by stereotypically romantic imagery. The narrator is seated beside Armand, her mute madman, watching the sun setting in the distance:

> Like a lookout at the prow of a ship of fools, I put my hand to my forehead and squinted toward the sun into the distance. I could spy with my little eye the roof of the shed, partway down the hill, and sparks like tiny fires in the low water in the creek, and the woods like a curtain with everything beyond darker than ever, sucking up the light. Soon the sun was setting enough that it was past the time when the pieces of the world are sharp and distinct from each other and on to when everything becomes one fuzzy mass. Our eyes saw and then didn't see the forms we knew were in there, and then saw again for a second, and then were just making it up. Okay, that's what my eyes were doing, anyhow. (*OHA*, 48)

Vision and understanding, look hard though she might, somehow fail to come to the narrator: the "curtain" only frames darkness, and what light remains is immediately "suck[ed] up," leaving but "one fuzzy mass" behind in what appears to be mere child's play (*I could spy with my little eye*). By then, revelation, should it have come, is irremediably "past the time."

"At some point," the narrator eventually acknowledges, "I was going to have to say something to [the madman], and if he had a voice he was probably going to say something back. Maybe something would change then" (48). The narrator's left suspended in time, between past (*I was . . .*) and future (*. . . going to*), unable it seems to tune one onto the other, apocalyptic-style. "Instead of saying something, I thought about the weathervane, spinning, because I wanted the moment to last forever" (48). Probably knowing it wouldn't. For the cycle is only beginning. Rather, associated with mutability and change, the weathervane proves incapable of freezing time, thus in fine pointing to the collapse of the symbolic as the world—a world that unshakably keeps turning on its axis—seems to have lost all symbolic value and meaning in the narrator's eyes, which in the setting darkness don't *see* anything so much as they are "*doing*." Doing what? Hard to say—compensating or "making up" for what, perhaps, they've failed to see or catch.

•

50   Sightings

The way she frames it, the narrator in Corin's "Madmen" is not the one who sees, or fails to see, but her eyes, acting independently of the character's volition— or so it seems. Alone with her madman, what the character is somehow witnessing, but cannot as such register, is the slow eradication of the world and its forms around her, whose only counterpart is to be found in the abolition of the narrator's *I*, which she can only reclaim, or try to, through the use of italics stressing the pun eye/I—"*my* eyes." "Madmen" thus closes while raising the issue of correlationism.

Markson's *Wittgenstein's Mistress* might itself be playing a similar drama— the metaphorical drama of correlationism. For as Kate herself realizes, the list of anecdotes that she's compiling may or may not be connected, both together and to her life story; in other words, they may or may not weave a bigger picture to which she could relate, one made up of *co*-incidences, of resemblances accreting eventually to make a point or other that, unavoidably, keeps eluding her: "For some reason while I was peeing I thought about Lawrence of Arabia. . . . I can think of no connection between making a pee and Lawrence of Arabia" (23); "Though perhaps there is no connection there" (36); "I am in no way certain what this is connected to either, but I suspect it is connected to more than I once believed it to be connected to" (56). As she strives to discover connections amid her random or associative recollections, Kate may be trying to tell *a* story, after all, to build or find a narrative that could serve to make sense of it all, to weave every strand together into a bigger picture or *text* that would not be her own doing, in which some autonomous meaning could emerge, some purpose or revelation independent of her—the better, perhaps, not to have to tell *her* own story. Hence Kate's more and more frequent avoidance of the first person to disengage herself as much as possible from her own text, swapping on crucial occasions the subjective "I" for the impersonal "one":

> There being surely as many things one would prefer never to re-
> member as there are those one would wish to, of course.
>   Such as how drunk Adam had gotten on that weekend, for instance,
> and so did not even think to call for a doctor until far too late.
>   Well, or why one was not there at the house one's self, those same
> few days.
>   Being young one sometimes does terrible things. (*WM*, 225)

Kate's initial concern for meaningful connections somehow mirrors ours, as we know or suspect early on that Kate's own narrative lies in connecting dots. But as we do, or try to, we're slowly realizing that how these dots connect may not form a picture so much as delimit a void or absence. If some revelation transpires in the end, it is precisely to be found in the text's gaps and what it leaves unsaid.

As Wittgenstein's conclusion to his *Tractatus Logico-Philosophicus* famously put it, a conclusion that Kate, quite significantly, does *not* recall: "What we cannot speak about we must pass over in silence" (Wittgenstein, 89). Which might very well be what *Wittgenstein's Mistress* is all about: given that the world ends and, ending, leaves one utterly alone, stranded in the midst of all these absences, how does one cope? What is left to say or "speak about"? How does one not turn mad, that is, absolutely deprived of reason, in the face of such radical impossibility to *relate*? What are Kate's messages, "in the beginning" and in the end, if not the half-hearted refusal of that impossibility?

Here, then, lies the truly speculative dimension of the novel: its ability to make the reader feel this radical absence, to make one think that which experience prevents them from thinking *about* at the cost of renouncing reason, to inhabit a language that, following the early Wittgenstein, may be purely logical yet absolutely void.[5] A world in which narrative as such is made de facto impossible. No wonder then that Kate's left with a number of (pseudo) facts she doesn't know quite how to handle, thus seeing herself as the last historian on earth (*WM*, 189), whose task consists in merely "curating" the world for no one:

> But then what is there that is not in my head?
> So that it is like a bloody museum, sometimes.
> Or as if I have been appointed the curator of all the world.
> Well, as I was, as in a manner of speaking I undeniably am. (227)

As such, Kate is slowly burying or putting an end to (hi)story by compiling and listing things, names, facts, anecdotes, or "data" confirming all but the emptiness of her residual world. Claims D. F. Wallace: "Her world is 'empty' of all but data that are like the holes in a reticular pattern, both defined & imprisoned by the epistemic strands she knows only she can weave" (Wallace, 226). Yet if, for Wallace, "weave she does," it seems that that is not quite the case—she does *not* "weave" but merely lists, enumerates, posits, remembers, distorts, forgets, mistakes, jumps, switches, reiterates, skips. Perhaps Wallace is right, after all, when a few lines down he claims that "Kate makes 'external' history *her own*" (Wallace, 226). Yet for that matter does she truly tell her own story, "weave" together the elements and events that make it up? The lack of emotional engagement—which, true, might be a telltale sign to the contrary—somehow tends to show how Kate acts as an "objective witness," a sheer recorder of so-called facts more than a storyteller or historiographer weaving them into a story proper.

52 Sightings

Hence her acknowledgement at the end that perhaps she could or should have been writing a *novel* instead of just typing everything she's been typing:

> So that what I realized almost simultaneously, in fact, was that quite possibly I might have to start right from the beginning and write something different altogether.
> Such as a novel, say. (*WM*, 229)

The novel—"an absolutely autobiographical novel" (230)—that Kate eventually contemplates is precisely the one she does *not* write, one in which the reader would be made to "just imagine how the heroine would feel . . . and how full of anxiety she would be" (230). That is, we are asked to imagine what she has deliberately left out of her account in the preceding pages, never indulging in any pathos in the course of her typing and thus leaving in the end her feelings and anxiety to be *imagined* indeed, for they're never actually woven into the fabric of the text.

Of course one question at this point is what would "an absolutely autobiographical novel" consist in. Kate provides some clues before admitting that writing one such novel would leave her no better off than she actually is.

So perhaps she *did* write it in the end. Maybe *Wittgenstein's Mistress* is nothing but that: "an absolutely autobiographical novel"—a truly autotelic, solipsistic novel cut off (*absolutely*) from all possibilities of ever relating one's life story when the world, everything that was the case, has ended. Thus ending all stories in the process.

•

For what sort of "stories" are there to be told at the end of the world? How can such stories make sense, or even pretend to, when sense *is* what is being radically shattered in the event—a question also raised by Doten's *Trump Sky Alpha*? For "sense" and "world," as argued in Jean-Luc Nancy and Aurélien Barrau's *What's These Worlds Coming To?*, might be coextensive concepts indeed. Hence, if not quashed altogether, these stories of/at the end of the world cannot but appear dubious at best—which is what Blake Butler's fiction often suggests.

For the worlds depicted—a problematic word—in Butler's works are no longer such, no longer "worlds" as usually conceived. In the words of Nancy and Barrau: today "the sense of 'world' is not only undecided and multiple: It has become the crucial point where all of the aspects and stakes of 'sense' in general become tied together" (Nancy and Barrau, 1). This radical dissociation—the ruin of both "world" and "sense" as concepts—is what Butler's fiction might be about, at least to the *problematic* degree that there can be any "aboutness" with regard to such dissociation, the obvious effect of which is precisely to ruin representation. The postapocalyptic devastations of *Scorch Atlas*, the dystopian setting of *Sky Saw*, the (onto-)logical aberrations of *There Is No Year*, the extreme violence lodged at the heart of *300,000,000*, or the radical acts of disappearance at the vacant heart of *Alice Knott* all say as much. Given such context, then, Butler's "worlds" or what remains of them are pervaded with an unavoidable sense of chaos; disorder, ruin, wreckage, loss, confusion all suffuse the texts both thematically and conceptually.

A case in point might be found in *Scorch Atlas*. As early as its title page, something appears irrevocably amiss and points to the deregulations at the heart of the texts that make up the book. Subtitled "A Belated Primer," *Scorch Atlas* is wedged in a paradoxical time frame, halfway and irreconcilably between a sense of belatedness and inchoateness. Something is about to happen that is already over; unless something that already played out is just about to play again. Once the end has happened, who's to say in what direction time flows? If it flows still. If there is still time.

Coupled with its reprise, the title—that is, the starting point or the origin from which the text unfolds—is made to stutter. On the very "threshold" of the text, as Genette called it, the reader is made aware that something is already out of order; the threshold somehow caves in underneath the reader's feet and, instead of propelling them forward, arrests them in their tracks. Another subtitle farther down the page reads *"no window,"* thus suggesting no point of entry into the text while alternate titles proliferate and all unavoidably point to the bankruptcy of naming. One already senses that language can no longer adequately designate its object, nor can it properly refer to the real, thus from the outset severing sign from referent and stressing the problematic, unrelatable nature of the reality that the language aims to cover in the pages that follow. How and what can language signify if the world in which it stems from has ended? What kind of "atlas" can this book draw in the absence of "world"? The catastrophe the book feeds on is also, perhaps first and foremost, one that befalls language and disrupts the mechanisms of sense-making and representation.

•

While California's burning in the distance, Patrick in "Godzilla versus the Smog Monster" is faced with his parents' imperturbability as they hardly leave their plush bedroom upstairs. The third story in Corin's *One Hundred Apocalypses and Other Apocalypses* is the one that gets closest to the usual apocalyptic setting. Yet the sense of threat and destruction that has been raging in the background and that momentarily seemed to benumb the world—"The fire is

54 Sightings

spreading. It's past Fresno. It's consuming the state but has yet to cross over its lines. Suspects accumulate, worldwide. The anchor chokes up, waxes and relates" (*OHA*, 60)—is at once defused by the growing apathy around Patrick: "Two weeks and two days later California is kaput. It's a heaving, flattened, blowing, billowing mass of ash and soot and toxicity. It's Saturday morning, and Patrick's parents are eating breakfast side by side in bed, kind of an ordeal because they had to go downstairs, make it, and then carry it up on trays" (68). With California wiped off the map of the world, the sense of the word "ordeal" absurdly changes to include such petty everyday acts as making breakfast. The ostensible apocalyptic event featured in the background is treated in the same way as Patrick apprehends the movie, in which the Smog Monster is but "a wad of wet-looking gray cotton with static red eyes" and "the Holocaust landscape" is designed with "bodies making a pattern you could turn into wallpaper" (52).

The apocalypse is here processed as mere decor, emptied of all narrative momentum. Even when Patrick's friend Sara vanishes, voluntarily heading to California or so it seems, Sara's drawing comparisons with the Smog Monster in Patrick's imagination. The mystery surrounding her disappearance is once more defused when the story goes back full circle as Patrick asks his dad why the Godzilla video was hidden in his sweater drawer, convinced that "a person doesn't just hide things for no reason" (71).

Maybe in the end that is the truly apocalyptic peak the story has been building toward so far, which takes Patrick's dad by surprise yet leaves Patrick himself paradoxically vulnerable, an umbrella in his hands that "shift[s] in his grasp so that it's pointing at the bed, and the way he's holding it, he's shocked to notice, is like he's holding his dick" (72).

> It's the first time Patrick's looked at his father and really seen himself there, in the past and the future at once. It shakes him. It makes a little dust rise. He tries to think of reasons to hide a video, other than what's recorded on it—ways it could be symbolic as an object. He thinks, *Something he watched when he cheated on my mother.* He thinks, *Something he never watched because the day he rented it he embezzled money at work and got away with it ever since.* And that's the limit of his imagination. For years, when he dreams embarrassing dreams of Sara, she's the Smog Monster, swooping over hills and valleys, a friendly toxic pollution freak from outer space. But one day when he's a man, out there living in a freezing city, such as it is, working at a job, playing in a band at least for now, he looks out his window through the frost forest and what he sees, finally, does not feel like land that is his or belongs to him in any way. (72–73)

The way the story ends again points to the same sense of discrepancy between past and future: the gap or *epochè* rent by the apocalyptic event—here as inconsequential as the presence of an old sci-fi, postapocalyptic videotape in a father's dresser—cannot be mended; nor can it mean anything to which the protagonist could relate, faced instead with the end of his own imagination and the absence, as at the end of "Madmen," of any symbolic intent, other than Patrick's eventual and final ("finally") sense of alienation and unbelonging.

•

As philosopher Jean-Luc Nancy claims in *After Fukushima*, today's regime is one "of general equivalence" (Nancy, 5). Each new catastrophe doesn't necessarily impact the world in equivalent ways, though: "Not all catastrophes are equivalent, not in amplitude, not in destructiveness, not in consequences" (3). Yet the interdependence of the social, economic, technological, and political realms makes this equivalency inescapable in any catastrophe's aftermath, whatever its scope and scale, as it "absorbs . . . all the spheres of existence of humans, and along with them all things that exist" (5).

Scorch Atlas, by multiplying catastrophes and replaying diverse ends-of-the-world from one story to the next, may literally depict this "regime of general equivalence," rendered visible as early as the book's title page, which offers thirteen alternate titles or subtitles rendered equivalent by the semantics of the conjunction "or" that lodges between them (see Fig. 3).

A general sense of interchangeability and hesitancy is thus immediately made manifest, reinforced by the presence of the *Contents* page (*SA*, 15), which like the title page comprises thirteen titles, referring to the thirteen full-length stories *Scorch Atlas* is composed of—with the exception of the intercalary one-page pieces wedged between each, not listed in the *Contents*. Incidentally, "Want for Wish for Nowhere" appears twice, both as a story title on the *Contents* page and as one of the book's thirteen alternate subtitles on the title page. As for the story "Bath or Mud or Reclamation or Way In/Way Out," it intrinsically repeats the same renaming gesture deployed on the title page, thus toying with a similar sense of equivalence. This move implicitly suggests that each story's title, as well as being provisional and arbitrary, could be used as subtitle to refer to some other reality beyond the text it supposedly and unmistakably designates, while the subtitles may be extending beyond themselves too, to riff on the contents of the listed stories, again creating a sense of reciprocity and homology.

Such equivalence and interchangeability already enact a catastrophe of sorts while contributing to the book's *critical* operations, from the start undermining its signifying regime. As Nancy explains, catastrophe finds its roots in Greek tragedy and seeks resolution at the end of a play through catharsis

56 Sightings

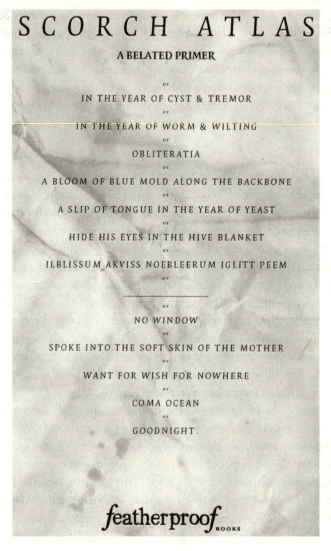

Figure 3. Table of contents ("A Belated Primer") from Blake Butler's *Scorch Atlas*

(Nancy, 7). Apocalyptic fiction, by playing out the human obsession with its irrevocable finality—in an age of blind terror, widespread pandemics, global warming, and the threat of nuclear annihilation—no doubt partakes of something cathartic, even tragic, to the extent that this doom promised to humankind and the world may be born of our own hubris. Yet with the contemporary "equivalence of catastrophes," Nancy explains,

We live no longer either in tragic meaning nor in what, with Christianity, was supposed to transport and elevate tragedy to divine salvation.[6] Nor can we take refuge in any sort of Confucian, Taoist, or Buddhist wisdom: Equivalence does not allow it, despite all our good intentions. We are being exposed to a catastrophe of meaning. (Nancy, 8)

Scorch Atlas could be seen as the acting out of such a "catastrophe of meaning." The implication to be derived from the book's title page and its play with equivalences is precisely that reference and meaning are at stake, which is also implied by the iterations of the same motifs ("In the Year of Cyst & Tremor"/"In the Year of Worm & Wilting"/"A Slip of Tongue in the Year of Yeast"[7]) or variations (*Scorch Atlas*/"Bloom Atlas"), as well as the assonantic or paronomastic intimations ("A <u>Bloom</u> of <u>Blue</u> <u>M</u>old Along the <u>Back</u>bone," "<u>Hi</u>de His <u>Eyes</u> in the <u>Hi</u>ve Blanket," "<u>W</u>ant for <u>W</u>ish for No<u>wh</u>ere"), all drawing attention to purely literal effects detrimental to meaning as such. The disintegration of meaning is further made clear with the alien subtitle "*Ilblissum Akviss Noebleerum Iglitt Peem*," which somehow harbingers the breakdown of communication that the diverse stories all stage, while riffing with Butler's novella *Ever*, published the same year and also pervaded with similar incomprehensible language. Such gibberish, passing itself off as foreign language, will incidentally resurface in such texts as "Seabed" or "Bath or Mud or Reclamation or Way In/Way Out":

"BUGMERMENNUNMMEM USSIS LUMMMM." (*SA*, 81)
"Blassmix buntum veep?" (83)
"YHIKE DUM LOOZY FA FA, she said. ZEERZIT ITZ BLENN NOIKI FAHCH." (120)

Before one even starts reading the texts composing *Scorch Atlas*, then, the title page somehow orchestrates the dissolution of meaning, thus intimating that something has already taken place that makes it impossible for the reader or anyone to keep playing the same interpretive game. Unsurprisingly, after nonsense and gibberish, the next logical step in the process appears to be none other than the eradication of language altogether, as registered mid-page in the form of a blank or missing phrase, an erasure or cancellation, a withdrawal, a line drawn in lieu of subtitle: "_____."

•

Stuck there on the text's threshold the reader already feels its foundations shake, its edifice wobble. One hardly knows how to handle the book, turn a

58   Sightings

grayish ruined page only to witness the same decay spreading at them, spilling from the book like some contagious disease. You hesitate. Then begin reading, tentatively. A couple of sentences. You stop. Reflect. Reread. Something's not quite right. You don't know what really. The language is simple enough. The grammar holds. Yet from the outset, it feels like there's something malevolent, a replicant germ infusing the air around the reader. The page is mottled gray, streaking. Words hardly stand out. You read again. They seem to curdle on the page, and as you try to understand them, you realize, just an impression, that they don't mean or convey so much as ooze or cough up their poison—pure performativity, harsh rhythm and baleful sound:

> We watched our dirt go white, our crop fields blacken. Trees collapsed against the night. Insects masked our glass so thick we couldn't see. The husks of roach and possum filled the gutters. Every inch mucked with white film. All spring the sky sat stacked with haze so high and deep it seemed a wall, a lidless cover sealing in or sealing out. Those were stretched days, croaking. I don't know what about them broke. I don't know why the rain came down in endless veil. It streaked the cities, wiped the wires. It splashed the dust out from our cricked knees. It came a week straight, then another. (*SA*, 20)

Thus opens "Water," the introductory vignette that sets the pattern for the whole book to follow: short, one-paragraph/one-page texts describing some (super)natural disaster, unlisted in the *Contents* page and thus acting in *Scorch Atlas* as spectral reminiscences, flash visions, shattered anonymous recollections, that preface the story that follows in their congealed tracks, offering devastated contexts or backgrounds against which the narrative as such can detach itself, like a scrap of loose skin from a bruised and diseased body.

Although titled "Water," there seems to be very few fluid elements in the text, unless the use of sounds replicating through assonances and paronomasia mimics some contagious, spreading seepage. Yet the rain itself pours "in endless veil" before turning to ice and "gaggling slicks of solid liquid" (20). The oxymoronic tendency immediately stresses the displacement or canceling out of meaning. Words on the page—black on (more or less) dark gray—are barely visible, and their contradictory associations (*go white* vs. *blacken, masked* vs. *glass, sat* vs. *so high, lidless cover*) gesture toward opacity. The harsh sonorities and the prevalence of plosives (*our crop fields blacken, insects masked our glass so thick*), the breaking up of the sentence into one-syllable words (*Every inch mucked with white film*), the alliterative doubling of consonants (*All spring the sky sat stacked with haze; It streaked the cities, wiped the wires*), all showcase the text's performative, material dimension. Words do not fade or lose their edges in favor of meaning or sense to which they would give a transparent access; instead, they materially clutter the page, saturate it, pour and fill and muck it up. Style and content fold back upon one another in recursive fashion, instantiating the same sense of opacity and saturation throughout.

Similar effects, collapsing style and content, can be found everywhere in *Scorch Atlas*. In "The Disappeared," for example—the first registered story in the collection—the narrator suffers from a strange skin disease: "I slept in fever, soaked in vision. Skin cells showered from my soft scalp. My nostrils gushed with liquid. You could see patterns in my forehead—oblong clods of fat veins, knotted, dim. I crouped and cowed and cringed among the lack of moonlight" (23–24). Here again the language reverberates through the rhythm of a truncated iambic pentameter (*I slept in fever, soaked in vision*—) before it thickens, founders, generates static (*Skin cells showered from my soft scalp*), breaks up into one-syllable words that invert (*oblong clods of fat*) and unsettle the rhythmic pattern (*veins, knotted, dim*), eventually coagulating around hard, stop consonants (*crouped, cowed, cringed, lack of moonlight*) that enhance a staccato rhythm whose effect, in colliding words and sounds, is to discontinue the syntax, rather than to make it smooth and flowing, in the wrecked course of sentences that often appear on the verge of collapse.

Content seeps into style; style feeds back into content. The geography of *Scorch Atlas* is a desolate one, rendered in, or *as*, sapped language.

●

Meanwhile *One Hundred Apocalypses and Other Apocalypses* multiplies small-scale apocalypses, mapping the concept onto fictional scenarios that barely fit the grandiloquent ends-of-the-world the genre usually indulges in. The second half of the book depicts one hundred so-called apocalypses whose destructive and revelatory power seems, more often than not, to be held in check. You go through them one at a time, expecting perhaps some momentum to gather, wondering if, one after the other—whether intimate, nonsensical, banal, spurious, insignificant, anonymous, or revelatory in their own strange terms—they might not pave the way for *the* apocalypse, a final and truly grandiose one that could up the ante and match generically codified expectations. But somehow they all repeat the same vexation: "soon the cries of leftover apocalypses were all that remained," concludes the last one quite enigmatically, endeavoring to draw on mere remains, or remains of remains. "Some of the things we knew were true. I'd only wanted to keep the bells ringing" (*OHA*, 183). And that's it. It's all over with, with the lingering suggestion that even the bells have stopped

60   Sightings

ringing. The concept has been exhausted, deflated, discarded, ringing no more bells. Maybe the apocalypse, rather than a shattering, irrupting event that puts an end from which everything is made to cohere, is what remains after all is said and done, pure remainder that changes nothing to what was known and true, that acts as mere, disappointing confirmation. In that sense, then, the apocalypse does stress a lack of imagination indeed, as one apocalypse suggests— "According to renowned experts, apocalypses, utopias, and the persistence of capitalism are all due to a cultural failure of imagination" (171)—showcasing its inability to lift the veil of indeterminacy: "*Something will provide*, I seemed to be thinking, but who knows anymore, I haven't had to think in so long I don't even know when I'm doing it or not" (183). As such, the apocalypse, or what passes for it, is sheer perpetuation outside thought, outside certainty and knowledge; or, in a word, it is speculation. It appears as what cannot be put an end *to*— continuance for continuance's sake. "Let's see where this is going" (158). But by this time, one knows very well where this is going; the pattern has been clearly established from the start. "Rate this apocalypse" (176), begs the title to one of the last ones, teasing its reader somehow, before treating the apocalypse as a commodity to be chosen, selected, "rated"—hence, yes, somehow *critiqued*:

> He led her to a long table, so clean, so cold, so bare, but for the apocalypses laid out in grid formation, uncountable, bouncing like icons waiting for updating, little puff of smoke in the grid, little lightning bolt, little funnel cloud, tiny tsunami, dancing flame, microscopic viruses magnified to match the rest, matchstick aliens, monsters like the figures on coins, anything you ever wanted. He said choose. The large print said to rate them but the small print said, in bed. She thought about choosing one of each, but he said it was one for each of us on Earth. (176–77)

To each according to their own private apocalypse, then, to be tried and enjoyed individually, for there might even be a kick to be gotten out of it. "The efficient orgasm is the most productive moment of the day," says another, "because, apocalyptically, it has wiped the slate clean, and no one will ever know about it" (136). The apocalypse may well be unshareable, that is. Not to be related to in any way, not to be known by anyone but the person going through it—a moment of private revelation whose only value is to leave a clean slate, for it all to start over. And again. That might be, too, what artists do in the end: "When artists transport the furnishings of a family room into a gallery space and paint everything white, they are trying to transform contents into ash without using fire" (126). Or how to burn things with words.

> Artists do this all the time—cover the surface, cover like news, like the opposite of oil. These artists with their white paint are signifying ash to make a post-apocalyptic space. . . . Coating the things with paint erases and exposes them like you can't make your mind up. . . . As painted things float further from their meanings, we can too. (127)

The text, printed words coating or covering white paper, might provide the very negative of this artistic postapocalyptic space; a charred, blackened wordscape. If apocalypse, as (religious) concept, aims to offer meaning, then artists may be concerned with what comes *after*. After meaning has been expunged. Covered in white or blackened with empty language. The multiplying apocalypses spreading from page to page might indeed speed up the moment when a new story can begin, usher in new spaces, those blank white spaces separating one apocalypse from the next, devoid of meaning as such, that come to signify not destruction so much as the possibility for something else to start, right there and then in the midst of this "postapocalyptic space" between stories. A white page waiting to be filled. Spaces—distances—to be covered. *Like news.* New things, that is, what one doesn't know yet but may still learn or discover once meaning, tethering the object in place, has evaporated, been painted over, covered, struck out.

If *One Hundred Apocalypses and Other Apocalypses* is apocalyptic in any usual sense, it might be in its shifting resistance to meaning as such, in the way most stories both thematically point to and formally instantiate bafflement and puzzlement, vexation and disappointment. Revealing nothing, covering everything, in black and white, black on white. Ashes to ashes. And back again.

•

The stories gathered in *Scorch Atlas*, much in the same way as in Corin's book, somehow fail to end or close in any proper, final sense—and thus to deliver some meaning that can be authoritative or enlightening—and instead refract themselves endlessly, always pointing either beyond or below meaning as such. They do not aggregate into a bigger, coherent ensemble or *world*. For in the process, verisimilitude is often baffled, logic is undermined, coherence is brittle. The stories dip into several genres and categories at once (horror, bizarro, dystopia . . .) that do not aim or pretend to follow mimetic strategies.

The world(s) depicted in the texts—if "world" and "depict" indeed are apt concepts for whatever scraps remain in, or as, the stories' ruined backgrounds— do not hold, nor do they pretend to. They're punctured with representational holes, and whatever consistency they may have is perhaps poetic rather than mimetic.[8] When they indulge in more conventional mimetic techniques, as in "Water Damaged Photos of Our Home Before I Left It" or "Tour of the Drowned Neighborhood," for instance—two pieces that adopt a highly descriptive, even ekphrastic, hence hyperreferential, mode—their operations are blatantly gainsaid by the radical absence of the very objects they're supposed to be attached to:[9] the narrator's neighborhood in one instance is drowned out of sight, while the remaining photos in the other are, for the most part, worn down, discolored, blistered, moldy, blurry, their content barely perceptible or recognizable, as suggested, among them, by the narrator's own portraits: "Each copy of me offers a slight variety of spoil—some so warped you can't even read me—some where there is nothing left to hold" (*SA*, 133). But further, as items, the photos are left out of the text; they are literally absent—all, that is, but one, whose content is blackened out of recognition (135). In other words, in the absence of the objects it refers to, the mimetic gesture is immediately belied, a mere illusion rendered null and void, turning the text itself into a mute, indecipherable object. For as Timothy Morton says in *Realist Magic*,

> ekphrasis is precisely an object-like entity that looms out of descriptive prose. It's a hyper-descriptive part that jumps out at the reader, petrifying her or him . . . , a bristling vividness that interrupts the flow of the narrative, jerking the reader out of her or his complacency. . . . In strictly OOO terms, ekphrasis is a translation that inevitably misses the secretive object, but which generates its own kind of object in the process. (*RM*, 133)

Some stories even bypass the usual narrative layout, formally presenting themselves as a loose concatenation of texts, a mere catalogue of descriptive features. Such is the case with "Tour of the Drowned Neighborhood," whose litany of "This is . . ." enhances the iterative stance that jams the narrative understood as a sequence of interlocking events. The same is true of "Water Damaged Photos," "Bloom Atlas," or "Damage Claim Questionnaire," a piece penned on a questionnaire as a list of possible, albeit quirky answers to no less quirky questions that loosen the content of the story rather than make it cohere.

Whether in its rejection of traditional mimetic moves or in its fragmentary, discrepant approach, *Scorch Atlas* loosens and disrupts the narrative line and the teleological framework dictated by apocalyptic thinking. The end of the world, in Butler's experimental treatment, also spells the end of story in a traditional sense, that is, the possibility of relating it and turning it into some significant event. The chronological framework, the usual cause-to-consequence pattern, is rendered inoperative. Hence the general absence throughout of rational explanations or attributable causes to whatever catastrophes occurred: things are what they are, and, in the "world(s)" of *Scorch Atlas*, they happen without any reason or justification; or if there might be any, they can only appear in a twist of logic or reversal of chronology, as in "Bath or Mud or Reclamation or Way In/Way Out": "She said if I kept walking there would be a reason" (*SA*, 122).

As Morton contends in *Realist Magic*, "Causality is . . . distributed. No one object is responsible for causality" (*RM*, 121). Object-oriented ontology as propounded by both him and Graham Harman treats causality indeed as a purely aesthetic, rather than as a "clunk," phenomenon: "Causal events never ever clunk, because clunking implies a linear time sequence, a container in which one metal ball can swing towards another one and click against it. Yet *before* and *after* are strictly secondary to the *sharing* of information" (*RM*, 120). In other words, causality is not what leads from one object or event to the next in an orderly sequence but all that happens in-between, meddles, or surrounds them, "a plenum of objects pressing in on all sides, leering at us like crazed characters in some crowded Expressionist painting" (*RM*, 122).

This might be embodied in the very aesthetic of *Scorch Atlas*, in the way its basic (post)apocalyptic components are "distributed" throughout and suffuse the text rather than account for and/or make its world(s) up. Narrative no longer forms prescribed or pre-ordered sequences but rather instantiates an endless drift, swapping narrative continuity for mere juxtaposition and non sequitur. As defined by Nancy, "'struction' would be the state of the 'with' deprived of the value of sharing, bringing into play only simple contiguity and its contingency . . . a 'with' that is uniquely categorial and not existential: the pure and simple juxtaposition that does not make sense" (Nancy and Barrau, 49). Each piece in the book works *with* the others in a "structional" sense, enhancing contiguity rather than continuity, juxtaposition rather than logic, contact and friction rather than sense—elements themselves exacerbated by the material dimension and format of the book that turn it into an aesthetic object per se rather than a transparent medium, an object in multiple shades of gray and layers of opacity that further complicate and obfuscate more than mediate or give access to whatever redundant contents the book may hold.

•

The same imagery proliferates from story to story. The same degradations, the same incomprehension, the bizarreness, the horror, the same tonality and hues. Floods and fires. Dust and muck. Death and destruction. Swollen diseased bodies. Animals gone feral. Children turned threat. As you read *Scorch Atlas*, a sense of redundancy grabs you.

64   Sightings

The book's regime is indeed one of equivalence and repetition. Characters, hardly individualized, often appear interchangeable. Most of them bear no names and seem mere avatars of one another. They suffer similar infirmities, share identical functions, have the same status, thus paving the way for Butler's later fiction: a father, a mother, some children, whose relationships or ties can no longer be vouchsafed. They barely talk to one another ("Smoke House"). Husbands leave or were never there ("Want for Wish for Nowhere"). When they are, they're removed from their authority ("The Disappeared"). Mothers cope while they can ("The Gown from Mother's Stomach"). When, that is, they don't leave or were never there in the first place ("Seabed," "Exponential"). Or if they remain, they are beaten up by their children ("Television Milk"). Unless the children themselves are lone survivors ("Bath or Mud or Reclamation or Way In/Way Out"). Butler varies the pattern, but the pattern remains the same.

For it may be the same story over and over again. The world is ending or has ended already. Most didn't make it. Those who did have no clue what part they're still to play, wonder what the hell they're still doing there. Like the narrator of "Water Damaged Photos of Our Home Before I Left It," who says he's "hating [his] skin for not getting paler. [His] teeth for not rotting out. Wondering why [he] would have to be the one to hold the camera" while his mother lies there dying (*SA*, 134). As is the case for him, the configuration all these characters have always known, the structures that held their world together—marriage, family, school, the media—have all fallen apart. Everything is ruined. Nothing makes sense anymore. Yet life goes on. Amid unspeakable diseases and wreckage, stink and rot, scorched land or flooded neighborhoods. Someone is still there in order to keep on. Looking. Searching. Speaking. Showing. Digging. Walking. Feeling. Naming. Trying.

To relate, perhaps. What cannot be; where and when it cannot be.

In that sense, *Scorch Atlas* doesn't tell so much as reiterates. Upping the ante—in an all too literal way.

·

What goes on in a story like "Seabed"—nothing, precisely; mere continuance for continuance's sake—epitomizes what *Scorch Atlas*, as a book or collection, does. Or doesn't do: it refuses to tell a full-fledged, postapocalyptic story, with (new) beginning, middle, and (final or revelatory) end; a gesture that is summed up, or rather fully retracted, in "Manure," one of the book's intercalary vignettes, which consists of a single sentence: "I will not speak of this day" (*SA*, 116).

Posited in the wake of a catastrophic ending, yet continuing into a mysterious, wrecked, unknowable aftermath, *Scorch Atlas* appears as pure middle, an endless extension not unlike the chimney of the house stumbled upon by Randall and the girl in "Seabed," which "stretched so far into the sky Randall couldn't tell at all where it ended and where something else began" (89). Such a description could somehow fit the way the texts follow up on one another. The consistency of their postapocalyptic themes and echoes indeed tend to blur them all into one indistinct textual mass that keeps morphing, whose pieces are constantly reshuffled and prolong each into the other.

Interspersed between the stories are short vignettes that act as buffers of sorts, false starts or remnants, fragments or pieces of larger, crippled data generating interferences, noise, and feedback. These pieces act as materials out of which new attempts are born and to which, after having somehow faltered, they inevitably return, thus embodying a constant move from an attempt at narrative construction to its immediate deconstruction or fragmentation.[10] Hence, the stories in the collection do not gather momentum, do not spell a bigger story or draw a larger picture. They no longer construct a textual edifice that would or could stand on its own. Each of the thirteen stories as such repeats or rehearses, with variations, the ones preceding and following it, sometimes quite explicitly taking its cue from the vignette introducing it, as in the transition from the ending of "Caterpillar"—"In the end, the great unveiling: ten billion butterflies humming in the sun, fluttering so loud you couldn't think" (58)—to the opening of "Television Milk": "Moths and blackbirds flooded the front yard" (61).

Because of the iterative propensity of Butler's writing, neither the book as such nor any of the stories on an individual basis seem concerned with making up a fictional world, building it up from scratch and ruin, and developing or fleshing it out to the end. Instead, the book maps the wreckage, circumscribes the remains, dives back into the ruins, but eventually leaves everything as it was, intact—mere ruins, broken pieces, rotting heaps. The book may as such exemplify the shift away from construction and de(con)struction toward mere *struction*, what conceptually supersedes both of these notions when ends proliferate for their own sake without any sense of "constructive finality" anymore, according to Jean-Luc Nancy. *Scorch Atlas* thus appears "structional" indeed, its apparent structure dissolving into "struction" to exhibit instead "an assembling that is labile, disordered, aggregated, or amalgamated rather than conjoined, reunited, paired with, or associated" (Nancy and Barrau, 49).

This structional quality is in part exemplified in the visual disintegration of the syntax in a story like "Want for Wish for Nowhere," where paragraphs appear to break up and decompose in various places, thus piling up lines on top of other lines as pseudo verses:

> We glimpsed the charred valley where the sun rose sometimes
> and the bulb of maggots over McDonald's
> and the crisp crust of something unknown on the cold sand where
> I and his father had dug our dinner. (*SA*, 54)

> At first I'd fast-forward through those sent from late night, the
> 1–800 numbers with women moaning, but then I began to find
> that in those moments
> he seemed most pleased,
> most still and God-blessed,
> and so I let him go on watching,
> while outside the tides broke and swallowed cars,
> and on the beaches the bloated continued rolling in, rotting even
> in the sun's absence, clogged and ripped and lined with tumor. (56)

When such dislocation is not visible, sentences and paragraphs pile up in a semblance of progression; yet they lead nowhere really, toward no final resolution: the ending of "Caterpillar," for instance, may be referred to as "the great unveiling," that is, a bona fide apocalypse, but it nonetheless translates as noise "so loud you couldn't think," ironically abolishing thought rather than revealing any truth or knowledge proper.

A similar ironical ending may be found in "The Gown from Mother's Stomach," a story that reads like a fairy tale and as such is quite different in tone from the other, more conventionally postapocalyptic pieces. Yet its singularity is belied by the fact that, like the other stories, it fails to conclude in a definite way. As Deleuze and Guattari imply, unlike the novella or short story, the tale is clearly oriented toward an ending, since it aims to answer the question "What is going to happen?" Yet the story's end is here marked by its sheer discrepancy with what was expected and announced: not only does the bear that the girl encounters not talk (contrary to what the girl's mother told her), but it eats her up. If this could have served as a proper, final, albeit ironical ending, the story doesn't end there and propels itself past what could have appeared as the tale's cautionary moral: the girl indeed "became a strange fluorescence and she exited the bear— she spread across the wrecked earth and refracted through the ocean to split the sky: a neon ceiling over all things, a shade of something new, unnamed" (75).

Paradoxically, then, the cycle continues as the ending morphs into "something new, unnamed"—if this could at first be seen as a positive note, a rebirth of sorts, this peculiar "something new, unnamed" is however posited beyond story and language, a mere "shade" further extending the wreckage as it "split[s] the sky" and covers all things. The end thus undoes itself, it seems, by stretching beyond itself into what, again, appears as sheer, unstoppable continuance or "refraction." As Nancy claims: "We have come to a point in which architectonics and architecture—understood as the determinations of an essential construction or essence as construction—no longer have value. They have worn themselves out by themselves" (Nancy and Barrau, 50–51). The end, here, in similar fashion, has worn itself out, leaving the story as story, the story the girl had set out to find in the first place,[11] wobbling on the brink of meaninglessness.

•

Kate in *Wittgenstein's Mistress* might withhold some of the main narrative elements in her story and refrain from venturing into things that count, deliberately turning herself into a mere "character"—not to say caricature: that of the "mad woman in the attic" once the house has burned down—imagining herself as the "heroine" in "an absolutely autobiographical novel" she hasn't written, or not as such at any rate, yet one does relate to her predicament and senses or feels that her apparent detachment from whatever "world" remains around her belies, points to, is the sign of *something*. Some disaster, real or imaginary, grand-scale or intimate, that undoes language, turns it back upon itself to investigate or stake its own limits.

As Blanchot put it in *The Writing of the Disaster*, "The disaster is separate; that which is most separate" (Blanchot, 1). The disaster, in other words, is that which holds me irrevocably apart, is absolute in that sense—that which has no relation to me and what, as such, I cannot think, let alone speak about, for "to think the disaster (if this is possible, and it is not possible inasmuch as we suspect that the disaster is thought) is to have no longer any future in which to think it" (Blanchot, 1). Which might be what Rachel, in Doten's *Trump Sky Alpha*, is impossibly trying to do: think (through) the disaster, which in her case is both collective (the destruction of the world) and intimate (the deaths of her wife and daughter), to a future that no longer exists, to a space crammed up with and stifled by empty, obtrusive, provisional language, language that impedes story as such because it flattens everything, fails to discriminate and bring relief to words and events, make them count, make them matter—language that, following Kenneth Goldsmith in *Uncreative Writing*, can thus only appear

> temporary and debased, mere material to be shoveled, reshaped, hoarded, and molded into whatever form is convenient, only to be discarded just as quickly. Because words today are cheap and infinitely produced, they are detritus, signifying little, meaning less. Disorientation by replication and spam is the norm. (Goldsmith)

68 Sightings

Which is indeed what Rachel is experiencing as she's permitted, in order to research her piece on "internet humor at the end of the world" commissioned by Galloway, to scavenge through what was saved of the internet as she knew it before the world ended, that is, as we know it now, with its viral memes and infinite retweets, serial quotes, trolls, GIFs, #hashtags—empty messages indefinitely and instantly replicating, dislodging meaning and only serving the spurious, illusory sense of so-called belonging.

Maybe what Rachel needs in the end is the same as Kate in Markson's novel, who's been desperately trying to "[leave] baggage behind" (*WM*, 15) and empty her head of everything she's carrying around in it; and maybe this is what Birdcrash, the cyberterrorist Rachel has hunted down in *Trump Sky Alpha*, has to offer her as he drills holes into her skull: an empty, uncluttered space, a clean slate, a blank page. That onto which, come the end of the novel, with Galloway at her side, she finally steps, obliterating herself as she does. Along with whatever stories she, with Galloway, possibly had to tell.

•

What all these stories or nonstories have in common, in the end, may be their kernel of resistance; their refusal to tell whatever trauma, event, catastrophe they all originate in. What defines them best is perhaps their degree of implicitness, their blatant rebuff of both explanation and signification. What happened happened outside the text and is presented in the text as an unquestionable given. Or if there's a hint of explanation, as in "Seabed," for instance, it is immediately and authoritatively dismissed:

> Randall had a head the size of several persons' heads—a vast seething bulb with rotten hair that shined under certain light. Several summers back he'd driven to a bigger city where smarter men removed a hunk out of his skull. They'd said the cyst grew from the wires hung above the house. Randall's son hadn't ended up so well off. The crap ate through the kid's whole cerebrum. Radiation. Scrambled cells. *One had to be mindful of these things in these days*, the doctors said. Now, though, with the woman gone and the baby dead, Randall kept on living in that old house with the mold curtains where his guilt breathed in the walls. He lugged the kid's tricycle all over, the handlebars shrieking with rust on account of how he even brought it in the bath. (*SA*, 79)

The opening paragraph of the story says it all regarding Randall's condition: "Radiation. Scrambled cells." And the caution offered by the expert doctors that goes with it: "*One had to be mindful of these things in these days.*" The use of italics suggests a direct quote, yet the past tense sends Randall, the lone protagonist, back to an uncertain time that could be aligned with the "several summers back" or refer to a later, undetermined period in his life, when Randall had to face it all again with his son. The confusion is further enhanced by the use of "these" instead of the expected "those": the time frame is blurred, the individual is rendered impersonal ("one"), and everything in the end contributes to rendering the explanation quite dubious—an explanation that may not be one as such insofar as "these things" and "these days," in their generality, could apply to just about anything and can only make sense in a specific and shared context. Be that as it may, Randall has no choice but to "keep on living in that old house" with a sense of inexplicable "guilt breath[ing] in the walls," until he leaves the house in the second paragraph, never to come back. The rest of the story follows Randall, shortly joined by an orphan girl, through a ruined landscape and dump-slash-charnel-ground, and ends when they reach the evaporated sea.

If its opening, with the departure of the protagonist, can seem to be following quite a classical model, "Seabed"—like most if not all the stories in *Scorch Atlas*—doesn't tell or recount much in terms of peripeteia. If it sometimes sifts through the character's recollections, the text merely posits; it describes, it enumerates and repeats:

> Sometimes the sky would open up. Storms would appear out of nowhere, without thunder or a cloud. The only thing that didn't rain was water. Lather. Crickets. Lesions. Seed. Sand drenched in thin torrential pillars, poured from above by erupted hourglasses. Blades of grass came whipped by wind and sliced the thin skin of Randall's wrecked head. Peapods, pine straw, even plastic—sometimes they had to dig themselves out of what'd come down. Worse were the insects—gnat, mosquito, aphid—wriggling at their eyes. They picked the shit out of one another's hair. (*SA*, 86)

Randall and the girl keep walking through insensate repetitions (as suggested by the use of *would*), with no apparent sense of purpose, direction, or finality. When they arrive at the beach, "With nowhere else to go and under such stench, they continued on along the seabed" (88). Eventually they reach another improbable house, part-miracle, part-mirage, that should have been underwater in (so-called) normal circumstances. Before it starts raining, Randall and the girl take refuge there, the story thus coming full circle, impossible house to impossible house. If "Seabed" told anything, nothing truly happened; no significant event in any proper sense befell Randall and the girl, no peripeteia, nothing

70 Sightings

prone to rupture, modify, complement, or resolve their life stories. Instead, as the narrative voice repeats throughout, they merely "continue on":

> When the road ended where the town did, Randall continued walking on. (80)
> They continued on together in a straight line beneath the scratched lid of the sky. (85)
> With nowhere else to go and under such stench, they continued on along the seabed. (88)
> They continued in a short trench out into the heart of where the wet had been. (88)
> He continued on regardless, warbling. (89)

"Seabed" then may be just that: a (non)story of mere continuance—Randall's, after his son's death and his wife's departure, but also the girl's, bereft of her parents. Yet "Seabed," which might in that regard be quite representative of the whole book,[12] could also be about, or instantiate, the continuance of story after story's end.

"Inside," the text indeed concludes, "the song continued, drawing upward, its long calm chords vibrating the air, his hair, the house" (92). The rain may be pouring, the water ineluctably rising around the house, thus trapping the characters inside and somehow putting an end to their story, but something does continue beyond (the) story, a song picked up at random on a broken transistor through the noise made up by the radiations, "a soft-sunned song [Randall] could not place—throbbing and monotone and wordless" (91).

Whatever happened happened; the rest continues on, beyond words, beyond language, beyond story.

Mere speculation.

Narrative is what is at stake. The construction of story, of a spatiotemporal frame within which events could take place and connect sequentially, one after the other in orderly fashion, one leading to the next, accounting for it, explaining it, relating to it, all in order to make sense. Sense as product, as derivative, as what is to be gotten out of story through interpretation—once, that is, I have stepped out of it, reached the text's conclusion and safely retreated. The End.

Yet speculative fiction would precisely be what prevents narrative as such from developing; what collapses narrative onto alien modalities—modalities that may not have to be anti- or nonnarrative for all that. For narrative doesn't need to be utterly discarded; traces of it can remain and prosper, at least as a possibility, or virtuality, in the midst of different instantiations, or iterations. A narrative that I would fail to decipher somehow, not necessarily because of my lack of skills, nor because of any limitations inherent in my hermeneutical tools, although this of course remains plausible. But it might simply be that this narrative, loose and broken, may never have been addressed to me in the first place. I remain alien to it, or it to me—complete strangers with no language in common; or a language I cannot speak anymore. "This is not for you," reads the dedication of Mark Danielewski's House of Leaves. *"For no one," reads the dedication of Blake Butler's* There Is No Year.

Or maybe, as I'm opening the book, I realize that I'm entering a foreign territory that doesn't comply with mimetic rules of depth and perspective, where space and time are rendered in alternative ways—where simple basic questions like "What is happening?" have lost much of their significance. As suggested, for instance, by the proliferation of lists and catalogues of facts in Blake Butler's or David Markson's fiction, the speculative terrain is usually a flat one indeed, where objects/facts/events all have equal value, where no one single thing or occurrence matters more than another. Which indeed makes it all the harder for any narrative element to stick out and gain traction, to turn into a good old peripeteia prone to inflect the narrative course and propel the story forward toward its logical conclusion. For the conclusion may have already been penned. The end already taken place. What I'm reading, after all, may be what survived the end of narrative.

Where am I, then? What happened? And if something did, dear Incomprehension, *how and in what words can I relate?*

Speculative Topologies, Or "This Is Not for You"

With *Scorch Atlas*, Blake Butler may have been trying to discard (conventional) narrative, to do away with the beginning-middle-end pattern in favor of a more flattened, uneventful, or unaccentuated, often matter-of-fact presentation of things. Indeed, Butler's fiction often counters or resists attempts at ordering or organizing its contents in a (chrono)logical sequence. In doing so, it eradicates all perspective and distancing, in favor of what Gilles Deleuze, in *Logic of Sensation*, suggests is the shortened, intimate "plane of a close, haptic vision" (Deleuze, 135). And if such is the case, you are forced to close read, somehow—to read with your eyes up close to the text, thus in a way *seeing* nothing. Or seeing that there *is* nothing to see, facing what French philosopher Georges Didi-Huberman, after James Joyce in *Ulysses*, refers to as "the ineluctable modality of the visible": you may not see anything, but something could be looking back at you, may even be concerning you—something that you do feel "as a work of loss" (*une œuvre de perte*). In other words, what you do see, when not seeing anything, is that "something ineluctably eludes you."[1] Something to which, somehow, you've failed to relate.

•

To a certain extent, *The Flame Alphabet* by Ben Marcus frames this speculative dilemma. Plagued by a mysterious language disease, the novel in part reads like a "work of loss," as its characters are faced with the sheer impossibility of relating to their loved ones. The disease baffles everyone, spreads without anyone being able to comprehend it.

Of course, the conundrum it exemplifies could always be explained away epistemologically: one could hold that with the outburst of the speech fever,

74 Sightings

science as such may not be nullified altogether but merely facing its own limitations; what cannot be rationalized *now* could always find a subsequent explanation, much as "Hippocrates, Avicenna, a long list of experts . . . knew without really knowing that our strongest pollution was verbal" (*FA*, 82). If no one knows *yet* why human language has suddenly turned lethal, scientists in *The Flame Alphabet*—and chief among them, "smallworker" Sam, the narrator—keep looking for answers and experimenting with solutions in the hope that a cure might be found in due time. And the end of the novel does point to ways of curbing the disease, at least momentarily. Yet as the narrator enigmatically specifies, loath to get into details at first, those come with a steep price . . .

However, if an epistemological reading of *The Flame Alphabet* could plausibly be ventured, the novel also trades in metaphysical issues—the direct allusion, with "the flame alphabet," to Jewish mysticism, along with the place occupied more generally by religion in the text, says as much. The disease conveyed by language thus raises questions that go beyond mere epistemological ones regarding the limitations of knowledge and science and confers upon the novel a speculative bias, since by removing access to language it implicitly interrogates the very nature of human interaction and of any relation to the real—a real ever harder to pinpoint and define. With language in any form causing people to physically whither and decay, communication and, beyond, all human interactions become de facto ruled out from the world of *The Flame Alphabet*—research and science included. What Sam, in the second part of the novel, does at Forsythe—a school turned into a research facility under LeBov's supervision—is nothing short of a grotesque parody. "Are you serious?" asks LeBov of Sam in a moment of shared induced immunity. "You're sitting here creating fucking *alphabets*? How small exactly is your mind?" (198) Even were anyone to find a miraculous answer to the language toxicity, whether new alphabet or medical cure, they would be faced with the sheer impossibility of sharing it eventually. As Sam realizes:

> The days of understanding were over. The question I could not even formulate was this: What was it we were now supposed to do if it was medically impossible to even understand each other without a rapid, ugly sickness taking hold? This was not a disease of language anymore, it was a disease of insight, understanding, knowing. (196)

The disease as such is thus *not* to be known or understood. It affects the very foundations of knowledge and understanding—the grounds upon which they could be elaborated in the first place (*I could not even formulate*). Knowledge and comprehension are thus not just limited or suspended in the present—they're done away with utterly.

As a consequence, the novel's constant preoccupation with the notions of meaning and understanding, if derived from Marcus's own reading and interpretation of Jewish mysticism and Kabbalah,[2] cannot but endorse a metafictional or critical turn:

> "Understanding itself is beside the point," Burke said, more calmly. "Do not make of it a fetish, for it pays back nothing. That habit must be broken. Understanding puts us to sleep. The dark and undesired sleep. Questions like these are not meant to be resolved. We must never believe we know our roles. We must always wonder what the moment calls for." (46)

In many ways, then, *The Flame Alphabet* is a novel that vehemently resists understanding and targets any critical readings that would purport to explicate or derive meaning from it. Which does not necessarily imply that, as such, Marcus's novel is entirely devoid of meaning altogether or that it deliberately courts nonsense but that any attempt on the critic's part to find meaning and justification in the world depicted by Marcus is from the start, and de facto, if not utterly invalidated, then at least seriously challenged by the novel's own premise. Sam's aggressive tone throughout—"Do the math on that" (10), he says early on, thus urging his reader to draw self-imposing conclusions—does evince his unwillingness to tell his story as much as his reluctance, by the time he has lost touch with both wife and daughter, to relate.

In short, following and adapting Didi-Huberman, the "work of loss" Sam gives himself over to in *The Flame Alphabet* points to "the ineluctable modality of the readable."

·

Blake Butler's work might be the perfect embodiment of such an "ineluctable modality of the readable" according to which *to read would be to experience loss* or experience the fact, if fact it is, that something does elude one's grasp. Both published in 2009, *Ever* and *Scorch Atlas* are indubitably more narrative, in a traditional sense, than Butler's later fiction. Yet, whether through those first two books or the later ones—*There Is No Year, Sky Saw, 300,000,000*, or *Alice Knott*—the reader is slowly made to realize, as they read them, how often it is that they end up switching off, stumbling over the sheer opacity and impenetrability of some passages that appear to bypass conventional meaning in favor of more abstract and/or performative assemblages, which openly abstain from delivering immediate, if any, sense. It is as though in reading such blocks of text, one has read nothing indeed—nothing, that is, with or through which it could be felt that one's been *gaining* something, *getting* somewhere:

> Inside the wet, her body blinked and blinked. Behind her lids the years were strobing—she spoke their image on the air—they made more white surround them—they burned it open. With each syllable spent uttered, her body grew another creaming yard—yards of lash and lung all overflowing. (*SS*, 205)

Words in themselves are not abstruse; the syntax is pretty adamant. Yet the blatant lack of semantic or logical affinity between syntactic components makes meaning, insofar as it would appear to be that which could reward the reader's effort, opaque. At best.

Sometimes words (and sounds) collide more than they flow on the page: "Blood drying against concrete slathered baking in such daylight as glass shattered in metal crunching bone beneath bright planes banging bullets on the fields of women and men until the pilot too turns on the party of himself" (*3HM*, 228). Rather than a carefully structured and ordered grammatical unit, Blake Butler's sentence more and more appears as a blurry space with no real sense of direction. In the words of Jean-Luc Nancy, such syntactic assemblage appears "labile, disordered, aggregated, or amalgamated rather than conjoined, reunited, paired with, or associated" (Nancy and Barrau, 49). Whether on the micro level of the sentence or the macro level of the book, what such "struction" indicates might be a paradigmatic shift from a time-oriented, teleological conception of fiction—spanning from beginning to end along a linear, chronological axis—to its spatial translation, thus moving away from classic "optic" modes of textual apprehension to more "haptic" ones.

•

Space is a key feature of Butler's fiction, as suggested by the prevalence of houses and rooms to be explored and navigated, most notably in *Ever* or *There Is No Year*, a novel whose main action—or lack thereof in any traditional, plot-driven sense—revolves around the family's acquisition of a new house that the mother will want to sell back immediately after moving in. Similarly, *300,000,000* focuses, at least at first, on mass killer Gretch Gravey's house where Flood's investigation takes place. Yet such locations are not stable mimetic spaces; they are characterized by diverse levels that appear and disappear, that morph and distort, recede or draw near. In other words, just like the spaces it depicts, Butler's fiction is one that does not follow a linear, systematic arc but that is laid out more spatially and that somehow dismisses time more or less explicitly, as suggested by the titles *Ever* and *There Is No Year*, for instance, or time's absurd compression in *Sky Saw*: "Before I was born inside the mother I slept inside the wound for 37 years" (*SS*, 65). Hence the apparent sense of discontinuity favored by lists and iterations and recursions rather than narrative episodes (chrono)logically leading up to, and merging into, the following ones—all the way down the line to its logical and conclusive end. Instead, the text can be seen and apprehended as "navigable space," one of the key aspects of new media as delineated by Lev Manovich.

The focus on the texts' material dimensions, as well as their formats and visual layouts in the cases of both *Scorch Atlas* and *There Is No Year*,[3] make of them true avatars of what Katherine Hayles defined as "technotexts." Characterized by their lack of continuity and their iterative strategies, Butler's texts loosen up their (properly) narrative dimension. A story as such, one that could be summarized or retraced along major events prompting the characters' actions, never quite fully develops—the sense of quest in *300,000,000* for instance, cued by Flood's investigation into Gravey's murders, is exhausted as soon as Flood disappears into the margins of the text/house. In *Alice Knott*, the plot set in motion by the destruction of artworks hovers above the text more than it truly provides it with a structural backbone, as its protagonist, Alice, is assailed by images and memories from a life she may never have lived as such. The idea of narrative proper is bound to remain broken up into its mere constituents—a vague setting, character functions ("the mother," "the father," "the son" in *There Is No Year*; Alice, her dubious parents, mother, father, "unfather," and no less dubious "unbrother" in *Alice Knott*)—that never quite cohere. In other words, based on the dichotomy Manovich adapts from Panofsky, the space that Butler's texts open up isn't a fluent, "systematic" one organized according to linear perspective but more of an "aggregate" one (Manovich, 254), as further suggested by the sheer prevalence of the verb "parse" in *Alice Knott*.

●

Michael Joyce's *Was: Annales nomadique* builds on an immediately visible sense of discreteness. The text seems to be floating and drifting around on the page without any recognizable narrative markers apt to make it cohere into a greater, unified whole, as intimated by the novel's opening:

> was thought not were the yellow the irrepressible ever who said who said ends Ashtoreth one Wednesday, one Wednesday in June the damp the dampness in everything (light, profusionist, no I mean heat)
>
> forty times now, bowing, clogs along foggy bottom news from the front, wooden boxes neatly in rows
>
> the last the lost wandering *allées* (lips pressed to the neonate's skull, powder scent) willows all now gone from their ripeness

78   Sightings

> and what of the stipple, the limp, the lost what-was, despite the damp
> odor of canvas, the salt-cracked lips, inordinate corridors? Who can
> say who can say (*Was*, 11)

Thus launching from the book's margins, sentences lack both initial caps and periods. As supposedly consistent and self-enclosed grammatical/syntactic units, sentences no longer hold but dissolve into the blank interstices that separate and disjoin them, underlying their defective, shifty, or ongoing aspect in the absence of any main identifiable clause that is apt to ground them. And so it goes, comes and goes, for the duration of the whole book. It is as though the text underwent ceaseless topological transformations or translations devoid of apparent finality, forever fragmenting or veering abruptly. The novel's narrativity collapses or never quite fleshes out, a mere textual assemblage of free-floating, unanchored utterances that, at least in the book's layout, may recall David Markson's late novels. Yet unlike, say, *Wittgenstein's Mistress*, *Was* appears to be deprived of any cohesive center—"errors and wrecks cannot make us cohere," a fragment reads (Joyce, 113), reminding the reader of the ephemeral nature of her responses and interpretations, as well as of the disseminative nature of the text itself, its obtuse refusal to be grounded as story in the space and time of the traditional novel. In a sense, such "errors" and "wrecks" may be prompted by the basic, albeit corrupt material of the conventional story, such as characterization, plot, and setting, elements that, if not altogether absent from *Was*, collide and contradict or, rather, never logically follow or accrete—it "doesn't add up" (85), nor can it with "all references lost" (43).

As its title indicates, *Was* in its turn enacts a "work of loss" and can be read as an elegy of sorts to what is no more, pure fleetingness and elusiveness, "the last the lost"—that is, to that which has no presence, being-in-the-past, the irretrievable. Unless the title should be read in German—which, in a novel foregrounding polyglottism, doesn't appear utterly incongruous—thus drawing attention from the outset to the very nature of the text, its "whatness" or quiddity, while openly calling it into question. In both cases, the contents of *Was* remain highly problematic, mere fragments "tethered by memory" only (111). Yet whose memory is it, in the absence of any clearly discernible narrative consciousness? In their constant fluctuations and dislocations, such fragments appear unavoidably loose, ever fleeting, (un)shaping a story that cannot be one, for its ever-shifting contours delimit an absence or, at best, a substance that resists re-presentation, a pure empty or evanescent form that cannot be grounded or contextualized.

Subtitled *Annales nomadique*, the novel indeed foregrounds its plurality, its documentariness, and above all its sitelessness, which all finds an echo in the generic tag affixed by Joyce—"a novel of internet," thus revealing part of the novel's composition process.[4] As Stuart Moulthrop explains, *Was* may not be "a flarf project and was written in the traditional, inventional way, not by any process of direct appropriation." Yet for all that, "at some stage in the writing, Joyce made use of internet affordances, perhaps to research locations, check addresses, maybe to troll for inspiration and narrative leads. *Was*, published in 2007, is thus genuinely 'a novel of internet'" (Moulthrop 2013).

The result is a loose concatenation of story residues taken from nowhere, that is, everywhere, as the locale keeps shifting and extends all over the globe, embracing in the process multiple languages that inscribe at the heart of the text its radical otherness or dynamic (un)translatability. As such and beyond the opacity that the text exudes, what is thus foregrounded is the fluid transformation or melting down of narrative and conventional story material into pure motion and processuality, or its move away from a purely, static, print paradigm to a dynamic, new-media interface/database paradigm, according to Moulthrop. That is, "the reeds and the water, for instance, flow and potentiality, the basket snagged on a cattail, all history in the balance" (Joyce, 96). And in the balance as well is therefore the impossible development of the story itself, a story thus rendered deliquescent, effaced by blurry, unstable edges made visible in all those blank gaps unhinging the text, tearing it apart, undermining its progression and cohesiveness—not to say *mining* it altogether.

The fragments of text that flit throughout *Was* eventually appear as mere discrete remnants or relics indeed, or fallout perhaps, after a violent aesthetic blast.[5] That Joyce chose print as a medium for *Was*, thus pitting its textual dynamics against the fixity of the page, only exacerbates its disjointed aspect and the violence inherent in its composition, as though the book itself, in its materiality, had resources of its own to resist story and linearity in ways that hypertextuality had perhaps failed to,[6] if only because at its core lay a linking process and mechanism whose outcome could always be the actualizing of *a* story, however indeterminate—as suggested by *afternoon*'s subtitle. But because *Was* is delivered as print fiction, thus (not) taking place within the supposedly clearly delineated contours of a story bound and fixed between immutable covers, such actualization is rendered at best problematic in the absence of logical connectors or linking operators other than a mere arbitrary turning of pages: unlike *afternoon*—out of which it is always possible to draw *a* story by connecting various dots, since the planting of hypertextual links and hence directionality into the

80 Sightings

very fabric of the text indeed generates some continuity—*Was*, in its adamant refusal to "take" or bring its diverse components together, is claimed back by the virtual; or, following Moulthrop, instantly withdraws from its interface (the page) back into the database from which it originates as "a novel of internet."

In other words, in its constant departure or withdrawal, the text fixed on the page can only point and be assimilated to a disjointed series of *traces*— that is, "the appearance of a nearness, however far removed the thing that left it behind may be," according to Walter Benjamin's definition in his *Arcades Project* (447); such unapproachable nearness is, in the case of Joyce's unstable and fuzzy poetics, what literally de-stabilizes the text, dis-integrates it, tears it apart, and dis-seminates it. It is as though the text had eventually inverted the internet-mining process that generated it, turning itself into a virtual core or matrix to generate allomorphic bits and pieces of intractable story in its turn, moving along pages in a textual ebb and flow of sorts or a quasi-random sequence of folds. What prevails in the end is writing as pure *lifting* gesture, to borrow from Moulthrop's essay title, or language as mere passage on a page relentlessly folded and unfolded; a page upon which virtual traces merely flit and flutter but never connect—sheer evanescent vestiges, ghost notes already evaporated when heard:

> wishing language were a knot?
>
> Music anyways (*Was*, 123)

•

Was does away with almost everything that could denote the essence of the novel, stripped down to its bare virtuality. Joyce's "novel of internet" is dispersed in its blanks and gaps and appears as pure virtual space insofar as the latter, as characterized by Lev Manovich in *The Language of New Media*, "is fundamentally aggregate, a set of objects without a unifying point of view" (258). This "unifying point of view" is indeed absent from the text, and it might be up to the reader to bring everything together somehow. Yet in the absence of identifiable characters, of a set of events that could shape a distinctive plot,[7] this proves quite impossible. Because of the text's disseminative (or nomadic) nature, each element composing the final work is apprehended as a fragment cut off from its original context; the texture of the novel is regularly discontinued, and if echoes or occasional returns are discernible, the page of *Was* eventually, and visibly, remains an open, "aggregate" space of discrete, distributed items that cannot be merged into a greater whole.

Love Hotel by Jane Unrue employs a similar strategy. Unlike *Was*, however,

Love Hotel retains a few narrative elements contingent upon the chronological framework affected by the text. Chronology, as a consistent and logical sequence of events that would aggregate into a clear-cut plot and its eventual resolution, is however invalidated by the text's obsessive retracings. A story thus never quite settles on the page, where diverse, jarring elements or time frames tend to overlap and consequently blur the narrative picture. Linearity and narrative consecution are quickly replaced with another motion, rendered all too visually and hinted at by the novel's title; the hotel may indeed act both as an organizational premise and as a metaphor of a storied and transitory space.

Verticality thus trumps horizontality, as suggested by the text's layout. Paragraphs tend to break off into lines piling up and down the page. Navigating through the text thus requires an incessant, vertical motion along the page to access the different levels or floors upon which the narrative is layered or storied, with no guarantee, though, that those ever connect anywhere:

> The night we met
> *One day a man and his wife*
> as I proceeded down their hallway
> second floor
> then down their staircase
> main
> *were working in the*
> down the hallway
> ground floor
> passing three closed doors
> I felt so homesick for my *bed*
> my *windows*
> *floors*
> *were working in the*
> even for my *walls.* But at the same time just as soon as I had seen them
> seated in their study I
> *we'd both completely understand* he said to me when five nights later
> we had moved to the verandah where she said to me *If you feel*
> *you can't do it*
> etc. (*LH*, 17)

The sentence is here shattered on the page into a series of embeddings and breaks along a vertical axis. Around it, several possible actualizations seem always to be circling. If the initial move of the text is to underline chronology and linearity—*Love Hotel* opens page 3 with the heading "DAY 1"—reading *Love*

82 Sightings

Hotel rather constitutes a vertical plunge into the multiple strata of the narrator's memory. One progressively suspects or infers that something may have happened whose harmonics keep haunting the text without ever truly sounding. As suggested by David Winters in "Patterns of Anticipation," his review of *Love Hotel*, "Unrue's narrator can't turn back to the source of the story, nor can she bring it to a resolution: hers is a motion of incomprehension."

As is often the case with speculative fiction, incomprehension indeed prevails. For such texts often choose for themselves layouts, modes, or apparatuses that bypass meaning in favor of alternative grasping schemes. With regard to new media and electronic literature, Katherine Hayles intuited that criticism of such works is viable only to the extent that it seizes the material specificities of its objects:

> Understanding literature as the interplay between form, content, and medium, [media-specific analysis] insists that texts must always be embodied to exist in the world. The materiality of those embodiments interacts dynamically with linguistic, rhetorical, and literary practices to create the effects we call literature. (Hayles 2002, 31)

To put it differently, literary space is no longer exclusively delineated by text, merely—language and its effects more than ever meet with opposite logics inherited or transported from or committed to other practices or media. For that matter, so to speak, blanks in the text signify as much as words inked on the page, as revealed by Shelley Jackson's *Half Life*, a novel that reenacts and literally embodies the "black and white" drama of writing into its double narrative figure, the conjoined twin sisters Nora and Blanche. Searching throughout the whole novel for how to get rid of her sister, Blanche, who fell into a deep coma and who acts in the text as a supposedly white, blank, passive surface for Nora's identity quest, Nora will come to the following conclusion:

> I have spent my whole life trying to make one story out of two: my word against Blanche's. But we are only as antithetical as this ink and this page. Do these letters have meaning, or the space around them? Neither. It's their difference we read. (*HL*, 433)

Half Life, whose odd, right-hand pages are significantly not numbered—thus making Blanche's absence to herself and the text visible, all the while conferring upon her a paradoxical material presence—tends to turn this in-between space around in the course of a differential writing, where what you read is not so much the black *text*, what Nora has penned down in black ink, as its blanks, the white spaces, what has been silenced or withdrawn—what precisely, as such, won't be *read*. The allegedly silent, dormant surface is *not* as passive as the reader or Nora might have thought but yields to imperceptible transformations. In each blank, another story lies that challenges the text with erasure and ensures that what you read is not what you get.

●

Defined by Brian Massumi as "the science of self-varying deformation," topology implies continuity; it entails a "continuous transformation" (Massumi, 134). Yet this continuity cannot be grasped or felt, since according to Massumi it partakes of the virtual, which "is inaccessible to the senses" (133):

> it is impossible actually to diagram every step in a topological transformation. Practically, only selected stills can be presented. Once again, the need arises to superpose the sequencings. It is only in that superposition that the unity of the [topological] figure can be grasped as such, in one stroke. That one stroke is the virtual image center of the figure. It is virtual because you cannot effectively see it or exhaustively diagram it. It is an image because you can, for all of that, figure it, more or less vaguely, in the imagination. (Massumi, 134)

What Butler's fiction may give access to are those "stills"—figures isolated and abstracted from the flow—through which deformation or distortion appears *after the fact*, in a series of "infoldings and outfoldings" (Massumi, 133).

Be that as it may, topology may not be totally opposed to a sense of felt discontinuity, and Butler's fiction may not be foreign to topological variation, especially as topology also bypasses reference and representation:

> Incapable of directly referencing anything other than its own variations, [topology] is more analogical than descriptive. It is not, however, an analog of anything in particular. It is not an analog in the everyday sense of a variation on a model. Here, there is no model. Only infolding and unfolding: self-referential transformation. The analog is *process*, self-referenced to its own variations. It resembles nothing outside itself. (Massumi, 135)

By resorting to topological transformation—if indeed that is what they do—Butler's texts emphasize deformation and thwart all mimetic moves, closing the texts upon themselves in self-referential frenzy. Hence, perhaps, the prevalence of mirrors throughout—but mirrors that distort the images they reproduce and increase the gaps between the figure and its copy, one never quite matching the other: "The mirror, likewise, did not seem to hold him" (*SS*, 120); "In the

84 Sightings

mirror the son saw nothing. The silver surface had a little curdle" (*TINY*, 88); "Again Flood does not see himself reflected in the mirror" (*3HM*, 180); "The mirror's surface seems different now, she realizes; she sees something odd there about her eyes, or at least a difference in how she would expect her eyes to look" (*AK*, 53). Instead, mirrors often act in the texts as surfaces that characters bump into, that obstruct rather than enhance perception and understanding, that conceal more than they might reveal—sheer diversion: "Underneath the floor is a second floor, forming a cavity beneath the room, which the mirrors had kept hidden from investigation" (*3HM*, 155). Ironically, then, the omnipresence of mirrors and the ensuing proliferation of unreliable reflections—especially in a novel like *300,000,000*, where a room in Gravey's house is made entirely of mirrors—embody a refusal of representation or figuration. The image the mirror reflects often appears distorted, blurred, overlaid, changing.

What is at stake is no longer mimesis and the truthful, authentic depiction of an external reality or model.[8] As is the case in Ben Marcus's fiction too, referentiality is radically contested and turned back upon itself in ways that differ greatly from the by-now conventional postmodern self-referential process. Hence the claustrophobic rendition of space by way of infinite houses, boxes in boxes, rooms layered upon rooms in which the figures are trapped and which they can leave only to gain immediate entry back into other ones—the same always, yet never quite the same.

> He tried several times to go back to where the door he'd come into the house through had been—the stairwell unto floors unending—though where it had been before it now seemed not—only the continuing flat surface of where the house was, holding what beyond him there all out. It was as if the door had never actually been there—as if it were a door existing only ever somewhere in his mind meat, burbling with knots. (*SS*, 188)

The outside as such is always-already folded back onto the inside, quite inseparable from it, as suggested by the ambiguous phrase "holding what beyond him there all out," in the course of which, due to the absence of conjugated verb, *beyond, there, out* seem to collide into one indistinguishable spatial "knot." To a certain extent, the father's drives from house to work and back in *There Is No Year* betoken the same topological distortions:

> The next day it took the father six hours to get home from work. He took the same way he took home every day but each day it seemed to take a little longer. The streets went on a little further each time he drove them. There were new things on old streets. There were

> new streets with no signs for street names. There were traffic lights
> spaced barely yards apart. Certain lights would sit for many minutes
> red with the father edging the car further and further into the empty
> intersection. There never seemed to be any other cars. Ahead, the
> horizon of no dimension—limbless and suspended, several states
> away. (*TINY*, 77)

The outside is turned into an inescapable, morphing labyrinth entrapping the father, who is thus faced with a "horizon of no dimension," that is, an unmappable space "suspended" in-between altering "states."

However, contrary to a smooth, indiscriminate passage from inside to outside and back, Möbius strip–like, the "zone of indiscernibility" occurs in the rifts, or is made perceptible in what Massumi calls the "stills." The lists, the iterations, the "sequencings"—sequences cut out and isolated and frozen—all contribute to the distortion, the blurring, the obfuscation of the narrative picture. The story-as-story is unhinged, its components do not follow or enmesh in linear fashion but instead superpose, overlay spatially, warping one another. In other words, Butler's texts eschew *narrative* proper—do not actually *tell* a story so much as they shape, almost prismatically, diverse isolated moments floating around one another, drawing one another while withdrawing in the process, cutting the flow, reassembling, starting over, reshaping, reiterating.

·

On a more thematic level, discreteness shows in the isolation of most characters through Butler's fiction. The father, mother, and son in *There Is No Year*, or former wife (Person 1180) and husband (Person 811), along with the putative child (Person 2030), in *Sky Saw*, are more often than not treated as isolated characters whose interactions are scarce and minimal. Although supposedly members of a same family unit, the space they occupy always seems distant and unrelated, a move made literal in the case of *Sky Saw* as husband and wife are confined to remote locations, virtually losing all memories of each other. This is also true somehow of *300,000,000*, in which Flood and Gravey never cross paths—a detachment made all the more visible as Flood's presence in the text is at first limited to comments appended in the margins of Gravey's transcribed notebook, a separation clearly marked by a horizontal line that holds these two distinct textual spaces apart in the book. Lone Alice, in *Alice Knott*, also recalls her extreme isolation and estrangement, whether physically or mentally, from her family—her "unfather" secluded in a room reading books after having taken her father's place; her "unbrother" always locked up in the room beside hers, and later put away in jail.

86 Sightings

Because of their isolation and lack of communication, Butler's characters, all of them ill-defined, most unnamed, never quite form characters per se but rather may be akin to "figures" instead, not unlike the isolated Figures that Gilles Deleuze identifies in Francis Bacon's painting—an isolation that makes it possible for the painter "to avoid the *figurative*, *illustrative*, and *narrative* character the Figure would necessarily have if it were not isolated" (Deleuze 2003, 2).

This overall sense of isolation, enhanced by the bare, ruined, postapocalyptic settings of *Scorch Atlas* or dystopian surroundings of *Sky Saw*, *There Is No Year*, or to a lesser degree *Alice Knott*, somehow loosens the fabric of Butler's fiction, pushing toward "aggregate" space instead of traditional, systematic, narrative space.

As such, and like *Was*, Michael Joyce's "novel of internet," or like Danielewski's *House of Leaves* too, Butler's fiction challenges generic and ontological boundaries between media. Says Manovich in *The Language of New Media*:

> traditionally the world of a computer game is not a continuous space but a set of discrete levels. In addition, each level is also discrete—it is a sum of rooms, corridors, and arenas built by the designers. Thus rather than conceiving space as a totality, one is dealing with a set of separate places. (Manovich, 257)

This can be viewed as quite a good description of what a novel like *There Is No Year* does and looks like, since the house at its core is made up of several rooms that never quite seem to communicate. Or if they do, they do so through unusual channels while indulging still in separate, autonomous lives of their own, causing the house's space to be endlessly reconfigured:

> Sometimes the son would come into a room and swear he was coming into the room he'd just come into when coming into the current room from the one before, and sometimes the son would come into a room and swear he'd never seen the room inside the house at all, and sometimes the son would come and there would be nowhere else to walk, and the room would have no ins or outs or exits: windows, doors. (*TINY*, 165)

The characters' motions through this ever-changing house are not unlike the moves made by players in a game, an analogy the novel openly invites when the son finds, one morning, his old video game console and starts playing:

> In the game the son was represented by a figure. The son could cause the figure to move in one direction or another. The son could lead the figure to die. . . . The son watched the figure fall through a section of

block he'd believed stable, but in fact held nothing there. The figure fell down a lengthy corridor just wide enough to fit the figure's breadth. . . . The room the figure fell into was made of walls. There was nothing much about them. The walls went on and on. There was nothing for the son to make the man jump over. There were no balls of fire or enormous rabbits, no floating crystal that squirted liquid, and no moving splotch with eyes. The room was just a room. An endless room in one direction. And yet the son could not get more than a certain distance through the level. (224–25)

The video game is here explicitly thematized. Interestingly, its basic description somehow resonates with whatever might be going on in the novel itself—a slippage made plausible in the shift from "the figure" to "the man"—especially when, toward the end of the game, the son activates a sequence that causes "a small black square" to appear "across the screen" (226). A glitch then seems to occur that initially freezes the figure—"No matter what buttons the son would press now the figure would not respond"—before eventually setting it free from the material constraints of the game:

Above, the square spread rapidly across the screen, aiming to cover over all. The son saw the figure begin to wriggle. The figure turned his head toward the son. The figure was looking at the son now most directly and there was something written in his eyes—something carried in the figure all those hours—carried over in every replicated instance of his entire life[9] (226)

Incidentally, a hundred pages further, in the course of his perambulation through the "copy house," the father stumbles upon "a black box large as the whole room," suddenly realizing

The door the father had come into the room through was no longer there behind him, nor was there much of any space left for him to stand between the box and wall. He had to suck his gut in, skin into skin there, held not breathing, and still there was hardly room for him to move—as if he were underneath the box at the same time as above it, and beside it—nothing but the box—no room at all. (324)

The flush-right alignment of the text in that section suggests that the father may have stepped into another ontological dimension; the "black box" he is suddenly faced with harkens back to the "black square" in the son's game—the space the father is moving through is now strangely empty, eaten up entirely by the box that descends upon and pushes against him. The father, it seems, ends

88   Sightings

up progressively merging with his own superficial image as the box swallows him up:

> The father pressed his head against the surface, wanting. He listened harder, leaning in. The more he leaned, the more he had to—his spine took kindly to the curve—then, there he was leaning with all of him against the image, its surface adhered to his shoulder and his cheek. . . . The box pulled on his backbone, barfing through his body in reverse— warm milk, spit, rainwater, stomach acid, fresh blood—his body sticking to the seam, wherever. In his head he heard a hundred guns—a fall, a swallow, sinking—black cells—then, there he was above him, and beside—then, there he was below him, and between him, and overhead, within—he could see himself from every angle—he could see himself inside the box. (324–25)

Once inside the box, the father may or may not be wandering in (literal) computer space, a shift or translation somehow suggested in the next section, where the text is now laid out in a single, narrow, centered column (326–27), before the column moves left or right on the page, following the father's moves inside the box (328–29), and finally spreads back into wider blocks of text (329–30).

•

Mark Danielewski's *House of Leaves* also impinges on new media aesthetics. Simulation is lodged at its core and displays itself quite dramatically on the page—a page turned screen, upon which the text plays and lays itself out spatially. In that regard, *House of Leaves* is a novel in performance as well as a novel to be read in the usual sense. What the page eventually showcases may be the conditions for an exchange between the *readerly* and—perhaps more than the *writerly* in Roland Barthes's conception as expounded in *S/Z*—the *userly*, turning the reader into a "user" faced with whatever is going on on-screen or on the novel's interface. As such, then, the page verges on, or mimics a computer screen, sharing its haptic modalities as defined by Lev Manovich. For indeed what *House of Leaves* shatters in its multiple, compound layout is the fixed frame of the page as a stable, continuous, systematic space, dislocating the text into a series of discrete elements whose linking, hence reading, remains highly problematic. The main effect that the page-cum-screen may be trying to achieve is none other than a form of simulation, aiming at some mimeticism between what characters go through on the diegetic level and what the reader has to perform, manipulating the book in an all-too-literal sense as one reads along. The book as media thus foregrounds its own materiality, not to say its technicity, asking to be turned upside down or to have its pages flicked through at different speeds, losing the reader in a maze of footnotes or insisting on the reversibility of its pages. Of course this might be true of any book, since as an object it demands minimal interaction from its reader, if only through mere page-turning, as ironically exemplified in Blake Butler's *Sky Saw*: page 133, "I would feel okay if you did not turn the page"; page 134, "Why did you do that?" However, *House of Leaves* pushes this to an extreme and instantiates a ludic temporality split between various rhythms dependent on the interventions of a reader/user in whom the text—its every move—comes to be embodied and performed. If this could initially be seen as a redefinition or *re*drawing of the relationality between reader and text, or user and object, rather than its speculative *with*drawing or cancellation, it tends to complicate it in ways that remain hard to grasp.

For of course, despite its generic hybridity, *House of Leaves* abides by a hermeneutic code and sticks to a more conventional narrative approach, resting as the text does on an enigma to be solved. If to a certain extent the novel can be seen as a remediation of video game aesthetics, it also instantiates a classic interpretative or explanatory quest followed on different levels of embeddedness by the diverse characters: Navidson et al.'s experience of the house; the documentary film shot by Navidson; its scholarly commentary by Zampanò; the putting together of Zampanò's work by Johnny Truant; and the eventual anonymously edited version of the book that the reader is holding in her hands. This complex relay and media assemblage inescapably mirrors and somehow parodies any subsequent readerly commentary, this one obviously in- or precluded. In short, to read *House of Leaves*, sifting through it for meaning, is always possible yet condemned in advance by its own parodied version.

The same is true of Michael Joyce's *Disappearance*, another novel remediating video games, about which Stuart Moulthrop in his preface writes:

> No doubt someone could spend great effort sorting out the various layers and correspondences of what may be an entirely logical dream, explaining what its various detectives seek to discover, the conundrum of the dream-murder that may have been an actual death, the contours and limits of its episodes and fugue states. . . . And yet, perhaps such success would never be the end this text desires. (*Disappearance*, xxii)

That could very well apply to Danielewski's novel too, for which numerous hermeneutic hypotheses and theories have been proliferating on various fans' sites, blogs, or forums exclusively dedicated to *House of Leaves*.

Yet the question raised by Moulthrop concerns the appropriateness of such

90   Sightings

readings; or, in his terms, their *desirability*—what do such texts "desire"?[10] The premise here is to treat the text as an object from an OOO perspective. Instead of asking what the text means *to* the reader, in a correlational way, Moulthrop inverts the terms of the equation to wonder what the text, *as such*, might want for itself, thus leaving open the possibility that whatever terms the text dictates, it might bypass correlation and claim some independence from reading and readers. Which, in a way, is made explicit by the non-dedication of *House of Leaves*—"This is not for you." But if reading then, conceived of in traditional terms oriented toward meaning and interpretation, appears not to be what such texts desire, what is, or could be, the alternative?

In the case of *Disappearance*, Moulthrop suggests that the video game paradigm entices the reader to treat the text as a game. Yet, "If this book embodies a game," writes Moulthrop, "we ought to be able not merely to lose our way in it, but ultimately to win" (*Disappearance*, xxii). In both cases, though—conventional reading and game playing—the framing of the question in those terms keeps positing an end to reach ("ultimately"), whether such an end happens to be some signification or some victory over the text's machination. As long as there remains something, anything, to be gotten, extirpated, gained from the text, the correlational element is not discarded. The text's desires are replaced with, usurped by, the critic's. Still, Moulthrop does realize, albeit tentatively, that "perhaps such success would never be the end this text desires" (*Disappearance*, xxii). Neither a game properly speaking—critics like Aspen Aarseth or Markku Eskelinen would insist that referring to such books as games can make sense only metaphorically—nor a novel anymore in any traditional instantiation, books like Joyce's *Was* or *Disappearance*, Danielewski's *House of Leaves*, and Blake Butler's *There Is No Year* do raise the question of how to read or use them, the better to interrogate the very modalities of *reading* as such—questions that trace and furrow various, ephemeral paths and brittle trajectories through the text that take the reader ever further away from this final promise: the promise of a reward to be found in the text, to which fiction, in its contemporary, experimental, or speculative mutations, may never fully yield. So the alternative may indeed be reading as a game, perhaps, whose outcome remains uncertain and elusive—promising nothing, issuing nothing.

•

Turning pages, in other words, no longer equates a linear, straightforward motion through the novel toward its logical conclusion. Whether with Butler's *There Is No Year* or Danielewski's *House of Leaves*, we're not traversing a systematic, unified, mimetic space anymore but, like the figures inhabiting the houses, we seem to be navigating through a sticky, palpable, performative space that keeps morphing and whose continuity is never guaranteed, as experienced by Alice Knott herself, who, in many regards, appears as the baffled reader's virtual avatar in the space of *Alice Knott*. Coupled with the figures' isolation in the case of Butler, these dynamic shifts rupture the continuity and linearity of the texts and contribute to turning the novels' spaces into discrete assemblages. Reading such texts thus requires readers to attune their perceptions of them and take heed of the texts' discontinuity, to navigate their aggregate spaces in ways different from more narrative undertakings, to "parse" them rather than read them. For what is eventually needed, it seems, is a form of "haptic" reading, another name for "parsing" perhaps, insofar as "Haptic perception isolates the object in the field as a discrete entity, whereas optic perception unifies objects in a spatial continuum" (Manovich, 253–54).

•

In *The Pleasure of the Text*, Roland Barthes famously recalled the etymology of *text* to draw attention to its intrinsic process or "perpetual interweaving," which led him to compare the text's fabric, or *tissue*, with a spider's web (Barthes 1975, 64). For what it's worth, such comparison also entails the recognition of gaps and holes in the midst of the text's diverse lines of force, a web amounting as much to its intricate structure as to what the structure hollows out—its cracks and breaches, its fissures and chinks. Discontinuity then is as much part of the text's *texture* as continuity is. But as the gaps widen and gain space in the text, narrative is dismantled, broken up, severed into discrete pieces whose organic continuity is made brittle and dissolves through the text's aggregate space.

In short, reading such texts paradoxically implies not reading them—or reading them differently, *haptically* perhaps—reading for the cracks that show through the surface of the text, for the blanks or "BLINK"s (*SS*, 84–89) that dislocate, disjoin, rupture, puncture the text's fabric.

•

There might be very little on the surface to accommodate this book's definition of speculative fiction in Shelley Jackson's *Half Life*. If the novel can be said to be speculative, it is mainly in the basic understanding of the term. Like Mark Doten's *The Infernal*,[11] Jackson's novel indeed posits a classic "what-if" scenario imagining a uchronic America. Following historical nuclear testing in Nevada, a wave of radiation permanently altered the American ecosystem, creating in the population of the United States a new minority of "twofers"—conjoined twins, their subculture, their lingo. Nora, the narrator, is one half of a twofer, sharing

92 Sightings

her body with her sister, Blanche. Despite its bizarreness, *Half Life* doesn't stray that far from the plausible. Contrary, say, to a novel like *The Flame Alphabet* by Ben Marcus, whose premise rests on a mysterious disease lodged in language, the premise to Shelley Jackson's novel remains entirely rational and doesn't entail the collapse of scientific explanation. Within the bounds of this peculiar world, the twofers' bodies remain realistic and bear very little resemblance to the weird bodies populating the post-catastrophic world of David Ohle's fiction, for instance. *Half Life*, then, remains on the surface a science-fictional text in a conventional sense, complying with Quentin Meillassoux's opposition between science fiction and extro-science fiction.

On a narrative level, *Half Life* also appears to be standard issue when compared with the likes of Joyce's *Was* or Butler's *Sky Saw*—there *is* a full-fledged story recounting Nora's quest for what birth deprived her of: a self, a singular identity. Nora thus embarks upon a search for a secret organization and clinic to rid herself, surgically, of her sister, Blanche, who's been plunged in a coma for quite some time after a traumatic event that Nora's dual narration—her own quest in the present paralleled with her retracings of its origins in the past— progressively unveils. *Half Life* thus appears far less extreme than more overly topological novels in their open challenge to narrativity, which takes the form of a discontinuous, aggregate, hybrid space.

Yet discontinuity is not altogether absent from *Half Life*, either formally or thematically. Nora and Blanche, or their common body, indeed appear as a peculiar site for such discontinuity, as suggested by Nora's frequent blanks and her growing suspicion that, without her being aware of it, Blanche may at times regain control of their body. Theirs is necessarily a *split* identity, which finds its way into the very fabric of the text. Nora follows a double narrative thread or arc or circle, alternating chapters about her childhood memories and present quest. These are distributed according to the four Boolean operators— NOT, XOR, OR, AND—each composing one of the four parts the book is divided into; if Blanche is represented by one circle, Nora by another one, the novel investigates the various ways they intersect and can or cannot be whole and claim an identity of their own. If Nora is slowly writing toward acceptance, as implied by the AND operator that closes the novel, the very title of the book, *Half Life*—punning with the nuclear concept referring to the time it takes for a radioactive substance to disintegrate—ironically unwrites the unity or completeness she's striving for.

In other words, despite its apparent narrative conventionality, *Half Life* is a novel that underscores its own paradoxical (lack of) identity, or unity, irrevocably split as it is between antithetical units—Nora and Blanche, black and white,

the ink and the page, narration and silence, the message and the medium—
that appear both fused yet separate, conjoined yet different, amalgamated yet
discrete.

Such discreteness is enhanced by the intertextual layering of the text,
whose opening lines blatantly echo the incipit of Nabokov's *Lolita:* "Blanche,
white night of my dark day. My sister, my self. Blanche: a cry building behind
sealed lips, then blowing through. First the pout, then the plosive; the meow
of the vowel; then the fricative sound of silence. Shhhh" (*HL,* 5). The slow de-
composition of Blanche's name significantly programs the movement of the
text from utterance (*cry*) to silence (*shhhh*), from language to its subtraction
made manifest on the novel's last page (see Fig. 4).

Beyond this initial allusion to Nabokov, literary references abound
throughout *Half Life,* from Shakespeare to Melville, Dickens, Lewis Carroll,
Twain, Beckett, folk and fairy tales. Nora's voice is never quite hers and often
rings with foreign echoes in the same way as her story is interspersed with alien
material she collects in her "Siamese Twin Reference Manual"—songs, interviews, op eds, emails, flyers, even a napkin (*HL,* 72). The very fabric of the text
is thus othered, somehow, and discontinued—a patchwork of foreign elements
that never quite mix together, that never erase their own materiality, which also
manifests in the novel's play with different fonts.

All these strategies, more or less covert, more or less visible, aim to defamiliarize the reading of the text. What is it that one reads, in the end? As Nora
herself finally comes to realize, "This book has been so much erased that its
larger part, like an iceberg's, is invisible. I begin to feel that *that* is the real book.
The words you are actually reading are just a sort of erased erasing, a cautiously
omitted omission" (355). What Nora thus draws attention to is the inaccessible
depth of her writing/unwriting. Whatever *Half Life* is *on the surface* is eventually countered, offset by its unfathomable *depths.*[12]

How deep, one may wonder, could all those subtractions, omissions, era-
sures be? How much has been left out or withdrawn from the text? "So much,"
claims Nora. Yet her own account, spanning more than four hundred pages, is
far from insubstantial. Again, a possible answer is provided by the conceptual
framework of Jackson's novel and its focus on its materiality. Nora understands
this in her next diary entry when she writes: "I am forgetting what cannot be
erased: the spaces. An eraser wielded against a blank page does not further
whiten whiteness, but leave [*sic*] a mark" (355). The forbidden depth of the
text stops at the whiteness of the page then—at its own surface; a merely differential surface between the words and what they rest on, ink and paper. A difference that eventually collapses as Blanche silently awakens from her coma,

Figure 4. Blank page from Shelley Jackson's *Half Life* (437)

thwarting Nora's plans, undoing the text, unraveling and literally undermining its reading. The novel's last line, uttered in Blanche's voice, signals an unexpected, untrackable shift in perspective, a takeover that caught both the reader and Nora unawares. Whatever happened happened without either noticing it, thus calling attention to the irrevocably flawed aspect of one's reading. Whatever one read, was misread, was missed. The reader is now left facing her own inadequacy—what she read eluded her grasp. A potential reminder that what you read, ultimately, may never be addressed to you. *Half Life* is thus *half-text*—one half you read, one half you couldn't.

•

At the heart of Jackson's *Half Life* lodges an unreadable absence, an indecipherable mystery embodied in Blanche—the word "mystery," Agamben recalls, derives from "**mu*, which indicates the moaning sound when the mouth is closed" or, "in other words, silence" (Agamben, 60).

Shhh.

Unsettling the course of the text, a similar type of absence/presence can be felt at the heart of *Fra Keeler* by Azareen Van der Vliet Oloomi. The novel opens on the narrator's blunt decision to buy Fra Keeler's former house in order, he only comes to understand later, "to fully investigate Fra Keeler's death" (*FK*, 7). From the start, then, the (chrono)logical pattern is subverted, as the act, buying the house, precedes its motive, investigating its former occupant's death: "And it is the same thought since I left the realtor's office: some people's deaths need to be thoroughly investigated, and, Yes, I think then, Yes: I bought this home in order to fully investigate Fra Keeler's death" (7).

Hence a mystery, one reckons, must surround Fra Keeler—about whom nothing is specified, and whose death is described as "more than just a death" (6). For indeed it seems to trigger enigmatic, unspecified events said simply to be "of the *un*friendliest category" (6). The italicized prefix draws attention to the strange formulation and the so-called notion of *unfriendly events*—as though the narrator were trying to personify whatever may be happening, presenting events in a weirdly personal light or connection. Yet, if the phrase is not altogether incomprehensible, its meaning is somehow called into question by the constant italicization of the negative prefix throughout the novel, enhancing the negativity with which the word is charged while jarring with the use of the superlative form, which pushes meaning in the opposite direction.

And indeed, the events befalling the narrator are bizarre and hardly rational. Things appear in his backyard—a canoe, a yurt—a package is delivered; the phone keeps ringing, reassembles after having been shattered; the weather abruptly switches from perfect sunshine to pouring rain; a cactus transforms into a woman; the narrator suddenly goes blank and wakes up hours later with no recollection of what happened in-between; the narrator is beset with images of his mother, her face burnt off, claiming her son did this to her; or mysterious fragments of language besiege his memory. So much so that the narrator himself acknowledges the "senselessness" of it all and the pointlessness of an investigation defined in terms of sense-making:

96 Sightings

> One is compelled to do something. To take advantage of the things that don't make sense: the yurt, I thought, Fra Keeler, waking up in the bedroom as though all of a sudden. And to attempt to make sense in regards to all of this is senseless. Rather one must attempt to make senselessness. "Because senselessness," I whispered to myself, "is sense at its peak, sense when it can no longer bare itself." (70–71)

Such lines inevitably reflect back upon the critical activity. For with the help of the first-person narrative, one cannot but step into the narrator's shoes, sharing in his investigation. I too want to comprehend; I too endeavor to make sense of the perplexing narrative—to connect events together, retrace causes, anticipate effects, locate the parting line between the real and the dream or hallucination(s). Yet something in the process is not quite right; the narrative frame is subtly deregulated as similar motifs, patterns, images, obsessively reappear. The text more or less unravels into abstraction and mere empty thoughts, as suggested by the sheer prevalence of the phrase "I thought," whose recurrence (more than four hundred times in a 120-page novel) turns what was purported to be an event-driven narrative into mere speculation, indeed.

However, if one were to take the narrator's hint, how could they or anyone actually "make senselessness"? The antithetic expression is in itself telling in that it again subverts the usual order of things according to which *sense* is what is being *made*. In other words, it grows out of something that is supposedly deprived of initial sense. Yet here the narrator's phrasing rather suggests that sense is always-already there somehow; a pollutant of sorts to be gotten rid of in the same way as "images," according to Francis Bacon, are always-already present on a canvas in the form of clichés the painter has to discard before he or she can start painting eventually (Deleuze, 2003). Sense would thus have to be dismantled, ruined, obliterated, stripped in order to achieve *senselessness*—which, contrary to sense then, would not be a given but something to strive toward and assemble: "sense when it can no longer bare itself."

In that regard, the obvious interpretation of *Fra Keeler*, according to which the narrator would be mad and suffering from hallucinations, is perhaps too obvious to be entertained. Granted, the narrator is quite obviously not to be trusted. This—of course his madness *is* a plausible explanation supported in part by the bibliography Van der Vliet Oloomi provides in her acknowledgments—is perceptible early in the text when, after having claimed that all official records of Fra Keeler's death arrive at the same conclusion, the narrator admits: "But no: I lied. To be fair, I omitted, I didn't lie, there is one record that does not match the others" (9). It seems then that *Fra Keeler* is a classic case of narrative unreliability—except that the narrator eventually admits to it, which thus paradoxically subverts the interpretative logic and eventually turns him, willy-nilly, into someone worthy of some trust. Or, at the very least, someone whose perception may not be as estranged from reality as it initially seemed and whose understanding of the "*un*friendly events" may not be utterly devoid of acumen. Hence his realization when faced with the incomprehensible sequence of events he is trapped in, which in part matches the reader's: "How else, I thought . . . but with sheer madness could one explain?" (87).

Yet if madness appears as the only possible explanation for the apparent non sequiturs the narrator goes through—"One minute it is raining—devilish sky!—the next the birds are chirping" (88)—it obviously remains an easy trick to make sense of what, on the surface, appear as absurd, unrelated events. In other words, making of madness the key to the enigma confronting the narrator, an enigma that now goes beyond the sole investigation into Fra Keeler's death and evolves, more and more, into a personal, mental, or cognitive drama, is just another way to forcefully blow meaning into the narrative and somehow standardize it—or to eschew its "*un*friendliness," that is, its sheer reluctance to *relate* and conform.

●

The same reluctance can be found in Ben Marcus's *The Flame Alphabet*, in which whole passages are devoted to, and filled with, their own negations. A case in point might be chapter 2, which opens with the following, baffled assertion on the part of the narrator: "The day my wife and I drove away, the electric should have failed. The phone should have died. The water should have thickened in our pipes" (*FA*, 8). The rest of the chapter is in keeping with its opening, as Sam details the diverse ways in which the real, on that particular day, failed to conform with his own expectations, or retrospective understanding of what was then taking place—and what now feeds his sense of loss and catastrophe—as he and Claire were leaving their neighborhood behind and abandoning their only daughter. Willy-nilly, what Sam thus patiently elaborates in chapter 2 is a review of the staples of postapocalyptic scenarios:

> That day should have been visibly stained at the deepest levels of air, broken open, sucking people into oblivion. The neighborhood should have been vacuum-sealed, with people reduced to crawling figures, wheezing on their hands and knees, expiring in heaps. (8)

By drawing attention to such a lack of conformity, Sam of course enhances the emotional impact the scene had on him and his wife, as well as his frustration at the fact that so-called postapocalyptic fiction is eventually no match for reality:

98 Sightings

"What is it called," he asks, thus appealing to what turns out to be a purely literary concept, "when features of the landscape mirror the conditions of the poor fucks who live in it?" Not caring for the answer, Sam concludes: "Whatever it is, it was not in effect" (9). Whether or not Sam may have the concept of pathetic fallacy in mind, its omission from the text ironically points to its blatant fallaciousness indeed when gauged against the lived reality of the scene.

After the initial exposition of the language disease in chapter 1, chapter 2 thus already holds the narrative development of the novel in check by marking a pause in the chronological recounting of the facts—Sam, that early in the novel, somehow refuses to tell what happened and chooses instead to focus on what paradoxically didn't. The gesture punctures the narrative fabric, depletes the text of its so-called events, replacing them with empty pockets of nonfacts. In a way, Sam is literalizing the father's optical tricks in "The Father Costume" as a way of "creating a disappearance" (*LS*, 189). The math Sam aggressively urges his reader to do in conclusion—"Do the math on that" (*FA*, 10)—indeed suggests a list of operations that, in that case, turn out to be subtractions: rather than adding grist to Sam's narrative mill, the text folds back upon itself, slowly negates its own contents, thus signaling a larger narrative trend that consists in opening up various empty textual spaces that double, obfuscate, and/or drain the expected narrative development of the text.[13]

Like: "I'd put it in the refrigerator, is what I would do. The cake would be there for [Esther] when she was hungry. Perhaps when I was feeling better I would have a piece, too" (108). Yet Sam will never be feeling better.

Like: "When we got to the motel I would bathe [Claire], let her sleep, and go out and get us some food, if I could find any. Perhaps she would sleep for days. I would let no children into the room" (137). Yet Sam and Claire will never get to the motel.

Like: "I thought of Claire waking up tomorrow morning thinking *This is the day*, stepping over the badly slept bodies of her cohorts, and then getting led down hallways and corridors and through rooms and out, finally, into the sickening light of the courtyard, where she could finally, she just knew, run to Esther and hug her close, and even if they could not speak, couldn't they be near each other, maybe find a shelter somewhere to enjoy each other's company in silence? Why, after all, would anyone want to keep Esther from her?" (219). Yet it will *never* be "the day."

Or like: "Not if I can help it, I didn't say, whoever you fucking are" (69); "Spitting image of LeBov, I didn't say" (119); "*It's all right*, I didn't say" (230); "I'm coming for you, Darling, I didn't say. I'm coming to get you" (241); "Just not to you, I didn't say" (246); and so on.

If such passages obviously point to Sam's powerlessness, which in turn feeds his own wishful thinking, they're also part and parcel of the text's apophatic aesthetic and ontology.[14] For these (non)narrative moves, which consist in or enact a withdrawal from the text, may gesture toward that "ineluctable modality of the visible." If such modality proves "ineluctable," Didi-Huberman claims, it is mainly because it pertains to a question of *being* (Didi-Huberman, 14); as such, it is akin to some symptomaticity and recedes into an unreachable background constituted by "a work of loss."[15]

And loss, in Sam's case, is all too literal in *The Flame Alphabet*—loss of his daughter, loss of his wife, loss of language and the ability to communicate or to relate. No wonder then that Sam's account, in its constitutive reluctance, should be pervaded or inscribed with paradoxical moments that resist and elude narrativity by overtly fleeing from it, doubling and intensifying it in the same paradoxical way that Burke's sermons happen to be devoid of signification altogether, appear "skeletal, in bones of language that often could not be joined for sense. Such messages were often hammered flat, their meaning ripped out" (*FA*, 44), or, later, in the same paradoxical way that Sam's attempt at a new "flame alphabet" would turn out to be the very negation of an alphabet, a "nonalphabet, a system revolving around one symbol that could never be used in a word, a letter that did not even exist yet, a letter whose existence was merely inferred by the other letters" (210). An unreadable, invisible one—one that would indeed be an irredeemable, ineluctable work of loss, not to be shared, seen, or ever related to.

Such might be, perhaps, what Sam's narrative enterprise consists in, in the end. A nonnarrative. A "decoy" or mere pretense eventually—the negative of a text, written under or underwritten in ways reminiscent of Nora's attempts at concealment and erasure in Shelley Jackson's *Half Life*, for instance. The sheer insistence on decoys, doubles, fakes, secrecy, camouflage, impenetrability throughout *The Flame Alphabet*[16] does point in this direction and begs for a rereading of the text from its opening line in order to *see* to what extent one *cannot see* how this incipit cues the rest of the novel: "We left on a school day, so Esther wouldn't see us" (3).

·

"We left on a school day, so Esther wouldn't see us" (*FA*, 3). Not only are the notions of flight, evasion, and invisibility already scripted in the line that opens *The Flame Alphabet*—what matters here, in the novel's incipit, is for Sam (and Claire) *not* to be seen, for their move *not* to be witnessed, which of course can read as a form of necessary deception and betrayal given their condition and

100 Sightings

its origin in Esther—but the opening line in Sam's account, to anyone familiar with Ben Marcus's previous works,[17] cannot fail to look inconspicuous in its blunt declarative stance. A fact is stated and henceforth taken for granted: Sam and his wife, Claire, left their neighborhood, unseen by their own toxic daughter. This line will resurface several times through the first part of the novel in various forms, propagating the same apparent fact: "Once just days before we left ..." (6); "The day my wife and I drove away ..." (8); "In the months before our departure ..." (11); "We drove out the next morning" (134).

However, this version—though true in many respects: Sam and Claire did leave their home on Wilderleigh Street, they did part ways with Esther, who happened to be nowhere in the picture around them—proves eminently deceptive. In the subsequent reenactment and repetition of their departure, something somehow escapes you—something you don't or can't *see*. The fact is *ineluctably* split, rendered dual, doubled or lined by its own cancellation, as eventually revealed in chapter 22, which somehow picks up where chapter 1 left off. Resuming the description of that same departure day, Sam now adjoins the missing part—the withdrawn part, the part not seen, the *counter*-part: "When the departure horn tore open the New York air, and the cars started their slow crawl from town, Claire opened the passenger door and stumbled into the grass" (141). Never to return to the car. Sam may step out to chase after her, but he's immediately caught up by "the technicians of the quarantine" and shoved back into his vehicle: "They stuffed me in my car, shut the door, then banged a hand on the roof to tell me it was okay to go now. Join the procession out of here. Get going. *Without her*" (142).

Whether or not this twist can or should be seen as the result of a classic case of unreliable narration, it does set into motion the text's formally disseminative dynamic, in the sense Derrida gives to the word when, in a footnote to "Outwork," the (un)opening of *Dissemination*, he comments that "Everything, then, begins—this is a law of dissemination—doubled by a 'facing' [*par une doublure*]" (Derrida, 8). Such happens to be the case too of *The Flame Alphabet*, whose inconspicuous opening is similarly and already "doubled by a facing" that appears ineluctably deceptive. The split occurs in ways that cannot be reconciled, reduced, or synthesized,[18] as—this being another law of dissemination—it foils all binary oppositions along with their dialectical sublatings (Derrida, 25).

In other words, cued by this doubled, "ineluctably" split opening, the whole novel proves eminently duplicitous, built as a gigantic trompe l'oeil according to which what one sees is always traversed by this "work of loss" that Didi-Huberman identifies as "the ineluctable modality of the visible"—which here could be said to translate, somewhat speculatively, as *the ineluctable modality of the readable*: reading is thus necessarily unproductive insofar as the text, in its intrinsic formal nature, does not, cannot, yield or give access to anything that could be construed as an asset or a gain. Didi-Huberman writes:

> Of course, the familiar experience of what we see seems more often than not to lead to some gain [*un avoir*]: when we see something we usually have the impression of having gained something. Yet the modality of the visible becomes ineluctable—that is to say destined to a question of being—whenever seeing amounts to feeling that something ineluctably eludes us, or to put it differently: how to lose things by seeing them. That is all there is.[19]

•

Whatever mysteries the speculative text contains, they're bound to remain intact, intractable. Of this, the reader's immediately forewarned by the "Argument" opening Ben Marcus's *The Age of Wire and String.* The society and culture that the book is supposedly a "catalog" of is from the outset programmed to remain deeply and paradoxically hidden at the heart of its very disclosure. The antagonistic vocabulary—"prosecuted," "looting our country of its secrets," "a product that must be ravaged of bias," "by looking at an object we destroy it with our desire," "perish in blindness, flawed" (*AWS*, 3–4)—enhances the text's aggressive stance while showcasing its categorical unwillingness to cooperate with its readers and critics, "professional disclosers" practicing their nefarious "routine in-gazing," treacherously appropriating the exoticism of the textual landscapes they visit while drowning them under their all too "banal hues" (*AWS*, 3–4).

This "Argument"—the term ambiguously suggesting both an opening statement and/or a disputation—reads in part as a challenge to critical writing, warning readers like me, that is, readers with a view to understanding the text they're about to read, against interpretation while displaying its intrinsic resistance and opacity. The sheer absurdity—"Intercourse with resuscitated wife for particular number of days, superstitious act designed to insure safe operation of household machinery" (7)—or abstruseness of the vignettes—"Girl burned in water, supplementary terms *help* or *X*, basic unit of religious current. It is the fundamental spiritual object used with the *X*-water (burnable) system of units of the GOD-BURNING SYSTEM" (89)—indeed pleads against meaning or, if not, at least demonstrates its necessarily arbitrary, artificial nature. This resistance to meaning eventually becomes a leitmotif in *Notable American Women*,

102 Sightings

at the end of which, after recounting in the recriminatory letter she addresses her husband what could serve as a parable of sorts, Ben's mother bluntly states: "Understanding is overrated. To hell with it" (*NAW*, 228).

The very stylistics of both *The Age of Wire and String* and *Notable American Women*, their aggressiveness and radicalism, their anti-narrative streak, their absurdist bias, their overt fictionality: all of those eventually call the reader's attention to the texts' inherent efforts to withstand meaning, their reluctance to yield to interpretation, their withdrawal behind a screen-text that is nothing but mere trompe l'oeil or simulacrum. The "Blueprint" section in *Notable American Women* exemplifies this, since with each new occurrence of the phrase "this book"—"This book is unfortunately designed for people"; "Although this book is for people in general . . . " (46)—the text, in what amounts to an impossibly self-reflexive move, merely exhibits the absolute remove or utter discrepancy between sign ("this book") and object (the material book that contains the words "this book"): the whole section fills indeed with pages that ultimately deal with what the book supposedly is or should have been, "but for the limitations of space," for instance (47), thus further limiting the available space and ironically withholding the narrative proper.

Although the strategy appears different, the result is somewhat identical: much like Shelley Jackson's *Half Life*, then, Ben Marcus's early fiction unreads itself, as it were. The book I *am* reading never truly coincides or corresponds with what the book (says it) *is*.

•

To the extent that it abides by Barthes's "hermeneutic code," *Fra Keeler* may not be immediately speculative; nor does it consequently spell out the end of narrative proper. Right from the beginning, one is made to understand that a sequence of events must have unfolded that culminated in Fra Keeler's death, which provides the narration with its starting point—a sequence that the narrator purports to retrace when moving into Fra Keeler's house. *Fra Keeler*—or so is the expectation that the text raises in its opening pages—is thus bound to account for the character's death, to solve its mystery by unveiling what caused it and what truly happened. The narrator indeed suspects that Fra Keeler may have died in circumstances that drastically differ from the official cause found in the various records he claims he has come across so far:

> We are said to die of one thing on paper, but it is entirely of something different that we die, I thought as I left the realtor's office. And it is dangerous to take the discrepancy between the two for granted, what one

> actually dies of and what one is said to have died of on paper; there is
> hardly ever a correspondence. (*FK*, 6)

Fra Keeler, it seems, will thus embark on a quest for answers, in search of meaning and "correspondence."

Indeed, attention is immediately drawn to the "discrepancy" between the fact and what is said of it; between death as a terminal event and what is *said* to have caused it. If there is something to investigate, then, (official) language has to be part of the problem, to the extent at least that it cannot bridge the gap between the real and its representation or the ways of relating to it; a gap here made all the more problematic in this instance as one specific event in space and time—"I was thinking of Fra Keeler's death" (5)—is generalized into a universal truth ("<u>we</u> die"/"what <u>one</u> actually dies of"). Framed this way, Fra Keeler's death already recedes into an abstract, universal distance; Fra Keeler ceases to be some (unspecified) relation of the narrator and becomes instead representative of some general truth—albeit a truth made up on the fly: "I was thinking of Fra Keeler's death. . . . I thought as I left the realtor's office. . . . And I'm thinking now. . . . I'm thinking now, it isn't every day one comes across a death that is especially timely and magnificent, for example Fra Keeler's death" (5–6).

"Timely and magnificent," Fra Keeler's death is situated both in and out of time. It is both concrete and abstract, actual and receding, a fact and its aestheticization. Thus posited in the text as the initial mystery to be investigated, Fra Keeler's death happens to be the starting and ending points of the narrative, what launches the hermeneutic quest yet, also, what instantly freezes it—for the answer to the question is *already* provided a mere couple of pages later: Fra Keeler died of lung cancer (9). But such an answer proves unsatisfactory to the narrator, who cannot make sense of it: "The reasons given for Fra Keeler's death are nothing short of nonsense, and if they do make sense, their sense is limited" (8). In short, the character's death is unreadable to the narrator; it appears literally out of reach, out of bounds. It may set the narrative in motion, yet it also simultaneously thwarts it, impeding all attempts at "correspondence," proving utterly devoid of meaning. The whole novel, in other words, rests on a yawning gap—a blank never to be filled, between Fra Keeler's death and the way the narrator could ever relate to it, between what happened and what could ever be said about it.

Such discrepancy is pointed to in the very first lines of the text: "'It's on the edge of a canyon,' the realtor said, raising his eyebrows when I offered to buy the home without having looked at it first" (5). *Fra Keeler* thus opens on a blatant reversal, immediately signaling a flaw in the eventual chronology of its events: "without having looked at it <u>first</u>." To put it differently, the novel takes its cue from an original action that, as such, failed to take place. What logically, as much as chronologically, should have initiated the narrator's purchase of the house did *not* happen. Not only is the opening move of the text incongruous—the house is far from ideally located, on the edge of a canyon—it also appears to be literally noncongruent, belying the non-correspondence between the act and the context or background against which it takes place, thus arousing the realtor's surprise and incomprehension, an incomprehension further indicated by the narrator's baffled response: "'Fine,' I said, though I wasn't sure exactly what the realtor <u>meant</u>" (5).

Despite its overtly hermeneutic bias at first, *Fra Keeler* will never close its initial gap. Comprehension and understanding, to the extent that they suggest matching and correspondence, are modes of relating to the text that are bound to remain foreign to it. If understanding presumes the slow building of the narrative toward its own resolution, it is blatantly undermined by the text's progress or, rather, its slow unraveling process. Instead of moving forward and building momentum, the text indeed stagnates around diverse reiterations, obsesses over static thoughts, contemplates absences, ponders gaps in sequences that appear truncated or counterfeit. And it is precisely the idea of such impossible *sequences* that bothers the narrator, who finds himself caught up in dubious events and thoughts that do *not* follow any orderly or logical pattern: "some things are willfully intractable, I thought, some things go against the grain. One moment, and then the next, I thought, with no event in between" (51).

Such discontinuity in the narrator's lived experience is offset by the very texture of the narrator's thought process, which on the surface seems to develop smoothly, thought after thought in a ceaseless, uninterrupted flow. Yet this apparently seamless stream is often disturbed by the abrupt contradictions or about-turns in the narrator's thinking, at times convinced, for example, that everything connects—"The events, one after the other, a whole constellation of events connecting" (85)—and at times persuaded that nothing does[20]—"Just event after event: one event landing, another setting off" (73). And if there is something in between to ensure a semblance of continuity, it is a mere "phantom event"—"events out of nowhere in between" (51).

The picture is thus irrevocably blurring or distending. The further one reads into the narrative, the more estranged the narrator becomes from his own environment—his new home, the backyard, his neighbors: the gap that keeps him at bay widens more and more until he no longer even recognizes himself or his own thoughts, which, the narrator claims at some point, seem strangely to preexist him:

> Thoughts, you walk through them, they exist before you, I told myself, picking up the thought again, and by some trick of the mind you think it was your thought and you drag it out, a thought as long as your DNA, and you push at it with your finger and you say, "Ah, yes: This is my thought," and it breathes back against your finger, and you are very satisfied, you and the thought together, you thinking the thought is yours and the thought thinking back at you, right up against your finger. What an idiotic thing to think about, I thought, as I slammed the door shut. (39)

Whether or not this makes any sense, the narrator is here both actor and spectator of his own thought process, both caught up in the act of thinking while at the same time estranged from it—much like Alice Knott appears to be in Blake Butler's eponymous novel: "Alice is there. She can hear her thoughts as though in dictation, somewhere above her. . . . *I was watching myself as if from above, and at the same time as from inside me*" (*AK*, 59).

As is more and more apparent in *Fra Keeler*, the drama the narrator is absorbed in no longer has anything to do with facts and events so much as his own thinking process *about* them. The distance grows between so-called reality and its internalization by the narrator in the guise of "thoughts" circling around on themselves. What the narrator experiences, whether this indeed is madness or not, is his own aloofness from his mental landscape, as exemplified by the mirroring enacted by the second person—"they exist before you, I told myself" (39). Thoughts, as suggested here, possibly ironically or comically, grow autonomous and create another gap that punctures the narrator's experience of the real—a real that remains unapproachable, irreconcilable, forever distant and incomprehensible in its absoluteness, that is, its own unrelatability.

•

"Was it real? I thought, and looked down at my hands" (*FK*, 111). The novel concludes on yet another blank, as the narrator is arrested for an act that remains untold and whose reality eludes him. Having apparently broken into his neighbor's house by the end of the novel, the narrator is confronted with her mutilated body—a body barely evoked or described by the narration, however, both present and absent. "Could it be, I thought, and by whose hands?" (111) The narrator's question is significantly truncated and murder is never qualified as such; it only registers in the narrator's mind after his arrest, albeit as a general category whose reference remains uncertain:

> "Take a look at these," [the detective] said, "and tell me what you think." He tapped his index finger against the papers, as if to say look here, and I spied near his finger something very familiar across the page. The death-related papers, I thought, forgery, murder, and the lights went out in my head." (118)

A few lines down: "Blood, I thought, murder, the *un*friendly events" (119). In both instances, the reference to murder is ambiguous, unattached to any specific event, and it seems to strike the narrator only in relation to Fra Keeler, his "death-related papers" or the "*un*friendly events" surrounding his demise; the act is never quite registered as the narrator's own and is not explicitly mentioned in connection to the neighbor's death either, which is merely alluded to and immediately evacuated from the text as well as from the narrator's thoughts. In other words, the final, and possibly only, *event* to speak of in the novel is treated as though it were another of the "phantom events" coming "out of nowhere," an event that may or may not have taken place—a blank in the narrator's memory, a gap in the texture of the narrative.

Of course, such a blank could corroborate the narrator's madness and/or be interpreted as a traumatic event immediately repressed from his consciousness—thus rescuing the narrative from the "senselessness" it appeals to. But wouldn't that be, like the detective, perhaps too quickly "jump[ing] to conclusions"? Because the act is passed over in silence, registered as a blank or committed in a textual gap, it literally haunts the novel's ending instead of anchoring it firmly or resolutely. More than an actual event, it is present in the text as a mere possibility or virtuality that, rather, appears to be floating above reality and suspended in time: "How much time has gone by, I thought, since I have been here? Minutes, I counted, years. Anything in between" (116). The narrator appears radically alien to the world around him and further estranged from himself: "I looked down at my hands. I hardly recognized them" (116). "Hardly anything was making sense. I had the distinct feeling of having cut off various parts of myself. I am empty, I thought, my core is dead" (119). He ultimately realizes how far removed he is from whatever may have happened—a spectator again grappling with a performance that eludes him, surfacing amid mere reflections and echoes. Whether or not the narrator did commit the murder, the fact that it is left out of the narrative picture turns it into an act whose violence cannot be related or related *to*. What the narrator eventually brushes up against, thus coming full circle, is the radical discrepancy between the act and whatever could be said about it—an absolute lack of correspondence. "'Are you going to talk this time?' the man asked. . . . 'Nothing?' he asked, hanging his head from his neck. 'Nothing,' I responded'" (116–17).

Fra Keeler may be just that in the end—a novel that, despite all appearances to the contrary, severs itself from all modes of relating, cuts itself off, slowly dislocates, unravels into refusal and nothingness. "One moment, I thought, and then the next—and I couldn't tell if it was blood or water—I let everything drift away" (121).

Speculative fiction—as I conceive of it—may not be for me then. The speculative text is such, perhaps, to the very extent that it unweaves its own narrativity, dissolves in the midst of loose, haptic spaces, withdraws, retreats, crosses itself out, negates or simulates its own contents the better to resist appropriation and thwart reading. Meaning, or sense, insofar as they embody that which the critic strives for, that which supposedly lodges at the heart of the text, its depth to be fathomed, its secret to be pierced, is thus more or less overtly debunked in the process. Which does not mean that it is not *there, that speculative fiction does not* mean *anything—but that, whatever it may signify, it does so on my end only; I* make *the text* mean*, applying to it a language that is mine and remains foreign to the text as such. A text that eventually may beg for some different approach, that may desire something that I can't offer or won't see. Blanks, or blind spots; silences, or acts of disappearance. Perhaps,* dear Incomprehension*, it's time I came to terms with the fact that there is nothing to understand; that the text, as such and in itself, is not, never to be known but maybe simply acknowledged. Felt, touched. Manipulated. Handled. Fondled. Not so much for what it would stand for as for what, in itself, it* is*. The fact that it* is*. Which is mystery enough.*

Speculative Sublime, Or "_____"

As exemplified in "The Disappeared," the opening story in Butler's *Scorch Atlas*, the quest for answers and meaning—in which only the narrator's incarcerated father seems to believe, his son merely taking up after him mechanically at first—irremediably fails, just as doctors failed to account for the son's skin disease:

> My uncle sent for surgeons. They measured my neck and graphed my reason. Backed with their charts and smarts and tallies, they said there was nothing they could do. They retested my blood pressure and reflexes for good measure. They said say ah and stroked their chins. Then they went into the kitchen with my uncle and stood around drinking beer and cracking jokes. (*SA*, 24)

However, despite science and reason's bankruptcy, in ways reminiscent of what Quentin Meillassoux describes as extro-science worlds, the son's condition ends up unaccountably improving after a dream in which his mother appears to him:

> Another night I dreamed my mother. She had no hair. Her eyes were black. She came in through the window of my bedroom and hovered over. She kissed the crud out from my skin. Her cheeks filled with the throbbing. She filled me up with light. (24)

As depicted by the narrator, his dream is strangely transitive—the son does not dream *of* his mother but dreams her into being, or so the grammar suggests. The separation between the real and the dream is breached and the hallucination gains as much efficacy as the laws of science, if not more:

The next morning my wounds had waned to splotches.

After a week, I was deemed well. (24)

There and not there, an auratic presence bathed in light and brilliance —"clear and brimming, bright, alive" (29)—the mother defies the conventions of realistic representation throughout. As such, she might embody a form of sublimity not unlike that which Timothy Morton, in *Realist Magic*, opposes to horror and posits as a privileged aesthetic mode to try to account for reality from a speculative, object-oriented perspective: "What speculative realism needs would be a sublime that grants a kind of *intimacy* with real entities" (*RM*, 130).

Indeed, the disappeared mother could be seen or *felt* as a metaphor of the real understood along speculative lines and revealed, yet not explained, by a speculative sort of sublimity that Morton derives and adapts from the Longinian sublime, to the extent that the latter "is about the physical intrusion of an alien presence"—a presence that can be extended "to include non-human entities" (*RM*, 131). Of course, one could always argue that in this particular example the mother doesn't rank as a nonhuman entity and that whatever sublimity she manifests in the story proves not speculative enough; yet her disappearance, her absence, her "aura" (*SA*, 28), and, more generally, her association with radiance throughout "The Disappeared" somehow turn her into something both more *and* less than any human, correlational entity, positing her on a de facto "alien" plane of (in)existence or (non-)relation, rather than rendering her as just another full-fledged character. The dream the narrator experiences, in all its transitivity and directness, suggests that the hallucinated mother extends beyond mere mental phenomenon; her direct action, as intimately *felt* rather than decoded by the narrator, whose deadpan, purely descriptive account hints at some absence of relationality, further contributes to turning her into an "object" per se—as understood by ooo: "we define 'object' as that which has a unified and autonomous life apart from its relations, accidents, qualities, and moments" (Harman 2010, 199). The mother may act, yet she remains untouchable, spurring no apparent reaction in her passive son. Hence her luminous associations, given that, in the conception Morton expounds in *Realist Magic*, "Brilliance is what *hides* objects" (*RM*, 132). This in turn attunes the notion of brilliance to the withdrawn character of all objects as conceived by Harman's object-oriented ontology. As Morton explains, in words that could apply to the presence-absence of the mother in "The Disappeared":

> Brilliance is the secretiveness of the object, its total inaccessibility prior to relations. In the mode of the sublime, it's as if we are able to

taste that, even though it's strictly impossible. The light of this inner magma is blinding—that's why it's withdrawal, strangely. It's right there, it's an actual object. Longinus thus calls this brilliance an uncanny fact of the sublime. . . . For the object-oriented ontologist, brilliance is the appearance of the object in all its stark unity. Something is coming through. Or better: we realize that something was already there. This is the realm of the uncanny, the strangely familiar and familiarly strange. (*RM*, 133)

•

A similar type of light and brilliance traverses Butler's *There Is No Year*, a novel that does not overly partake of the same (post)apocalyptic conditions of (non) representation but that shares *Scorch Atlas*'s "speculative sublime" aesthetic, almost stating it as such in the novel's opening line: "For years the air above the earth had begun sagging, suffused by a nameless, ageless eye of light. This light had swelled above the buildings. It caked on any object underneath" (*TINY*, ix). Rather than revealing objects for what they are, the light that pervades the text leads to some material obfuscation, "cak[ing] on any object" it touches upon. The light itself, though acting in almost tangible ways, "unlike most other light, outside itself could not be seen, could not be felt impressed upon each inch of air and body. It had no length, no temperature, no speed" (ix). In short, it eludes all measures, exists outside of any frame of reference, thwarts all systems of representation without however shying away from what Morton calls intimacy with real entities: "Each day the light grew gently thicker, purer. Each day still felt the same. Its presence rode in ridges on the faces of the hours and in silent hair all down all arms" (ix). Unfelt yet not immaterial, the light is a jarring, sublime presence that underlines, in Morton's words, "the sensuality of objects" (*RM*, 131) as it courses on, or through, or against them, as suggested by such terms as "gently," "ridges," "faces," "hair," "arms"—a sensuality to be found in the language itself, through its rhythmic and alliterative patterns: "<u>ro</u>de in <u>ridges</u> <u>on</u> <u>the</u> <u>fa</u>ces <u>of the</u> hou<u>rs</u> and in <u>s</u>ilent hai<u>r</u> <u>all</u> down <u>all</u> a<u>rms</u>." The book itself is not devoid of such (dark) sensuality, its pages displaying various colors from pure white to dark gray in what resembles dynamic ink swathes, as though the light itself moved along the pages throughout the book, ebbing and flowing rhythmically, in cadences further mimicked by the visual layout of the text, which on the novel's opening page is arranged in six evenly spaced, two-line paragraphs.

As its opening suggests, then, in all its "strangely familiar or familiarly strange" associations, *There Is No Year* is a book—more than just a novel—that undermines mimetic representation and linear narrative in favor of a more

112   Sightings

abstract, more performative, and more sensual regime of writing verging on the speculative sublime.[1] What, according to Morton in *Realist Magic,* distinguishes the speculative sublime from horror as a mode privileged by "several speculative realists" for apprehending reality is that horror remains "too much of a reaction shot, too much about how entities correlate with an observer" (*RM*, 130). On the contrary, the speculative sublime as remodeled after its Longinian definition, eludes correlation; it manifests itself between objects, independently of any human reaction or observation. "What we need," Morton claims, "is an aesthetic experience of coexisting with 1+n other entities, living or nonliving" (*RM*, 130). In other words, the sublime is not limited to one's understanding of—or lack thereof—or correlation with the object that triggers the sublime experience, with its mix of "shock and awe" in its Burkean definition, for instance. It involves "1+n other entities"—that is, it goes beyond mere correlation to include an unknown, unknowable number of foreign elements that escape one's grasp, that retract into the background of one's perception and understanding—or withdraw, for Morton, into an *aesthetic* field inasmuch as causality pertains to aesthetics:

> This background is nothing other than an aesthetic effect—it's produced by the interaction of 1+n objects. The aesthetic dimension implies the existence of at least one withdrawn object. To put it another way, in order for anything to happen, there has to be an object in the vicinity that has nothing to do with the happening in question. (*RM*, 32)

Much like *Scorch Atlas,* and along with *Sky Saw* and even *300,000,000* to a lesser extent, *There Is No Year* may flirt with the aesthetics of horror—the proliferation of insects, the misshapen bodies, the gruesome depictions, the gory details seem to vouch for horror indeed. Yet Butler often blurs the generic picture, and something, at the heart of horror, resists it if, in Morton's words, horror is conceived of as "the limit experience of sentient lifeforms" (*RM*, 130). To the exception perhaps of *300,000,000,* whose take on the detective story suggests, at least at first, the possibility of a more hermeneutic approach embodied in Detective Flood, who acknowledges being baffled by the Gretch Gravey case under investigation, Butler's work does away with any human attempt at understanding whatever befalls the characters, whose blatant lack of emotional commitment points to their passive acceptance and resignation, at best.[2]

A father, a mother, a son may disappear in *There Is No Year,* but the family's interactions are so scant that they don't even seem to notice, as though they are living on separate planes of existence that barely intersect. The same is true of *Alice Knott* in which the sudden disappearance of Alice's father, replaced by an "unfather" she fails to recognize, is treated matter-of-factly by the mother who claims things are what they've always been. In *There Is No Year*, the result is cold, mechanical descriptions rid of any narrative peak, as no event ever seems to happen; or if something does, it is treated as from a distance that blunts whatever narrative edge the event could have had. In that sense, the worlds depicted by Butler appear irretrievably *flat*, with each element—whether a character, a change in scenery, an accident, a disappearance—given the same importance or, rather, *lack* of importance. In *Alice Knott*, the whole world around Alice, or what little descriptive landscape there is, shares in such conspicuous flatness: "Meanwhile, outside, unseen, the sun is razing down upon the open <u>flatness</u>" (*AK*, 46); "The world around them continues on its fat blank, scaling toward nothing, <u>flatness</u> in all directions, for forever, only waiting some day to be filled in" (135); "in the sky above she sees no sun, no cloud or plane, but endless <u>flatness</u>, so sharp it's hard to look at" (251).

Blake Butler's fiction can thus be said to be speculative to the extent that it depicts worlds of pure objectness, "flat world[s], where things are devoid of any kind of intensity"—"world[s] in which any thing, *sensu stricto*, is equivalent to another thing" (Garcia, 5). Insofar as human emotions would highlight some intensity or belie flatness through the delineation of some apparent relief, they never quite seem to make it to the surface of the text. Yet it might be this very absence of emotional impact or investment that bypasses conventional horror to usher in the speculative sublime and its "1+*n* other entities," with which it becomes possible to step out of the correlational circle to focus on *objects* as such. As stated by Morton: "The way objects appear to one another is sublime: it's a matter of contact with alien presence, and a subsequent work of radical translation" (*RM*, 131).[3] The "contact with alien presence" and the "radical translation" that ensues ensure that the sublime encounter doesn't boil down to mere correlation with an observer, the observer in question being incapable of ever relating to what is happening or failing to, which was the case with most narrators in *Scorch Atlas*, for instance, most of whom trade narrative accents for mere ekphrastic description, thus replacing, displacing, or aesthetically *translating* their non-experience.

This is also the case with the unnamed son in Butler's *There Is No Year*, who's been witnessing the slow progression of ants in the house. The event could easily morph into a scene of pure horror. However, the ants—appearing from nowhere and eventually disappearing from the text with no more explanation—may well act in the text as pure metaphor, or a *translation* of something, some other entity/-ies, lying beyond them. The ants, in other words, are not just ants but, following Morton, ants+*n* other elements constitutive of the

114 Sightings

larger textual background, an aesthetic manifestation of the house that the son and his parents moved into, which leaves the son with no reaction: "The son stood in the flood of influx with them swarmed around his legs. The son could not unfocus his attention" (*TINY*, 171). Not only is this sheer impossibility reminiscent of the "awe-inspiring" encounter with the (conventional) sublime, but it gives way to no response whatsoever.

> The son stood above the ants. The son stood watching. The son could not feel his fingers or his arms. The small reflective surface of each ant's head showed his head back into him, a chorus of him, gifted through the house. The son squeezed his phone so tight the skin in his arms and knuckles lost their blood. He could feel ants inside his organs, digging rings and ruts and lines. He could feel them eating in his lids, licking the color from his cornea and replacing it with something other, drummed, undone—something from inside the ants—something digested. The son could taste them in his mouth. He could feel them swimming in his bloodstreams, bathing. Through his colon. Threading his back. He could feel them in the center of his each tooth and hair stem. A black box building in his belly. The phone vibrating in his hands. (174)

The son shows no apparent reaction other than "squeez[ing] his phone so tight," which could be a *sign* of fright indeed. But fright is not registered by the narrative voice, it does not manifest itself, nor does any other emotion for that matter, dulled by the sheer, automatic repetition of the phrase "He could feel," as though the ants only translated as feelings and sensations to which, dreadful and weird though they might be, the son did and could not relate. Lodged at the core of his body and self, they nonetheless remain strangely external to the boy who may feel and taste them yet appears never to assimilate them.

In the section immediately following, the blunt iteration of the anticlimactic sentence "The ants were in the son" amid a list of where and what the ants have been up to, further rids the scene of all horror and signification. As Tristan Garcia claims in *Form and Object: A Treatise on Things*, "Signification is the disappointment of never managing to abstract things from the relations that we maintain with them" (Garcia, 14). It seems that the emotionless rendition of events in *There Is No Year* precisely aims to counter signification by removing things and events, or "abstracting" them, from all possible correlation. The ants draw in their wake the "+n entities" that all contribute to the "contact with alien presence" and its "radical translation," both of which are eventually conducive to the speculative sublime as the real radically showcases its inherent alien nature:[4]

The ants were in the son. Other insects also had come in, though unlike the ants they hid in layers. They spun in futures. They knew the mindset of a mold. Small white spiders small as pinheads hung jeweled along the ceiling of one room. The quilt the mother had been making for her one-day grandchildren—the dream of other children always in her head—had been ribboned through and through with mites. A flood of fluttered butterflies had collected on the velvet slide hung over the mantle, a wide piece of woolen fabric that had been in the house when the family moved in, and the family before them, and before them and on and on. The ants were in the son.... Grasshoppers in the rice cooker. Roach babies in the sink. Wormy blankets burped by spiders—enough to wrap your head. Termites bundled in a jacket. Chiggers in the coffee grinds. Beetles in the grease and vents and elsewhere, waiting to awake. Insects so loud they could not be heard, obliterating words. (*TINY*, 175–76)

The presence of the ants, along with all the other insects that follow in their wake, reveal or "translate" the very fabric of the house and the diverse elements or objects that inhabit it, laying bare the alien, sublime contexture of the real. This, as per Morton, comes with the son's realization—a realization that shows in the section's title, "what the son learned the ants had done" (175), more than in the inexpressive narrative per se—"that something was already there. This is the realm of the uncanny, the strangely familiar and familiarly strange" (*RM*, 133). A realm that extends through time, in "spun futures" as well as in the past history of the house's inhabitants, whose uncanniness becomes inescapable and yet strangely unattainable—in a word, unrelatable, as it "obliterat[es] words" and language.

•

Intercourse with resuscitated wife for particular number of days, superstitious act designed to insure safe operation of household machinery. Electricity mourns the absence of the energy form (wife) within the household's walls by stalling its flow to the outlets. As such, an improvised friction needs to take the place of electricity, to goad the natural currents back to their proper levels. This is achieved with the dead wife. She must be found, revived, and then penetrated until heat fills the room, until the toaster is shooting bread onto the floor, until she is smiling beneath you with black teeth and grabbing your bottom. Then the vacuum rides by and no one is pushing it, it is on full steam.

> Days flip past in chunks of fake light, and the intercourse is placed in the back of the mind. But it is always there, that moving into a static-ridden corpse that once spoke familiar messages in the morning when the sun was new. (*AWS*, 7)

This "Intercourse with Resuscitated Wife" opening the first section of Ben Marcus's *The Age of Wire and String* embodies another form that the speculative sublime may take. Beyond the sheer absurdity of the situation—somehow reminiscent of Robert Coover's "The Marker" in which the main character, Jason, is caught making love to his, unbeknownst to him, dead and rotting wife in *Pricksongs & Descants*—the text's explanatory or instructional mode quite literally betokens the "aesthetic experience of coexisting with 1+*n* other entities, living or nonliving," posited at the core of Morton's definition. Quite significantly, the whole scene or act is indeed described from an objectal stance that (almost) does away with any human intervention.

The "intercourse" as such is strangely and paradoxically one in which human intervention is minimal and marginalized in favor of a mechanistic act or art of "friction." The dead wife is acted upon, as made explicit by the use of the passive form ("She must be found, revived, and then penetrated"), whose grammatical function is to allow for the sidestepping of the active subject—"you" is mentioned once, though it is not used as the grammatical subject in the sentence, the role it plays as so-called actor in this improvised act being therefore implicit and radically decentered; by the time "you" appears in the scene, the wife is now fully active ("she is smiling") while "you" are ironically acted upon ("and grabbing your bottom"), more object than subject per se.

The intercourse is thus one that occurs not so much between "you" and "the dead wife" as between what Morton refers to as the 1+*n* elements constitutive of the greater picture called reality. The act here, albeit absurd and grotesque, is one of "radical translation" indeed (Morton), the energy—a possible literalization/translation of the libido—now freely flowing throughout the house, with unrelated, surrounding objects and devices operating on their own, as though moved upon by this sublime "contact with alien presence" that Morton evokes, or what Ian Bogost, for his part, calls metaphorism, for which, he says, *The Age of Wire and String* might act as a paradigm (Bogost, 82–84).

In the process, the sense of horror and repulsion that the scene could have fostered—which is fully noted in Coover's "The Marker" for instance: "Jason tries desperately to get free from her body, but finds to his deepest horror that he is stuck!" (Coover 1998, 91)—is here debunked and replaced or translated with the sheer humor resulting from the juxtaposition, not to say collision or "daisy-chaining" (Bogost), of diverse, disparate, alien elements that eventually intermingle: life versus death, subject versus object, intimacy versus electricity, eroticism versus domesticity...

Not surprisingly, given the ambiguous "Argument" prefacing the book, the whole act is said to be one of superstition; that is, one posited from the very start outside rational thinking, strangely operative yet at the same time exposed for its inadequacy and fallaciousness, the light or enlightenment it provides appearing only in cut-up "chunks of fake light" in the end. In other words, "Intercourse with Resuscitated Wife" complies almost to the letter with the program enacted in the book's "Argument," launching one of those "many forays into the mysteries, as here disclosed but not destroyed" (*AWS*, 4). Revelation is achieved yet nothing is explained away; bafflement, along with a sense of wonder, prevails: "But it is always there, that moving into a static-ridden corpse that once spoke familiar messages in the morning when the sun was new."

The Age of Wire and String, as exemplified here, may thus act out Morton's claim that "what speculative realism needs would be a sublime that grants a kind of *intimacy* with real entities" (*RM*, 130). If intimacy is rendered all too explicitly (and grotesquely) in "Intercourse with Resuscitated Wife," it also transpires in the generic inclinations of Marcus's book, which affects the explanatory, definitional, and knowing tone of the encyclopedia or instruction manual, hence on the surface eliminating all distance from the entities, objects, concepts, or events it depicts or defines. Yet for all those generic moves that place the reader in intimate contact, as it were, with the sheer presence of this "culture," or "life project," in the course of what is described as "a document of secret motion and instruction" (*AWS*, 3), the properly *alien*, untamable dimension of this "settlement" is never lifted; its mysteries never clarified, "strangely familiar" perhaps, yet always "familiarly strange" (Morton).[5]

For the ekphrastic leanings of *The Age of Wire and String*, to be found in its definitional, encyclopedic stylistics insofar as it affects "a bristling vividness that interrupts the flow of the narrative, jerking the reader out of his or her complacency," says Morton (*RM*, 133), somehow contribute to its sublime aesthetic to the extent that the language that obtains throughout the book is both eminently transparent—the lexical entries that punctuate each of the book's eight sections further gesture toward such transparency—and paradoxically opaque insofar as ekphrasis, according to Morton, is "a translation that inevitably misses the secretive object, but which generates its own kind of object in the process" (*RM*, 133), a different sort of object in lieu of the targeted one, which obfuscates rather than explains it. The language of the text eventually solidifies, congeals, becomes its own unyielding object in the very course of description or definition, short-circuiting reference at the very same time as it instantiates it.

"This is a picture window with no picture" (*SA*, 98). Toying with the common phrase *picture window*,[6] Butler's narrator in "Tour of the Drowned Neighborhood" draws attention not only to the inadequacy of language but also to the visual absence, or abstraction, that the text feeds upon. The frame delimited by the window appears empty, its contents void, and it can no longer enclose any picture or, as a consequence, anything picturesque. The absence of a "picture" points to the difficulty, not to say impossibility, for what remains of the world in a postapocalyptic context, such as the one *Scorch Atlas* thrives on, to form pictures or be pictured, to be organized and structured, represented in any constructive or significant manner, to be turned into an object *of*—representation, narrative, language. Instead, the material of the book is always somehow posited beyond or below, before or after, representation.

As a matter of fact, bodies abound in *Scorch Atlas*, but they're all misshapen, bent, swollen, deformed, discolored, blistered out of scale and proportion, skin crudded, ruined, and cracked, covered in cysts or lumps, leaking blood or pus—bleak, often graphic details that all point to monstrousness, to nonstandard portrayals that defy conventional norms of representation:[7]

> Where once [the child]'d had the father's features, his skin expunged a short white rind. First in his crevices—armpits, nostrils, teeth holes, backs of knees—then the chest and cheeks and eyes. . . . The thick white mush became a second skin. It smelled of burnt rubber and stung the nose. ("The Ruined Child," 107)

> The baby measured longer than a machete—his massive skull, ruined fruit. His chest and belly were splotched with something. His head of hair—blonde like Father's—grew over his ears across his cheeks. It'd spread over his eyelids. I could see him. He could not see me. ("Want for Wish for Nowhere," 52)

> Back at home, locked in my bedroom, my stomach began to swell. At first the water simply pooching, then bobbing outward, more rotund. The grinding turned to stretching. My abdomen ballooned. I wiggled with the heft of it, learning to negotiate the rooms. . . . Soon I couldn't stand. My gut weighed twice as much as me. I spread-eagled on the floor. I stuck sewing needles in my belly button. I begged god to make it end. In the mirror my face was licked with burns and incisions that formed another face, one the wall had drawn. ("Exponential," 142)

As suggested by the proliferation of all those "ruined" or diseased bodies, Butler's aesthetic is a violent one of defacement—disfigurement rather than figuration.

There would be in Butler's writing something akin to what Gilles Deleuze defines, in relation to Francis Bacon's painting, as a "logic of sensation" that goes beyond mere representation—"the figurative, illustrative, or narrative" (Deleuze, 2)—to achieve isolated Figures instead that detach against a ruined, unrecognizable background, one in which communication is no longer tenable, in which exchanges and the sharing of information can no longer be guaranteed. In *Scorch Atlas*, for instance, the scant attempts at dialogue often, if not always, fall short of meaning and comprehension:

> My brother spoke: YOU HAVE A NEW NAME. YOU WILL WANT IT. YOUR NAME IS AKVUNDTBLASSEN. YOUR NAME IS XICTYHIAY BLODDUM YAHF. YOU ARE HERE. THE NAME IS MINE. ("Exponential," 143)

> She hadn't spoke [*sic*] up clear in years. She sometimes croaked or cracked or gobbled, or sputtered gibberish, glassy-eyed: YHIKE DUM LOOZY FA FA, she said. ZEERZIT ITZ BLENN NOIKI FAHCH. ("Bath or Mud or Reclamation or Way In/Way Out," 120)

What the frequent irruption of gibberish tends to suggest is that meaning is no longer viable or possible. What remains of the world in *Scorch Atlas* does *not* make sense, nor does anyone ever truly try to derive some sense out of it, to make the catastrophe mean something or find signification and purpose to the wreckage. The destruction, then, the ruination, also affects language in quite a performative way. Language itself becomes enigmatic, sense vacillates, and when meaning or revelation does seem to transpire, when some genuine exchange seems to be taking place, as between gone mother and narrator at the end of "The Disappeared," sense as such appears to be replaced with sensation as the narrator "let[s] [his] brain go loose," hinting that the exchange takes place outside of mere intellection and is posited on a more affective level, "deep inside" the narrator:

> Together the whole map made a perfect picture of my mother's missing head.
> If I stared into the face, then, and focused on one clear section and let my brain go loose, I saw my mother's eyes come open. I saw her mouth begin to move. Her voice echoed deep inside me, clear and brimming, bright, alive.

120   Sightings

> She said, "Don't worry, son. I'm fat and happy. They have cake here.
> My hair is clean."
> She said, "The earth is slurred and I am sorry."
> She said, "You are OK. I have your mind."
> Her eyes seemed to swim around me. I felt her fingers in my hair.
> She whispered things she'd never mentioned. She nuzzled gleamings
> in my brain. ("The Disappeared," 29)

A mere collection of dots on a map, the mother is not truly there, a dubious ("*If* I stared . . .") emanation at the heart of absence ("*missing* head"), the ironical condition for the picture to appear "perfect." What she says and never before mentioned "echoes" inside the narrator only, who feels her liquid touch more than he registers the abstraction pouring from her as she "nuzzles gleamings" in his brain. Whatever revelation, radiance, and solace might be found in those lines quickly dissipate as the son's memories are drawn back to his father, locked away, "alone and elsewhere," and pull him back down into the dirt and water in search of his disappeared mother,[8] "[his] nose clenched and lungs burning in [his] chest," thus pushing the story to its matter-of-fact conclusion: "But I could not find the bottom and I couldn't see a thing" (29). Light yields to darkness, search to impenetrability—the picture of the mother evaporates as soon as formed and the revelation opens onto a dead end.

•

Kant defined the sublime—in Timothy Morton's signature phrasing—in relation to "a Goldilocks aesthetic distance" (*RM*, 130). Taking as an example the Egyptian pyramids, Kant argued that their sublimity could be registered only if the viewer stood neither too close nor too far away. Morton comments: "The Kantian aesthetic dimension shrink-wraps objects in a protective film. Safe from the threat of radical intimacy, the inner space of Kantian freedom develops unhindered" (*RM*, 131).

In his *Logic of Sensation*, Gilles Deleuze never refers to the sublime in relation to Bacon's painting yet associates Bacon's art with the Egyptian influence of the bas-relief, which is at the origin of the conceptual opposition between "optic" and "haptic" perception as expounded by Aloïs Riegl:

> Bas-relief brings about the most rigid link between the eye and the hand because its element is *the flat surface*, which allows the eye to function like the sense of touch; furthermore, it confers, and indeed imposes, upon the eye a tactile, or rather *haptic*, function; it thereby

> ensures, in the Egyptian "will to art," the joining together of the two
> senses of touch and sight, like the soil and the horizon. (Deleuze, 122)

The Egyptian bas-relief abolishes all sense of depth and perspective, pushing all elements to the flattened foreground—the eye cannot discriminate or gain a complete, unified, organic view of its object. Instead, it grazes upon its surface; it touches it, comes in close intimate contact with it. If this proximity would render the Kantian sublime inoperative—Kant has his eyes away from the bas-relief and on the whole pyramid instead—there might be something akin to a *speculative* sublime at work in haptic vision, at least insofar as the latter "grants a kind of *intimacy* with real entities" (*RM*, 130).

•

Shelley Jackson's body of work, from her hypertext *Patchwork Girl* to her latest novel *Riddance*, from *my body—a Wunderkammer* to her "Skin" or "Snow" projects, is one that may indeed endeavor to turn reading into an all-too-intimate act of touching. Not only is the human body copiously semiotized,[9] but the text is concomitantly somatized, as can be seen most notably in *The Melancholy of Anatomy*, which is divided into four parts reminiscent of the ancient humors ("Choleric," "Melancholic," "Phlegmatic," "Sanguine"), or the hypertext *my body—a Wunderkammer*, for instance.

In *my body*, Jackson affixes several texts and stories in the form of autobiographical memories, beliefs, and anecdotes to different parts of her own body. To access those texts, you initially have to select and click on the author's body— standing naked and whole in front of you (see Fig. 5). Yet the diverse oblong boxes framing most of her body parts already point to the inherent violence of the gesture one is about to perform if they want the text to offer itself up to their reading gaze. Choosing to enter the text amounts to focusing on specific body parts, to getting close up to them and, in so doing, to forfeiting a distant, unifying perspective. As you do so, you also inevitably carve up the displayed body. From the start, reading is thus set up to be a violent act of dismemberment as one tears, piece by piece, the body with which, as suggested by its title, Jackson's (hyper)text is equated. Although long decried for its perceived immateriality, the hypertext is here conflated with an all-too-physical artifact that you literally have to touch and "feel your way" into in haptic fashion. Reading on-screen is here almost literally touching, as made explicit by the intrusion into the text of the Mickey Mouse manicule[10]—you point as you read; you touch, you feel, you poke, you probe, you sense, you caress, you jab. You *manipulate*. In other words, dealing with the text is entering in close, intimate contact with it. Abolishing all distance

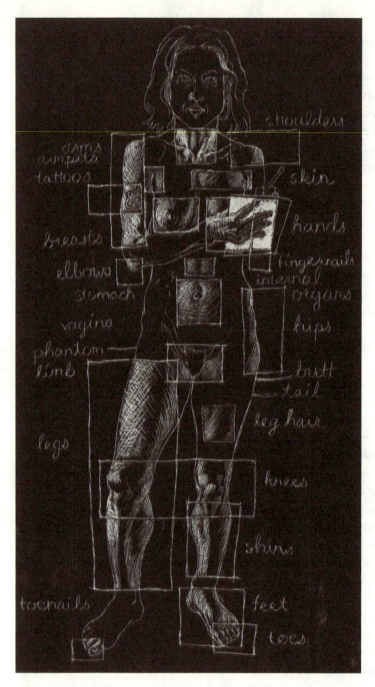

Figure 5. Screenshot from Shelley Jackson's *my body*

and sense of perspective; renouncing Kantian "shrink-wrapping" (Morton) in favor of a looser, closer, more disconnected *approach*. For, as Jackson puts it in the lexia "Cabinet," in which she likens her body to a cabinet of curiosities and to her own resulting text, "You will have to feel your way in." Into the text, of course:

> You don't approach a cabinet of wonders with an inventory in hand. You open drawers at random. You smudge the glass jar in which the two-headed piglet sleeps. You filch one of Tom Thumb's calling cards. You read page two of a letter; one and three are missing, and you leave off in the middle of a sentence. (*my body*)

Hence, into her body as well, from which the text is metaphorically indistinguishable: "I will hide secret buttons, levers and locks in my carved folds and crevices" (*my body*). However, despite or because of such intimacy, the text/body resists: "Some of those many recondite drawers slide easily out and whack you on the shins, some need a little wax and sandpaper." In the end, "there can be no final unpacking." No complete mastery or appropriation, no ultimate understanding. A sense of sublimity prevails, as suggested by the "cabinet of curiosities" metaphor, or *Wunderkammer*. Wonder and mystery eventually obtain, as betokened by the author/narrator's relentless insistence on representation's shortcomings and the fallacies of mimetic rendering: "Look too closely, I noted, and you will see monsters. Realism, and possibly reality itself, is reticence and fudging it" (*my body*, "legs").

•

Blake Butler's fiction may achieve similar haptic effects. Not only does its discontinuity, translating as aggregate rather than systematic space, favor what could be called "haptic reading," but the visual effects obtained in *Scorch Atlas* and *There Is No Year* in their material presentation somehow mimic a bas-relief touch as the pages' grayish background literally, visually, pushes against the text and collapses the usual black-on-white, ground-and-image distinction (with which, incidentally, Shelley Jackson's *Half Life* toys).

Hence the constant impression that one is reading too close to the text, that they remain incapable of ever achieving the right or safe distance from it, which would warrant the correct perspective—a perspective that would enable the reader to view the text in its entirety, in its organicity, to think it through, comprehend it, rationalize it—*explain* it. But explain it you can't, for you're never quite sure, because of the immediacy it forces upon you, what the hell is going on. That might be the point, actually—the painstaking blurring and muddying of the narrative dimension; the deliberate sabotage of story, as suggested

124   Sightings

by the falsely detective take of a novel like *300,000,000*. What is happening? What happened? What is going to happen? Those are all questions that, in the face of Butler's fiction, somehow appear irrelevant. The back covers of *Sky Saw* or *There Is No Year* don't seem to be more in the know than the reader, offering in lieu of "pitch" or "summary" mere lists of what is to be found between the covers: "Books that reappear when you destroy them, lampshades made of skin, people named with numbers and who can't recall each other, a Universal Ceiling constructed by an otherwise faceless authority, a stairwell stuffed with birds" (*Sky Saw*'s back cover).

It's in that respect perhaps that the logic presiding over some speculative works, like Shelley Jackson's or Blake Butler's, might partake of a logic of *sensation* rather than *sense*,[11] in ways not unlike what Deleuze theorizes about Francis Bacon and the painter's rejection of the figurative or the narrative in favor of the emergence of "Figures" on his canvas—Figures that are not mimetic or "figurative" but "figural" (Deleuze, 2).[12]

Yet as Deleuze explains about Bacon's painting, a logic of sensation does not entirely preclude representation: the Figures do not eradicate all figuration. Since Bacon explicitly chooses to forgo abstraction, figurative traces or touches inevitably remain. By confronting the chaos of his art, Bacon diagrammatizes painting so that out of chaos the Figure might emerge, thus achieving a second-order figuration: "Not all the figurative givens have to disappear; and above all, a new figuration, that of the Figure, should emerge from the diagram and make the sensation clear and precise" (Deleuze, 110). If "The diagram is indeed a chaos, a catastrophe," it should not engulf the whole picture or canvas: "It is a violent chaos in relation to the figurative givens, but it is a germ of rhythm in relation to the new order of the painting. As Bacon says, it 'unlocks areas of sensation'" (Deleuze, 102).

To the extent that an analogy is here possible, then, Butler seems to operate in similar fashion: despite their apparent anti-mimetic bias, Butler's texts do not dispense with representation altogether, nor could they utterly do so. The catastrophe at the heart of Butler's aesthetic and practice does not, and cannot, annihilate everything;[13] all narrative traces are *not* discarded;[14] elements remain that delineate the contours of a possible, or *virtual*, story,[15] if only with the presence of recognizable characters. A father, a mother, a son in a strange house (*There Is No Year*); Person 1180 (mother/wife), Person 811 (father/husband), Person 2030 (child) in a dystopian setting featuring a mysterious white cone (*Sky Saw*): these initially operate *as* characters in specific settings, even if their subsequent treatment turns them into blurry figures.

The same is true somehow of *300,000,000*, which focuses on E. N. Flood (detective) and Gretch Nathaniel Gravey (mass murderer) while innumerable voices start accumulating in the margins of the text and act as "witnesses" of sorts, both in the legal sense and the sense of *attendant*, a function Deleuze ascribes to the waiting figures in some of Bacon's triptychs. Yet Deleuze comments, "They are attendants not in the sense of spectators, but as a constant or point of reference in relation to which a variation is assessed" (Deleuze, 13). In *300,000,000*, such attendant voices, sifting through the text's margins, somehow bear witness, indeed, to the variations or deformations that the "figures" of Flood and Gravey will endure—Gravey yielding to the godlike Darrel who eventually swallows him; Flood progressively dissolving into his bizarre surroundings: "The language rips out of my mouth, though it is not actually me speaking" (*3HM*, 243).

What one at first takes for characters who would be playing, or so it is assumed, a narrative role are however quickly *deformed* or twisted in anti-realistic ways.[16] The sheer absence of names of course contributes to their initial vagueness or, in the case of most of Gary (now Garielle) Lutz's fiction, their mutability and interchangeability. As an (anonymous, gender-troubled) narrator has it, "Their names would just ruin everything" (Lutz, 234). In Butler's *300,000,000*, Flood and Gravey may be named, like the eponymous character in *Alice Knott*, but their cognomens already betray their superficiality—Flood will indeed be literally flooded by the case, while G.retch Grave.y's name points to the horrendous, sickening nature of his crimes. As for Alice Knott, if from the start her first name ushers her "through the looking glass" into a strange, nonsensical world, her last name, while pointing to the convoluted, tangled aspects of her life (Knot-*t*), places her under erasure (*K*-not-*t*).

Like Butler, Jackson plays in *Half Life* with onomastics by recalling the fictional, material, and bookish existence of her characters, the twin sisters Nora and Blanche, turning them into a dual rendition of the dramatics of writing: black, boisterous ink (Nora) on white, muted page (Blanche). Names in Ben Marcus's early fiction have similar blurring effects. Characters first appear in *The Age of Wire and String* and eventually resurface in *Notable American Women*; however, the distortion or lack of continuity from one appearance of the name to the next points to the referential instability, not to say hollowness, of such cognomens as "Ben Marcus," "Sernier," "Thompson," or "Burke"—the latter two also featuring in other texts by Marcus, like *The Flame Alphabet* or *Notes from the Fog*, in which Thompson becomes the name of a medical lab in the story "The Trees of Sawtooth Park."

In Alexandra Kleeman's *You Too Can Have a Body Like Mine*, the three main characters are referred to only with the letters A, B, and C, which, rather

126 Sightings

than give them some textual, referential substance, wrap them up in a shroud of anonymity and ease triangular permutations, enhancing the vampiric phenomenon the novel toys with between its female protagonists: A, the narrator, indeed fears from the start that she might be slowly becoming indistinguishable from B, her roommate, while outside their windows, characters mysteriously disappear under ghostly white sheets. Ironically, though, minor characters, like the ones appearing on TV or withdrawing behind masks that purport to render them anonymous, all bear first names, in a textual move that somehow blurs the definition of the novel: background pushing up against and contaminating foreground, which recedes into trompe l'oeil renditions. In the end, if cognomens traditionally act as mimetic, referential markers, they can also be used to unsettle the narrative picture, turning characters per se into vague, blurry, indistinct figures instead, or ones draining substance, as in Kleeman's novel.

Concomitantly, in all of Butler's novels, conventional psychology, as well as the characters' emotional investment, are scant, often neutralized by the flatness or matter-of-factness of the narrative voices. Eventually, most character descriptions, when there are any—often in terms of "meat" or body "liquids," leakages and deformities—serve a blatantly defamiliarizing function, spreading into what Deleuze calls "a zone of indiscernibility" that somehow turns the initial characters into literary avatars of Bacon's Figures—Figures whose bodies, Deleuze shows, are treated as mere flesh and meat independent of their bone structures (Deleuze, 22). Thus, in *Sky Saw*: "Inside her shape the mother found that she could both breathe and eat off of the liquid spurting there inside her and blurting from her body in the wash" (217); or in *There Is No Year*: "The son's forehead wormed with flexing meat" (312); or in *Alice Knott*: "When [Alice] turns to [Smith] for a reaction, some explanation, she finds he has begun to come apart: clusters of pigment foaming over where his outer façade won't hold together, with no real flesh or blood beneath the buzzing edges of his meat; all made only even hazier with her acknowledgment, as if where he is he really isn't" (270).

•

The depiction of the body as fundamentally alien in its very intimacy, whether because of its unconquerable, meaty materiality or its dogged resistance to representational norms,[17] gestures toward some form of (speculative) sublimity. This might be the case in the works of Shelley Jackson as well as in Sarah Rose Etter's *The Book of X*, in which the narrator was born with a "knot" that is both paramount to, and a negation of, her own identity, much in the same way as Nora, in Jackson's *Half Life*, feels threatened with erasure by her twin conjoined sister, Blanche. Not quite so incidentally in *The Book of X*, the narrator's name is "Cassandra X," though without specification as to whether this X stands for her last name or its crossing out in a visual rendition of the "knot" she was born with—itself a result of "a very rare gene resid[ing] on the X chromosome" (*BX*, 12). Cassie's inexplicable knot, a genetic aberration running in her family on her mother's side, turns her into a freak of sorts whose relationship to others is thus constantly impeded. This physical condition, lending to Cassie's body an accrued materiality and visibility—"'LOOK AT HER! LOOK AT THE FREAK!' . . . 'YEAH, LOOK AT ME!' I yell back" (18)—is eventually mirrored in the strange, sensuous, carnal landscape Cassie grows up in, on land mysteriously gorged with meat to be quarried up before being sold and consumed.

The comparison between Cassie and a piece of meat is made explicit early on in the novel:

> On Saturdays, my mother and I clean the meat in the big silver sink. On meat cleaning days, watery pink rivers rush off the flesh. The fresh piles of meat rise like bloody castles on the counter.
>
> On Saturdays, we must act very proper because we must take the meat into town. This is a ritual that requires preparation: I clean myself and put on my best dress. I am like the meat in this way. (16)

Because meat is strangely buried deep into the earth's entrails, it exerts some fascination but is, as natural resource, also prone to extinction, its price rising and dropping according to quantity as well as quality. The parallelism drawn by Cassie between herself and the meat turns her into an object of violent consumption, to be masticated and eventually spat out in one way or another. As such, though traditionally associated with union and bonding—"The knot was a symbol of the bond of marriage from the early 13th century" (64)— Cassie's knot marks her body as a site of unilaterality and eventually *unrelationality*:[18] most men she hooks up with end up renouncing physical intimacy with her as soon as they see her knot; when, on the other hand, they do engage with her physically, those relations prove either one-sided or a blatant, violent negation of their supposedly reciprocal nature. This is the case when Jarred, her would-be boyfriend at school, ends up assaulting and abusing her in the "Meat Quarry" owned by Cassie's father—thus symbolically reasserting the parallel between Cassie's body and some meat to be consumed and chewed up, digested and discarded.

Etter's novel of course may yield allegorical readings that in part prove *un*speculative, given that instead of impeding meaning as such, the plot, which

128   Sightings

can be viewed as Cassie's desperate desire to connect and belong, rather fosters interpretation—about body commodification, about female objectification, about desire standardization. Be that as it may, if *The Book of X* does not obfuscate reading the way, say, *The Age of Wire and String*, by Ben Marcus, or *300,000,000*, by Blake Butler, or *A German Picturesque*, by Jason Schwartz, or *I Looked Alive*, by Gary Lutz, often radically do, it nonetheless foregrounds its own materiality by questioning the work's *body* as such, grafting foreign elements onto Cassie's narrative in the forms of "Visions" and exogenous "Facts" that unsettle and loosen the narrative tissue, layering the text's fabric, doubling Cassie's life story with bits and pieces that jar, resist appropriation, or blatantly contradict the main narrative implementation.

Hence, perhaps, the proliferation of violent imagery involving fantasies of dismembered bodies in Cassie's "visions." If this enhances the novel's take on questions relating to consumerism, carnality, and (de)predation, it shifts it onto a surrealistic, dystopian terrain that mirrors the dysfunctional, patched-up aspect of the book/body. What *The Book of X* eventually performs is a radical questioning of the *use* bodies, and especially women's bodies, are put to, turning them into objects *qua* objects deprived of any affect; mere pieces of meat, pure objects to which relation, sought after, becomes problematic.

In that regard, the novel's ending remains ambiguous,[19] for if at first sight Cassie ends up patching things up a bit and finding what, on the outside, looks like true love, she ultimately decides to break up with Henry—whose married status initially compromised the viability of their relationship—after learning of her father's death. The novel closes with Cassie burying the urn containing her father's ashes and lying next to him, in the grave that she dug, thus in her turn surrendering to "the wide, bright mouth of death" (284). In other words, Cassie's last move is one of renouncement that resumes and perpetuates the objectifying, consuming cycle she has been submitted to from the start— "offering [her]self up" as a piece of meat shoved into the "mouth of death."

With Cassie's ultimate withdrawal from all relations, her severing of all knots as it were, the novel eventually questions the use it in turn might be put to, the same way the narrator's body is, or has been throughout, never up to the diverse expectations waged against it. What—allegorical, symbolic, interpretive—function does the novel, as novel and object, serve? Or put differently, is my attempt at *making* the text signify along hermeneutic, allegorical lines not, in the end, a violent, coercive gesture that refuses to take the book for what it *is*, rather than for what it *does*?

•

Alexandra Kleeman's *You Too Can Have a Body Like Mine* shares with Sarah Rose Etter's or Shelley Jackson's novels a similar concern for the body and its aesthetic representation. Where Etter's *The Book of X* however closes with its protagonist and narrator's body opening up onto the paradoxical acceptance and understanding of its alien, not to say sublime nature—"The brilliance illuminates each black cavern inside of me, smoothing the deep craters in my heart" (*BX*, 284)—Kleeman's novel instead opens with the radical discrepancy between a person and the body that can be said to be theirs on the surface only:[20]

> Is it true that we are more or less the same on the inside? I don't mean psychologically. I'm thinking of the vital organs, the stomach, heart, lungs, liver: of their placement and function, and the way that a surgeon making the cut thinks not of my body in particular but of a general body, depicted in cross section on some page of a medical school textbook. (*YTCH*, 1)

In tones reminiscent of Shelley Jackson's "Stitch Bitch" manifesto, what the narrator realizes before committing her story is how much her body is like anyone else's and as such blatantly eludes her grasp, thus turning into an object of sheer speculation: "Inside a body there is no light. A massed wetness pressing in on itself, shapes thrust against each other with no sense of where they are. They break in the crowding, come unmade.... Anything could be inside" (1).

From then on, A's story will recount the slow dispossession of her identity, prefigured by her lack of a name. Yet contrary to that of "C," her boyfriend, and "B," her roommate, "A"'s initial letter is not even given in the text, appearing only on the back cover of the book. If one were to take the novel's title at face value, the fact that "you too can have a body like mine" does not entail a goal to reach, a transformation to go through in order for the body to conform to a given model or ideal, so much as a stripping away of any external sign, any marking or re-marking, susceptible to *identifying* the body as individual or unique, of course starting with names. What the novel stages, in other words, is a going back,[21] rather than a move forward, to a sort of "degree zero" of the body—the scraping or erasing of all surface markers. Not so much *re*presentation as *de-* or *un-*presentation.

If, through Cassie's knot, *The Book of X* chose to flesh out the body's alienation from itself, Kleeman follows an opposite direction, working at eliminating all relation to the body's materiality instead, achieving in the process a sense of radical emptiness or hollowness, as exemplified throughout the novel by the diverse instantiations of the Kandy Kakes TV commercials whose almost paradoxical, counterintuitive point is to focus on the product's inaccessibility or exclusivity, forever depriving its main character, Kandy Kat—"the company's cartoon cat mascot" nonetheless (13)—of the cakes he's not only lusting for but eventually starving from. The Kakes, as such, are personified and depicted as products that *won't* be consumed, thus somehow perversely defeating, as such, the commercial's very raison d'être. No wonder, then, that when the narrator inquires after them in (what purports to be) a supermarket, it takes her ages, due to preposterous (anti-)commercial policy, to eventually find empty boxes:

> Kandy Kakes used to be in the back right corner of the store, then they were in the far left near the sugar cereals, but that was weeks ago. By now they'd be in the place that Wally Incorporated's team of programmers, statisticians, and behavioral psychologists had calculated to be the least thinkable location for the statistically average Kandy Kakes consumer. (114)

> Out of the corner of my eye, I saw the red-and-orange coloring of the Kandy Kakes logo. I was close! . . . There were dozens of boxes of Kandy Kakes stacked on top of one another on the shelves, red-and-orange boxes with the neon-green lightning bolts that signified snack cake bliss. . . . I saw my bony arms sticking out in front of me as I maneuvered them over to the shelf and picked up the nearest box, which was suspiciously light, because it was empty. . . . All the other boxes were empty, too. (124)

In the process, A has powerlessly turned into a double of the infamous Kandy Kat, the caricature of a caricature: "I remembered that I was starving. . . . My body felt small to me and light, and I walked to my Kakes with a cartoonish energy in my limbs, as though one giant leap could carry me all the way to their shelves" (124).

Placed under the tutelage of Deleuze and Guattari, *You Too Can Have a Body Like Mine* thus toys with notions of mimeticism, mimicry, parasitism, and simulacrum, as exemplified in the ambivalent relationship between A and B, who does her utmost not only to look like A but eventually to become and *be* A—cannibalizing her, as suggested by the novel's second epigraph from the (interestingly enough, apocryphal) "Gospel According to Thomas," or, which amounts to the same thing, enacting the "capture of [her] code," to quote from the novel's first epigraph, borrowed from Deleuze and Guattari. The world of the novel is thus one in which it's increasingly difficult to tell the original apart from its copy; a world of mere, apocryphal surfaces that belie their lack of singularity, in which the ideal to follow is one of so-called purity understood in terms of utter blankness, absence, and hollowness—in short, pure commodification and, eventually, sheer *flatness. A, B, C*: the novel's literal logic, which is redeployed throughout the novel—<u>K</u>andy <u>K</u>akes & <u>K</u>andy <u>K</u>at; the "<u>D</u>isappearing <u>D</u>ad <u>D</u>isor<u>d</u>er" (38); or B's alleged ex, whose name A can't remember specifically but which has "something standardly male like <u>B</u>rendan, <u>B</u>rady, <u>B</u>rian, <u>B</u>ob" (118), or perhaps "<u>T</u>om, or <u>T</u>im" (121)—already points to the lack of differentiation, to motifs of subtraction, withdrawal, erasure courted by the parodic cult of the Conjoined Eaters A stumbles upon, whose followers only eat to famish their bodies, hide underneath blank sheets in their absurd *becoming-ghosts*, as it were, which appears as nothing short of an attempt to "capture the code" of ghostliness—the code of what, in a way, has *no* code, therefore achieving a grotesque "zone of indiscernibility" taken in an all too literal, self-canceling sense.

You Too Can Have a Body Like Mine thus recounts what finally appears as a self-diluting story geared somehow toward its own effacement, a story that, courting the flatness of the page, purports to stick to its own fragile surface or "the thickness of paper" (2). In the process, Kleeman eliminates virtually anything that could stick out and favors an all-too-active *écriture blanche*, or *blank* (rather than transparent) writing—one that is not "a transparent form of speech. . . . a style of absence which is almost an ideal absence of style," in the words of Roland Barthes (Barthes 1981, 77), so much as it performatively works toward its own effacement or defacement.

•

The comparison with Bacon's Figures becomes almost literal in *Sky Saw* when the father figure[22]—presumably Person 811, now referred to as "the father"—catches sight of "a woman on the bed"—presumably Person 1180—whose body he fails to "decipher":

> There was a woman on the bed—the same woman he had seen before, from somewhere, though he could not decipher this, as her body had changed too: *her body less wrinkled in his presence than under any light.*
>
> By her reflection in the mirror over his shaving shoulder, the father could see the woman mostly did not have a face. That is, she had a head and hair around it. The snow stuck in her hair. It did not melt into the hair, just clung there glinting.
>
> The woman had a mouth of huge white teeth—this he could see. She had spent years caring for them, each, in full. But where the woman should have eyes and cheeks and nostrils, instead the father saw

132 Sightings

> something else. Staggered beads of wretched colors, rolling in and on around against their texture like pixels flailing. Bits and pieces of other parts of other bodies, collaged. Bodies he had known or not known and did it matter. No, it did not matter. (*SS*, 120–21)

The description here almost amounts to some sort of ekphrastic exercise in the course of which elements pinpointed by Deleuze as characteristic of Bacon's art are made prominent—the figure's transformation, her double isolation (on a bed, in the mirror); the absence of a face, replaced by a mere head devoid of all face-like, intimate elements (cheeks, nose, eyes), with only a mouth remaining, a grinning mouth that equated with its disproportionate teeth stretches throughout the absent face, Cheshire Cat–style;[23] the violent modulation of colors, "rolling in and on against their texture"; the indiscernibility of diverse body parts in a collaged, figural ensemble.

Representation per se is not abolished, nor do traces of narrativity utterly disappear from the picture—a virtual story lingers somewhere on the periphery or in the gaps of the text (the whole passage, like others throughout *Sky Saw*, is framed by the heading "BLINK"[24] that acts as a cutting, montaging, or isolating device): the father immediately remembers having seen the woman before, which signals time spent together, a connection that is accompanied with the vision of the woman "ha[ving] spent years caring for [her teeth]." This is not explicitly referred to as a clear-cut memory of the father's, but it nevertheless points to an intimate past in common, thus delineating fragments of a virtual story that hovers in the interstices of the passage. The descriptive, in other words, is tinged or blurred with narrative virtuality further relayed by the father's hesitation—"and did it matter"—then conclusion—"No, it did not matter"—which gestures toward differentiation or accentuation, with the hint that elements may or may not detach from an otherwise flat, static presentation. And so progressively, in flashes or samples, the father will be made aware of a narrative taking shape: "She, he recognized then, had been inside his home. *His home?* The phrase contorted in his flat mouth as he tried to speak it, spit it aloud. It wouldn't come out how he meant" (121). His connection with "the woman" thus slowly clarifies, despite the resistance of language, until the phrase at last comes out, italicized, as a revelation: "He tried to turn around and look upon the woman, *his young wife*" (122).

Interestingly, the whole passage stems from the father's impossible relation to the woman, described in terms of a critical failure or sheer incomprehension: "though he could not *decipher* this" (120; emphasis added). What is at stake throughout, then, is and remains an issue concerning signification—that is, how to relate to the picture or scene framed in his mirror. The whole situation is thus one that literally eludes the father's grasp from beginning to end, since his slow recognition, as narrative elements about his past are being extracted from the scene, is ultimately drowned under his own inability to voice it. Words not only resist him, but what the woman gains in precision, all the while disappearing as an object of representation—the woman is said to be enveloping herself in black film, leaving only "her screwed head" apparent (121)—the father loses in control over himself and his own body: "I still do not know . . . Person 811 said in someone else's voice. Still do not know . . . Still do not . . ." (122).

In the end, the father can only keep on shaving, alone with the woman, "*his young wife*," wanting to "ask her to help him say the words right, ask her to tell him where and when and who he was, but still he could not make his body work." And as he shaves on, the father is literally shredding his own body, "the hair and skin beneath him piling up in cold report" (122)—a "report" here condemned, or so it seems, to mere noise or an echo of nothing in the face of the father's slow impairment and impossible relation to the woman. His own body is deformed in the process, trimmed and turned into an indiscernible figure, "not shaving now so much as laughing, rubbing an apple on his face. A chubby wretched apple, stuck with aphids. Its crumpled skin clung to his skin" (122).

However, the intrusion of the apple at the end of the scene seems to point toward the possibility of a symbolic or oneiric interpretation. In spite of the cryptic strangeness of the whole situation, despite the figural deformation of both the wife and the father—interestingly, the woman is constantly referred to as "the woman," eventually "his wife," but never as "the mother" as elsewhere in the text, while the male figure is referred to as either "the father" or "Person 811," yet never "the husband," which somehow underlines their asymmetricality, their radical separation or isolation from each other—the whole episode does not eliminate all attempts at signification. Yet the apple proves resistant too, and if it could have conventionally served as a symbol for knowledge—whether literal or metaphorical in this instance—it encroaches upon the text and suspends its narrative development by diverting the focus away from the wife's enigmatic presence. Tasting it, the father finds it "tasted hot hair oil and bleach" while "inside his stomach he felt the pieces of the apple reconvening. He felt it stick in his throat width, holding certain words there" (122). As a potential symbol, then, the resilient apple yields no signification, and its mystery remains entire. Paradoxically, if it did serve a hermeneutic function, the only immediate sense it provides is that of its own inscrutability.

134 Sightings

When compared with *The Age of Wire and String* and *Notable American Women*, whose discontinuous aspects thwart any narrative impetus, *The Flame Alphabet* on the surface seems more immediately reader-friendly. Contrary to "Ben Marcus" in *Notable American Women*, Sam does tell a full-fledged story whose dystopian premises do not radically sever all ties with reality, not unlike the narrators of both Kleeman's *You Too Can Have a Body Like Mine* and Etter's *The Book of X*. Despite its extro-science inclination, the aesthetic of *The Flame Alphabet* is not averse to some form of realism; on the contrary, it even seems to thrive on it.[25] The novel's dips into the real are numerous indeed, one of them being the naming and depiction of the Jewish faith.

The novel's take on questions of impenetrability, misunderstanding, or inscrutability displays the same speculative—that is, elusive, refractory, paradoxical—logic as elsewhere in Marcus's fiction and is perhaps nowhere more suggestive than in the formalization of the peculiar branch of Judaism that the novel depicts and that, in part, confers upon it its metaphysical slant.

As "Reconstructionist Jews," Sam and his wife are said to follow "a program modified by Mordecai Kaplan, indebted to Ira Eisenstein's idea of private religious observation, *an entirely covert method of devotion*" (41). If the point or raison d'être of any religion is, etymologically speaking, to unite people in the same set of beliefs, to integrate and bind them into and as a community—what a figure like Jane Dark in *Notable American Women*, despite her apparent lunacy, vehemently strives to do—this fictional reworking of Jewish Reconstructionism, what with its "idea of *private religious* observation," appears almost as a contradiction in terms. The religious theme in the novel thus echoes its main topic—that of toxic communication and the ever-increasing isolation of characters who, as a consequence of the language plague, are estranged and severed from one another.

This is illustrated in the private way "forest Jews" like Sam and Claire are taught to worship—in private groups of two, a husband and a wife, in a secluded cabin hidden in the midst of the forest. Secrecy is the key here; so are silence, incommunicability, and unresponsiveness. The idea of community—a group of people with shared interests—is thus ironically replaced with a sophisticated, albeit grotesque, network of underground cables and wiring that broadcasts Rabbi Burke's sermons through a "listener," that is, an implausible technological device with weirdly animalistic traits. The community, and the collective relationship and interdependency it instantiates, are here abstracted into a mere technological framework:

> The practice derived from Schachter-Shalomi's notion of basements linked between homes, passageways connecting entire neighborhoods.

> But our sunken network existed solely as a radio system, feeding Rabbi
> Burke's services to his dispersed, silent community. Tunnels through-
> out the Northeast, stretching as far as Denver, surfacing in hundreds of
> discrete sites. Mostly holes covered by huts like ours, where two mem-
> bers of the faith—the smallest possible *chavurah*, highly motivated to
> worship without the *pollutions of comprehension* of a community—
> could privately gather to receive a broadcast. (*FA*, 41)

Reconstructionist Jews like Sam and Claire are thus part of a paradoxical "silent community" asked to "privately gather," the members of which are never to
meet or talk together or share in their experiences: "The experience would not
be rendered in speech, you could not repeat what you heard, or even that you
heard anything.... You would not know who else received worship in this manner, neighbors or otherwise" (42). "Forest Jews" thus problematically participate, if that is the right word, in a community shunning itself and dodging "the
pollutions of comprehension" that it would necessarily foster and breed were
that not the case. Ironically, the religious "broadcast," with its implications of
mass (*broad-*) communication (*-cast*), appears so in name only, in a paragraph
riddled with jarring semantic interferences and oxymorons between what pertains to networks, connections, community, and linkages, on the one hand, and
to seclusion, isolation, discreteness, and privacy, on the other.

The *Flame Alphabet*, in that regard, may be working toward some form of
absolutization—or radical separation from thought—in part supported by
Marcus's realistic inscription of the novel within the Jewish folklore. If, like
Kleeman in *You Too Can Have a Body Like Mine* with her invented, spurious
"New Christian Church of the Conjoined Eater," Marcus "could have called his
hole-worshipping 'Jews' the Listeners, Hearbrews, Hutites, or the People of the
Cabling," as Joshua Cohen remarks, the fact that he insistently refers to them as
"Jews *qua* Jews" (Cohen) somehow enables him to push his critical, speculative
agenda. For what lies beneath the issues of faith and their inscription within the
Jewish context, as here represented in the novel, is none other than the kabbal-
istic tradition recalled by the very title of the book. Marcus explains:

> Kabbalah, as I understand it, both chases after and tries to protect what
> can't be known, what can't be thought, what can't be understood. It's
> not hard to see language itself as a kind of folly, in this light. At times
> I didn't feel that the language plague was much of a stretch. Judaism,
> at least in terms of its mystical side and Kabbalah, seemed to accom-
> modate, or at least not forbid, some of the crises that arise in the book.
> It seemed that we could persuasively devise a mythology in which we

136   Sightings

> are punished for our use of language, for presuming to know anything, and there are days when I think that all I've done is illustrate and dramatize some of the warnings I've read.[26]

Seen this way, Kabbalah may be defined by its speculative underpinnings in that it, at least in Marcus's view of it, aims to articulate, preserve, and think "what can't be known, what can't be thought, what can't be understood," thus opening onto specific forms of sublimity. Marcus extrapolates from this premise to view language itself—in its referential claim to match reality, to shape meaning, to channel understanding—"as a kind of folly" not much different from kabbalistic endeavors. Which, in *The Flame Alphabet*, translates as the following belief:

> The secrecy surrounding the huts was justified. The true Jewish teaching is not for wide consumption, is not for groups, is not to be polluted by even a single gesture of communication. Spreading messages dilutes them. Even understanding them is a compromise. The language kills itself, expires inside its host. Language acts as an acid over its message. If you no longer care about an idea or feeling, then put it into language. That will certainly be the last of it, a fitting end. Language is another name for coffin. Bauman told us the only thing we should worry about regarding the sermons was if we understood them too well. When such a day came, then something was surely wrong. (44)

Despite obvious aesthetic differences, *The Flame Alphabet* consequently meets both its predecessors, *The Age of Wire and String* and *Notable American Women*, on their own grounds, pursuing their downplaying and undermining of understanding and of meaningfulness. In a way, *The Flame Alphabet* could be seen as the flipside of the same coin, aiming to tackle the same issue from the perspective of verisimilitude, looking for accommodation in ("seemed to accommodate," says Marcus) or authorization from ("at least not forbid") the real, whereas *The Age of Wire and String* and *Notable American Women* somehow worked at devising the "mythology" Marcus speaks of, one according to which people would be "punished for [their] use of language," hence Silentism in *Notable American Women* and the banishment of the father into the language hole at the beginning of the text, or "for presuming to know anything," hence the warnings against such easy, specious knowledge evinced in the "Argument" opening *The Age of Wire and String*. The blatant flight from reality into the nonsensical, the absurd, the grotesque, the farcical, the incoherent, the illogical, betokens the artificial, invented, tinkered, and arbitrary aspect of signification, of interpretation. The result—which itself is the problematic product of such interpreting gestures that Marcus's writing wards off—are highly comic texts that in part read like parodies or pastiches of learned, expert documents: encyclopedia or dictionary entries, historical chronicles, statistical studies, instruction manuals, FAQS, legal documentation, or even interviews in *Leaving the Sea* . . . If the texts resist, they also showcase their conspicuous lack of (mimetic) realism; the sheer comedy they entertain may concomitantly defuse them, blunt their edges, pass them off as gratuitous acts disconnected from any reality other than their own.

This parodic dimension is far less pregnant in *The Flame Alphabet*, which indulges in a more conventional narrative approach and which at times even openly invites its reader to dabble in hermeneutics—"Do the math on that," Sam challenges early on (*FA*, 10)—whereas Marcus's previous books rather warned them against, blocked, or rendered such interpretive moves incongruous. The borrowings from the history of philosophy and medicine in chapter 13, or of religion when it comes to explaining what Jewish Reconstructionism consists in, as practiced by "forest Jews" in chapter 8, may at first sight serve as an epistemological and aesthetic safeguard, since, according to Roland Barthes (and provided the role they're meant to play remains minor and oblique), historical names and figures—Hippocrates, Avicenna, Falloppio, Boerhaave, Laennec, Auenbrugger, Pliny in chapter 13; Kaplan, Eisenstein, Schachter-Shalomi in chapter 8—act as "superlative effects of the real" that "equaliz[e] novel and history" in order to "give the novel the glow of reality" (Barthes 2002, 102). In the midst of such names, cognomens like "Rabbi Bauman," "Jacob Gallerus," "Hiram of Monterby," or "Albert Dewonce" sound all too real and easily pass off for real historical figures in their turn when, in all likelihood, they're mere inventions. Because all those names appear in the issues of *The Proofs* Sam peruses, a pseudo-scientific magazine peddled by Murphy, they could initially be dismissed as the result of Murphy/LeBov's own mystifications. Yet things may not be as easy and clear-cut as they seem, since what *The Proofs* operates—a dubious mix of historical facts and fiction—also obtains elsewhere in the novel, most notably in the depiction of Jewish Reconstructionism; as Cohen points out in his review of the novel, Marcus's "Jews bear such slight resemblance to even the craziest who claim that identity" at large. To Cohen, then, what Marcus has done in *The Flame Alphabet* eventually amounts to this:

> He has exiled the public name of the religion from its past in order to imbue it with private meaning. He has turned "Jew" from appellation to word to pure intellection: fictile, unfixable, rootless. This is a variation on what Marcus earlier did with toasters and vacuums, "weather" and "sleep" [in *The Age of Wire and String*]. It's also a kabbalistic technique. ("How So Very Dear")

138   Sightings

A technique whose aim in the end may not be so much to *reveal* meaning and knowledge as to obfuscate it, render it unapproachable, incommunicable, unrelatable.

In brief, *The Flame Alphabet*'s apparent reader-friendliness, supported by the techniques of verisimilitude and narrative realism, may be just another "decoy" in the end—a deceptive and pernicious trick to lure readers into believing in an impossible tale, one according to which "the language itself was, by definition, off-limits" (*FA*, 65). Much like the bastard letter to the flame alphabet Sam is devising at Forsythe, the book itself may turn out to be a nonbook, after all—one that you cannot relate to; one that recedes from your grasp, whose story may be nothing more than sheer trompe l'oeil effects, valuable not for what it says so much as for what it *doesn't*—what it leaves out of the picture, conceals or dismisses, cloaks or screens out. In that sense, *The Flame Alphabet* may be secretly working toward the delineation of a nonbook, a nonstory, an absolute object bound to elude and remain non-understandable, saturated with non-meaning—like Sam's new secret lettering, "It would require redundancy and nonsense built in, ligatures that expressed merely noise, to soften the harshness of meaning, extend it, disguise it. I saw it as a foam I needed to add to my system, a cloaking agent" (210). A book in disguise, then; a nonbook passing itself off as one that projects qualities behind which it can safely retreat or withdraw. That is, a book-in-itself perhaps, the access to which may be denied—or, if not, then eventually revealed to be delusory.

•

Incidentally, when in *The Flame Alphabet* Sam leaves Forsythe at the end of part 2, when he flees an ailing LeBov and abandons Claire a second time, he does so passing by an elderly man who is secluded somewhere in the facility, underground—a possible variation on the impotent father figure at the outset of *Notable American Women*—singing in a microphone "with Rabbi Burke's voice. A perfect imitation" (*FA*, 250). So perfect indeed it might well be Burke's very own voice.

> I stroked the man's hair and he looked up at me with a face I'd always wanted to see. I did not care if his words were from decades ago or today. I did not care if he spoke a decoy service to deceive people like LeBov, whether his sermons were real or fake, because what was the distinction again? It didn't matter to me. He was still mine. And now they'd gotten to him, too, reduced him to a crooning role in this underground work site. Or else he'd always been here, had never left, and it took me this long to find him. (250)

Whether or not the old man is Burke, Sam is unable to say. The novel will not clarify this point—the distinction between "real or fake," the authentic and the decoy, already seriously undermined by the Murphy/LeBov's antics, has finally collapsed; in fact, by propagating "the same shade of doubt about the same unknowable deity" (249–50) and favoring a constant "relationship to uncertainty" (42), by entertaining a radical secrecy along with "a great awe for what could not be explained" (48),[27] such distinction is bound to appear ultimately ungrounded: "'Understanding itself is beside the point,' Burke said, more calmly. 'Do not make of it a fetish, for it pays back nothing. That habit must be broken. Understanding puts us to sleep. The dark and undesired sleep. Questions like these are not meant to be resolved'" (46).

Fair enough. They will not be.

Because it in part undermines interpretation, as classically defined, speculative fiction may at times open onto some form of sublime experience—one in the course of which what is perceived, or felt, or sensed can never completely be read or understood. Once I've closed the book, I'm faced with the haunting impression that something always remains—a remainder in the form of questions whose answers elude my grasp, which of course can partake of the very essence of the literary as such, whether speculative or not, that is, its inexhaustibility. Which is here, or so it seems, somehow magnified, made pregnant, all too concrete in the bafflement that follows reading. Its part maudite maybe. Who knows, dear Incomprehension. *Something perhaps fundamentally alien, yet all too intimate for that matter. The speculative text is thus one that never truly coincides with itself, traversed by contrary currents, whose language may be deceiving, luring me toward ruined shores of understanding, from which, and from afar by necessity, may be glimpsed fragments of a receding reality. Despite its flagrant lack of conventional mimeticism, because of its blatant absurdist leanings at times, speculative fiction may remain, at core, a realistic endeavor.*

Speculative Language,
Or "Understanding Is Overrated"

Speculative fiction does not merely attempt to construe speculative situations—scenarios in which the correlational circle is broken, in which rational thought collapses on itself, or in the course of which reality appears to contravene or contradict physical laws in ways that cannot be accounted for: *"when the son had stayed alive the doctors seemed more nervous than relieved—how peculiar, they kept saying, it's against science"* (*TINY*, 17). Like the postapocalyptic sketches of *Scorch Atlas*, what the son went through in Butler's *There Is No Year*—the mysterious disease he weirdly recovered from, never described or named and thus significantly left out of the narrative—is one unexplained/inexplicable element among the many that tilt Butler's fiction toward the speculative indeed, along with the strange, ever-shifting topography of the family's house and its surroundings, as well as the uncanny appearance of mundane objects (an egg, a black box) that yield no function, no apparent purpose, or no visible explanation. Such occurrences pervade Butler's fiction and convey a general sense of inscrutability or "weirdness" that sets Butler's work apart from the staples of science fiction. The "White cone" featured at the beginning of *Sky Saw*, for instance, could at first be seen as a futuristic device framing the novel as a science-fictional one, estranging the text from its immediate, mimetic inscription into the everyday real. The overly dystopian shades of the novel, with characters going by numbers instead of names, is a further sign of such estrangement. Yet again Butler's writing obfuscates the generic picture to sketch what the book's back cover describes as "a post-Lynchian nightmare" in which what matters is not so much the narrative that the text instantiates[1] as the way narrative as such is rendered problematic. In other words, the speculative is not

142 Sightings

merely an outcome of the text's narrative renderings but also a direct manifestation of its very language—a language itself turned speculative in its poetic functioning or, rather, *dys*-functioning.

In that regard, Butler's language is highly performative, doing more than it says. The broken, staccato rhythm of a sentence like this one, from "Dust" in *Scorch Atlas*—one example among innumerable others—upsets the image of a seamless, harmonious syntactic flow: "Each inch sat spackled, crusted over. Each inhale brought a mouthful" (*SA*, 30). Language often becomes such a mouthful indeed, forcing its materiality down the reader's throat, and it may at times be difficult to stomach it. It is as though words were piled up one against the other like inert material—not unlike corpses in *Sky Saw* that keep accumulating, "the state ha[ving] claimed use of the bodies to build a wall" (*SS*, 31). The result at times can be a massive, chaotic block of text or an abstract, directionless wordscape not unlike the wall suddenly sprouting up at the beginning of "Exponential" in *Scorch Atlas*, "a huge flat black on the horizon . . . monolithic, blue and edgeless, stretching forever out at both ends and upwards into wherever" (*SA*, 139).

The lists that proliferate through the texts, the numerous iterations, as in *300,000,000*, for instance, all point to the same deconstruction of narrative continuity. As Ian Bogost writes in his *Alien Phenomenology*, "The off-pitch sound of lists to the literary ear only emphasizes their real purpose: disjunction instead of flow. Lists remind us that no matter how fluidly a system may operate, its members nevertheless remain utterly isolated, mutual aliens" (Bogost, 40). In Butler's case, however, the system never quite seems to operate fluidly to start with, and the lists merely repeat on another scale the texts' recursive process.[2] Linearity and chronology are disrupted, and the time frame is often impossible to establish. The sheer reluctance of *There Is No Year* to make use of pronouns now and then where "the son" is concerned is also suggestive of the text's inherent disruptive or disjunctive nature:

> The son walked. The son crawled a little. The son's legs began to ache. The son tried to hail a long white taxi that barreled past him but the taxi did not slow or stop. Through the taxi windows the son saw no one. The son felt hungry. His hair was itching. The son licked his wrists. The son looked into the light. The night was scorched and streaked in lines. The son could hardly see. (*TINY*, 238)

The repetition of the phrase "the son" from sentence to sentence achieves a paratactic feel that undermines the integrity of the paragraph. As a unit, the paragraph appears discontinued, broken up into sentences that, in the absence

Speculative Language   143

of pronouns whose function would be to perform continuity and aggregate the paragraph, do not blend. A similar effect can be produced at the sentence level as soon as clauses start piling up, causing a sense of juxtaposition rather than coordination:

> The rough lining around the muscle was melted under flamethrower and used to tease the dogs who would run from the stench of it into a deep woods; then the men, who'd never meant to feed the dogs with this gray meat regardless, could chew and choke themselves and taste the silence where words pocked into the mashy pockets of the brain and down the fingers of a man suffused with light from machine screen and buzzing bells reminding human contact and the words that time had altered in their unpresuming meaning beforehand as he placed his fingers on the buttons to again be misread by whomever beyond his own misreading as should all things be until they no longer are. (*3HM*, 340)

If the sentence starts in a conventional fashion, alternating signs of punctuation (a semicolon and commas) to balance its diverse clauses, it ends up doing away with any syntactic tool capable of hierarchizing its components, flattening everything into a mere sequence of words crammed one after the other without ever fully amalgamating into a whole; although some coordinators remain ("and"/"as"), it's getting harder to tell how the clauses are embedded while meaning becomes more and more tenuous. In the end, the impression lingers that, despite having reached a period, the sentence is not quite complete and doesn't really hold, being imperceptibly flawed while grammatically correct on the surface.

In the course of such concatenations, language is indeed subtly deregulated, as though diseased, becoming prone to errors and glitches that, whether voluntary or not,[3] disarticulate the syntax, unhinge the text, impede narrative development. As in: "She could not stop her body coming with it. She opened <u>and</u> her eyes and closed her eyes and opened them and <u>watch</u> the pattern of the texture change" (*SS*, 58). As in: "This is an art project, someone stutters, and the teeth fall out of their mouth onto the ground and are eaten by the starving some days layer" (*3HM*, 212).

A similar glitch occurs, as pronouns get mixed up in *There Is No Year*, when "the son" starts being referred to as a girl:

> Had someone been around to see the son come in, perhaps, they might have stopped him, touched his hand. What's in that package, they might have said. Let's make it open. You are so young to receive

mail. Instead the son went into <u>her</u> room and closed the door and locked it and turned around and set down the package and took off his clothes and faced the wall. (*TINY*, 52)

The error is somehow signaled or programed by the chapter's enigmatic title, "HIS," which could read as an advance correction. It will recur several times in the novel, here, for instance: "Most days he went to bed and slept hard from the moment he got home until it was time to get up again for school the next day, unless the mother or the father woke him up and made <u>her</u> come do something nice like eat" (122). The mistake is eventually pointed out and commented upon by the mother later on: "This is where on the weekends my son likes to sit and tan <u>her</u> skin, the mother mentioned in the kitchen, pointing through the door glass at the yard and swimming pool. *His skin*, she corrected, not *hers*. My son is a boy" (123).

Similar gender glitches occur in Gary Lutz's stories, most ostentatiously in "The Boy," where the character is apprised, one day, that "it would be in the best interest of both the boy and the school if, for the remainder of his tuition, he were enrolled as a girl" (Lutz, 245). Although such change is immediately validated in the rest of the story, the text never registers it grammatically, as the boy—now turned girl—remains "the boy" throughout, even through *his* marriage to *his* guidance counselor. In "The Summer I Could Walk Again," the narrator's gender identity is never quite revealed until a conversation occurs when a car stops by the road where the narrator is standing: "'<u>She</u>'s not looking at us,' the woman says" (Lutz, 236). However, the female identification is blatantly negated a couple of pages later when someone inquires about the narrator, who locked up in the bathroom overhears the conversation:

"Are you the mother?" It's a woman's voice.
"I'm who the mother pays," my cousin's voice says.
"What about the boy—he's here?"
"Can't say. I might have dozed off." (Lutz, 239)

Male or female, gender instability or character misconception—the text does not say.

Not only do such errors stress the ontological instability and/or flatness of the character, who in the case of *There Is No Year*, like his father and mother, remains unnamed and surrounded by "copies" of himself throughout, but they also draw attention to linguistic disorder and language breakdown, suggesting that words do not *refer* to anything outside themselves, nor do they attempt to convey meaning that could or should be deciphered and interpreted once and for all; rather the texts' language implements its own tangible, opaque, autonomous reality, independently of who speaks it. Or to put it differently, the speculative language of Blake Butler's fiction does not aim to convey or shape signification but instead forges, in an all-too-transitive way, a sense or sensation, rather, of ungraspability and impenetrability—reinforced, in the case of *Scorch Atlas* or *There Is No Year*, by the grayish texture of the pages.

•

Ben Marcus's work has been focused on language from the start, whether through the (re)definition of words as propounded by *The Age of Wire and String* or the interrogation of language's performative power in *Notable American Women*. In *The Flame Alphabet*, arguably the most straightforwardly narrative of his first three works, Marcus depicts a world in which it is no longer possible to make any use of language, whether orally or in written form, without suffering severe physical impairment. *The Flame Alphabet* thus portrays characters who cannot interact with one another through language and who, therefore, can no longer relate to one another, as dramatically experienced by Sam, the narrator, who powerlessly witnesses the slow, distressing breakup of his family. Because speech, communication, and the verbalizing of emotions are actions that literally kill, Sam, his wife, Claire, and their daughter, Esther, irrevocably grow apart, painfully estranged from one another.[4]

With its mysterious language disease that spares children but affects adults, Marcus's novel could serve as an apt enough exemplar of Meillassoux's extroscience worlds, worlds in which science is bankrupt and fails to account for and make sense of whatever bizarre events might be happening in them. Sam recalls: "The early diagnostics were sad and random, experts holding forth confidently on the unknown, using their final months as language users to be spectacularly wrong" (*FA*, 15–16).

No explanation can or will be provided about the origins of the toxicity whose only precedents are tentatively listed in some copies of *The Proofs*—a dubious magazine put together by no less dubious LeBov, which "resembled a university newspaper, except blown strange, its histories slurred, its facts effaced" (81). The issues appear in Sam's mailbox and flaunt historical names (Avicenna, Pliny, Hippocrates, Falloppio, Boerhaave, etc.) in the midst of apparent inventions (Jacob Gallerus, Hiram of Monterby, Albert Dewonce). Among those names resurfaces the name "Perkins" (84), already found in Marcus's *The Age of Wire and String* and *Notable American Women* (along with Sernier, Thompson, and Burke). The overt reference to Marcus's earlier works sheds a parodic light on the whole passage, whose "historical anecdotes" (82) recall

146   Sightings

the spurious historical references disseminated throughout *Notable American Women*, and short-circuits the historical grounding purported by the mention of real, authoritative names. Sam himself is aware of the doubtful nature of *The Proofs*:[5] "Throughout *The Proofs* were phrases lifted from as far back as the medical spookeries of Laennec and Auenbrugger, sometimes misattributed, sometimes attributed to medical scientists I'd never heard of, because, I suspected, they had not actually lived" (82). "I knew my Pliny pretty well and I was fairly sure this was wrong, hadn't happened to Pliny. Or anyone. Yet the tone was assured, hardened in the rhetoric of fact" (85). In other words, at the very same time that the novel is alluding to so-called (scientific) authorities in order to ground its fictional contents into the real and substantiate the disease that sets the plot into motion, a parodic undercurrent—"like a writing erupted under skin" (81)—collapses the authoritative edifice, questioning and hindering language's referentiality. Far from acting as a sanction of verisimilitude and the rationalization of what remains, at core, an absurdist fiction, historical names and references here deregulate the language of the text and suggest that what is at stake, in *The Flame Alphabet* as elsewhere in Marcus's fiction, is a crisis in reference and authority that renders all forms of learned, expert, scientific discourse moot[6]—this one necessarily included.

·

To a certain extent, *Notable American Women*, Marcus's second novel, starts where *The Flame Alphabet* ends, exposing the conditions Sam is reluctant to acknowledge: "I offer this message under duress," writes the narrator's father, "hungry, winded, and dizzy, braving a sound storm of words meant to prevent me, I'm sure, from being a Father of Distinction" (*NAW*, 3). "Michael Marcus," the father of "Ben Marcus"—"the improbable author of this book" (3)—is buried somewhere in his backyard while "language poison" is being hurled at him. Words are used as a weapon; language is a threat. What in *The Flame Alphabet* is the slow, bizarre, unaccountable deregulation of verbal communication is here taken for granted—language *is* toxic, an airborne poison that disturbs the weather and kills off birds. Words are lethal. If not, or not yet, language at least has the power of hurting those to whom it is targeted through highly performative effects.

"Bury Your Head," the opening section of *Notable American Women*, purports to read as a cautionary tale of sorts, since Michael Marcus, not merely content to offer "corrections" to his son's ensuing narrative, urges readers to approach (fictional) Ben Marcus's account "not uncritically" (11). It is here made clear that reading is at stake; that distance is needed, careful attention should be

Speculative Language   147

paid, comprehension questioned. From the start, reading is thus channeled by the father toward his son's "distortions," "manipulations," "bias" (4), his blatant lack of "loyalty to the actual world" (6), and the "aberration" (8) that his text consists in, with its listing of "*events [the narrator] cannot possibly grasp*" (15). Not only does Michael, from his hole underground, undermine his son's narrative, but he also signals what is to be a problematic read by pointing to the discrepancies lodged at the heart of the text, challenging its inadequate or fraudulent aspect.

So doing, the father contests his marginal position, both in his son's narrative and in the refashioned world at large, and he endeavors to regain what his wife, along with Jane Dark and her Silentist followers, have deprived him of— his authority as a man and a father. From harsh critic, given the initial role of reviewing his son's work, Michael in virtually the same breath evolves to assume authorship of the text, claiming that his fathering of Ben Marcus entitles him to be seen "in no small way" as "the first author of anything [his] son endeavors to write" (5). Yet, given his constrained situation, such authority can only be recouped through the very language that he claims to be fighting, that is, by resorting to the same, rhetorical poison he is being forcefully fed while in his hole underground.

This paradox is enhanced by the fact that the father figure, one conventionally associated with authority—a symbolism the father ridiculously falls short of when first appearing in the subsequent chapter: "Everyone laughed when my father came into the kitchen," remarks Ben (39)—is given preeminence in the text, thus placing Michael in the untenable position of having to claim things that are immediately countered by the very fact that he *is* able to claim them. To put it differently, Michael's discourse, by supposedly being appended to the text as the introduction to the narrative that follows, opens up a speculative space in which language turns back against itself. For, as Ben's father decries the authoritativeness of his son's narrative—while paradoxically claiming authorship of it—and denounces the authoritarianism of Jane Dark's new sociopolitical regime and cult following, he is unwittingly deconstructing the very mechanics of his own discourse, a discourse replete with rhetorical ploys and a blatant degree of manipulation as soon as he aims his language at none other than "you," personally.

Indeed, by the end of his letter, Michael disowns Ben as his son and appeals instead to his readers, claiming that *he* is their true and legitimate father, "the overfather, the father of fathers" (17). "Your father," he even goes as far as signing his letter. Michael, in that regard, is not much different from Sam by the end of *The Flame Alphabet*, who in order to survive and pen his own narrative

148   Sightings

has to lure children to him and extract the Child's Play serum that immunizes him against language. In a rhetorical feat not unlike those of Orwellian Newspeak, and by way of an appeal to history, Michael has thus grotesquely written his way back to authority, turning his isolation and exclusion into signs of power and resistance:

> Throughout history, all important Command Centers—where key strategies have been decided and the Lost People of this world have been instructed through the haze—all of these Command Centers have existed underground, below the flow of the projectiles that reduce every other creature under the light into such shivering wrecks in need of protection. If your local father is not at the Command Center, *for I do not see anyone else here with me*—if he is sleeping, or tending the yard, or laughing and splashing in a pool—then I ask you how he can be an effective ruler. Is it not true that he has vacated his throne, and is now simply a boy who would cry like a child as soon as he saw me walking toward him? The minute I approached to take charge of the situation, your so-called father would collapse and fold into my arms with tears of relief and become simply one more of my children— *There there*—making him only a brother to you, an older brother who briefly thought he knew something and could lead the way. (20)

"*There there*"—what Sam, one imagines, could very well say at some point or another to the "little ones" he attracts to his hut after having fled Forsythe. "In every way I was a gentle guardian," he confesses. "I provided food and shelter, sometimes sat on the floor with them and played with the little sack of acorns I'd brought in for distraction" (*FA*, 280). "*There there*. All will forever be all right" (*NAM*, 21). Except it won't.

The "duress" Michael claims he is writing under in the opening line of the novel has thus been turned around as he, through flamboyant use of language (imperative forms, rhetorical questions, and various injunctions), is now exercising full coercive, performative power. What his note initially started to rebuke—a sense of wrongful authority, usurpation, injustice, fraud—has been grossly reappropriated as his, in the process turning him from pitiable victim to despicable victor.

The less than subtle way through which this reversal is achieved is of course self-annihilating and somehow legitimizes any move the "notable American women" of the title will have made to exile and bury Michael in the first place. The strategy, if it is one, used by the father to plead his case is in that regard self-defeating and his language of course ridiculously self-indicting.

What is at stake in the process appears to be the very mechanics of language—how language works, what it does. If, like most of (author) Ben Marcus's work, *Notable American Women* were *about* anything, thematically speaking, it would thus have to be this: language itself. Language taken as theme and object of the writing in ways that go far beyond the by-now conventionally stale metafictional turn. For the point might no longer be to demonstrate the artificiality and constructedness of the fictional process against realistic verisimilitude at a time when some have been willingly petitioning for a return to more transparent aesthetic practices.[7] Language, in Marcus's fiction, formally turns back upon itself in ways that, true enough, are often "entirely lacking in loyalty to the actual world" (*NAW*, 6), to focus instead on itself, in pure autotelic fashion.

Such a move, however, can at first sight appear to be belied by a story like "I Can Say Many Nice Things" from *Leaving the Sea*, which on the surface complies with every staple of the metafictional piece: Fleming, a mediocre writer, is hired on a cruise ship to teach a creative writing class, thus reflecting both on the mechanism of the literary artifact and on his own, failed writerly practice, all the while allegedly trying to steer the creative impulses of his students. If the locale—a cruise ship—appears strange enough, it does exemplify Fleming's sense of isolation and drift, his own incapacity to belong and relate to his surroundings and to connect to the people around him. Not only is he estranged from his own wife and daughter—Erin, Fleming's wife, projects a version of her husband that he fails to recognize—he also inevitably is estranged from his students, unable to understand, for instance, why one of them would openly flirt with him the way she does. The picture of himself that Fleming witnesses in the eyes of others thus happens to be one that he never acknowledges, one that never actually overlaps with his own self-perception. Eventually, Fleming is left alone, literally *at sea*, wandering a world that has lost all credibility, one in which events and facts, in their own banal hues, have shed all verisimilitude, appeal, and connection to him. In other words, what in its metafictional turn conspicuously remains a half-hearted, half-baked "old story about a story trick" (*LS*, 47) ends up veering and finally shifts the whole paradigm toward a questioning and deconstruction not so much of the mechanics of storytelling per se as of the very notion of realism and its grounding in a so-called real world that has been utterly depleted, faked, and rendered inoperative.

> Why was that so easy to believe, and it wasn't true, yet what was true was so finally impossible and unconvincing? The stars—close and dirty and shapeless and false, the sort a child might draw, and what did children even know?—were not credible. The sky, the whole night, his conversations. These things did not fucking ring *true* anymore, they needed

150   Sightings

work. What happened to him needed to be revised until he could find it believable. Or, *he* needed to be revised. Fleming. He needed to change himself so what was real did not seem so alien and wrong. Do you do that with tools, with your hands, with a bag over your head? Do you do that by standing on the ship's railing at night? (*LS*, 56)

In Fleming's eyes—and, ironically enough, in an all-too-realistic rendering, if compared with the aesthetic agenda of other stories in *Leaving the Sea*, like "On Not Growing Up," "My Views on the Darkness," "The Father Costume," or the very short pieces collected in part 5 of the book, along with previous Marcus texts like *The Age of Wire and String* and *Notable American Women*—reality itself is what needs to be edited and appears, to Fleming, in serious need of "work," a term that, if it echoes literary demands, gains a very material, pragmatic, not to say ontological dimension. What thus started as a classic, postmodern metafictional piece probing into the creative process—which the narrator wryly identifies as an "act of sheer violence to its audience" (*LS*, 47)—ends up being a realistic investigation into the nature of the real, its lack of believability, its own superficial, shifty, faulty aspect: the language of the text, from the start geared toward its own reflection and self-targeted as the very *object* of the text ("I Can *Say* Many Nice *Things*"), eventually changes course to tackle and paradoxically reopen the referential process instead, hoping to match the very experience of its protagonist, albeit one defined by loss, discrepancy, and withdrawal.

The dynamic reversal appears somewhat differently in *Notable American Women*, although it might achieve similar, self-obstructive effects in the end. The critical stance initially embodied in the father at the beginning of *Notable American Women* ends up bearing on itself much more than it does on the subsequent portions of the narrative. As often occurs in Marcus's fiction, an undercurrent runs throughout the text whose movement is inescapably dual: what is being said on the surface—for instance, the father's critique in "Bury Your Head"—is offset by contrary moves that inevitably collapse the textual edifice.[8] Or to put it differently, what seems at first sight to have been posed on a textual margin allowing for the necessary distance required by the critical discourse to gain validity and relevance, actually happens to have been set from the start right in the middle of the textual picture: the father's so-called introduction to his son's text exists only in his own spurious rationalization of it, yet is formally *included* in the novel, as its first chapter, and cued by its intrinsic, deceptive mechanics, Michael's voice just one among others (along with Ben's and Jane Marcus's). The distance claimed by the father's rhetoric is thus implicitly denied: the *object* of his text—what it refers *to*—turns out to be canceled in the process

Speculative Language   151

of its own utterance. The father's digression is in fine an implacable regression into its own vacuity: a discourse voided by its own rhetoric that not only stops *at* but *on* nothing, as language irremediably gets jammed on the page:

> I am aware that Ben Marcus, the improbable author of this book, but better known as my former son, can pass off or structure my introduction in any way that he chooses: annotate, abridge, or excise my every comment. He will have the final cut of this so-called introduction to his family history, and I'll not know the outcome unless he decides to share with me how he has savaged and defathered me for his own glory. He can obviously revise my identity to his own designs, change my words altogether, or simply discard them in place of statements he wishes I would make. I would put none of these distortions past him and will only caution the careful and fair-minded reader to be ever vigilant against his manipulations, to remember that he is a creature, if that, of inordinate bias and resentment, for reasons soon to be disclosed, undoubtedly intimidated by the truth only a father can offer. . . . I fully expect even this statement to be omitted, given how it might contradict the heroic role he will no doubt claim for himself, in which case, it is only you, Ben, my jailer, who will read this. (3–4)

None of the above seems to have taken place as stated—I'm not "Ben," yet I *am* reading these lines. Which, of course, does not necessarily imply that Ben's narrative stands blameless. However, the father's projection results in an obvious contradiction: the text's very existence, as such, belies the very point the father is trying to make. A sort of dissonance, as one reads, thus takes place between what the text says and what, or how, or even *that* it is. A radical discrepancy arises as the reader is faced with a textual reality that immediately withdraws or negates itself.

•

Compared with his earlier fiction, Ben Marcus's *The Flame Alphabet* strikes a somewhat different chord. *The Age of Wire and String* and *Notable American Women* indeed appear more overly "alien," in Ian Bogost's sense of the word, and their treatment of religious matters and questions of faith, for instance, prominent in *The Flame Alphabet* too, verges on the grotesque and is blatantly unrealistic.

In *Notable American Women*, a bizarre women-only creed is developed by part prophetess, part dictator, part comic figure Jane Dark,[9] whose aim and mission is to put an end to motion and speech. After settling with her army of

152   Sightings

Silentists on the Marcus family compound in an estranged Ohio, Jane Dark, in league with Ben Marcus's mother, starts utilizing Ben as her cohorts' inseminator in hopes of furthering the Silentist population and propagating "the New Behavior." The diverse precepts at the heart of Dark's cult offer a satirical occasion to tear the mechanics of religion apart:

> The first Jane Dark gods were invoked by members of Team Quiet in Ohio to solidify Dark's authority as a silence expert. Most organizations require a deity scaffold to boost their veracity with recruits. The deity referred to as Thompson has been used in fiction and nonfiction alike, and is not scheduled to die, or to suffer myth remission, until certain concepts have fully integrated the culture. The Jane Dark gods were never described physically, and they had no special powers. (76)

The godlike Thompson incidentally originates in *The Age of Wire and String*, a whole section of which is titled "God" yet bears very little connection to or resemblance with even the widest notions of religion or deity. Thompson —a name so unoriginal and widespread as to defeat the supposedly unique, one-of-a-kind, unapproachable nature of the divine as well as to discard the notion of the presumed unpronounceability of God's name according to some traditions—finds ways of embodying himself in/as "Perkins": "Term given to the body of Thompson, in order that His physical form never desecrate His own name" (*AWS*, 26). Perkins makes a brief apparition in *Notable American Women* too, where he's said to have "killed himself by vigorously repeating his own name" (*NAW*, 187). The use (and recycling) of recognizable, albeit not immediately identifiable, family names—Thompson, Perkins, Burke, Sernier—can be seen as a comic device to deflate the theological apparatus the books are purporting to implement, foregrounding the crafted, rhetorical, or technological nature of belief, as well as intensifying the fiction-making process at its core by reneging all claims to verisimilitude. The fact that these names recur from one book to the next, far from consolidating the *system* of beliefs they are supposed to be holding together,[10] further complicates the edifice, making it wobble instead through interferences and contradictions that prevent a global, consistent, realistic picture from emerging. Burke, for instance, a prominent figure of *The Flame Alphabet* in which he acts as a rabbi, is introduced as a language scholar in *Notable American Women* who is eventually murdered by rival Sernier (*NAW*, 140), himself first introduced in *The Age of Wire and String*. Ironically, the name "Burke," after his bearer's murder, is said to become a word-weapon shouted at people in order to "create 'a lasting wound to the skin'" (*NAW*, 141), thus acting as a harbinger of the language toxicity *The Flame Alphabet* later tackles.

If both *The Age of Wire and String* and *Notable American Women* eschew consistent references to any one faith grounded in reality, *The Flame Alphabet*, on the other hand, broaches and names the Jewish religion, making of its protagonists Reconstructionist Jews while portraying the novel's evil figure, Murphy/LeBov, as a potential anti-Semite archetype. The move, on Marcus's part, can be seen as a realistic one, which consists in setting his fiction against a recognizable, relatable background defined by verisimilitude, itself enhanced through the mention of historical figures. If the move, which at first sight seems quite at odds with Marcus's earlier aesthetic, has puzzled critics—Joshua Cohen chief among them[11]—it interestingly, and quite radically, shifts the grounds for the novel's reception. In other words, *The Flame Alphabet* appears to have been cast into a more realistic, more mimetic tradition, the result being that its frame of reference goes unquestioned and is immediately taken for granted. This in turn raises expectations that are foreign to books like *The Age of Wire and String* and *Notable American Women*. The "Ohio" of *Notable American Women*, for instance, has nothing to do with the New York background of *The Flame Alphabet*:[12] while the latter seems realistic, the former is a grotesque caricature, a mere name emptied of any real contents.

•

Whether in *Notable American Women* or *The Age of Wire and String*, the texts' weird, comic, absurd effects are achieved mainly through the immediate recognition, on the reader's part, of the sheer discrepancy between sign and supposed referent. For the very language of such texts in advance invalidates all pretenses to *reference*, and the aesthetic mode of both texts is one of radical anti-mimeticism, as suggested by the sheer impossibility of locating *The Age of Wire and String* both in space and time or of giving an approximate age to "Ben Marcus" in *Notable American Women*, who is at times referred to as a mere boy, at times understood to be a young adult. The name itself, "Ben Marcus," which features prominently in both *The Age of Wire and String* and *Notable American Women* but which the author significantly drops from *The Flame Alphabet* onward, is in that regard striking for its blatant lack of correspondence with the author that the name on the books' covers supposedly identifies: one Ben Marcus does not equate with another, and the texts' stylistics leave very little room for confusion:

> BEN MARCUS, THE — 1. False map, scroll, caul, or parchment. It is comprised of the first skin. In ancient times, it hung from a pole, where wind and birds inscribed its surface. Every year, it was lowered and the engravings and dents that the wind had introduced were studied. It

> can be large, although often it is tiny and illegible. . . . When properly decoded (an act in which the rule of opposite perception applies), it indicates only that we should destroy it and look elsewhere for instruction. (*AWS*, 76)

In *Notable American Women*, because "Ben Marcus" looks to be a more conventionally full-fledged character whose physical description in part matches the author's physique, the overlap with reality seems plausible at first; yet the novel's background, its overt contradictions and incongruities, the antics performed by so-called Ben and the other figures around him—among them "Pal," an unidentified creature, part-wolf, -dog, -boy—are so far removed from any mimetic rendering that the name "Ben Marcus" itself is immediately understood as pure trompe l'oeil. The name, as sign, has been gutted of any reference whatsoever, and its use in the novel cannot at any point be mistaken for some autofictional technique by which character and author would happen to be one and the same.

To a certain extent, what such novels do—and what *The Flame Alphabet* doesn't, or not as conspicuously—is intensify their own *fictionality*. Their literary anti-realism is achieved not so much via a blunt refusal of mimeticism as through its paradoxical amplification.[13] Marcus goes a few steps beyond the mimetic, which usually stops short of language itself: mimeticism indeed reputedly thrives on a transparent, self-effacing language. But what Marcus seems to be doing is precisely to turn the gesture around and include language in the process at the cost of the referent. Unlike any realist, Marcus doesn't aim at rendering, as faithfully as possible, whatever may lie outside language but shifts focus instead toward language as such in order to mirror or exacerbate some of its specific uses, turning the whole of language into a fiction of itself in the fake belief that, so doing, language and reality can be reconciled, that the gap between signifier and signified can be (parodically) bridged,[14] that words can be turned into *names* that entirely, exclusively cover, define, and match their referents.

The "Names" sections in *Notable American Women* are a case in point; the narrator surveys the effects that each new name once conferred upon his sister may have had on her person, with the Cratylian conviction that the name is fully constitutive of the person/object it designates: "A name, as the government instructs, can no longer be an accessory of a person, but must be her key component, without which the person would fold, crumble. She would cease, in fact, to be a person" (*NAW*, 91). Ben's sister will apparently die from the experiment, somehow grotesquely confirming the initial belief; with no more names assigned to her, she withers away:

When the names ran dry, my sister pulled up short somewhere in the heart of the Learning Room. The mail had ceased, and no one was sure what to call her. She slept on the rug and scratched at herself, looking desperately to all of us for some sign of a new name, of which we had none. No one, as I mentioned, was sure what to call her, a problem that proved to be the chief void in her identity, which slowly eroded. (*NAW*, 95)

Without a name of her own—"Out of sympathy, we reverted back to her original name, or one of the early ones. I have to admit that I'm not sure what name she began with. Nor were any of us too sure, to be frank, whom, exactly, she had become" (*NAW*, 95)—Ben's sister is condemned to the margins of a story (i.e., what *little* story there is) into which she, as such, never gained full entry.

Names also proliferate in *The Age of Wire and String*, which indulges in a naming frenzy in the course of which common words are treated like proper names and vice versa: "It oxidizes slowly in ALBERT and rapidly in LOUISE. It is attacked by solutions of RICHARD 3 and by concentrated or dilute SAMANTHA 7G" (*AWS*, 11); or: "JENNIFER The inability to see. Partial blindness in regard to hands. To jennifer is to feign blindness. The diseases resulting from these acts are called jennies" (*AWS*, 15). The process, which consists in giving new names/signifiers or concepts to unknown referents, is actually reversed in the story "First Love," in which familiar, standard language seems to have lost all leverage and transparency. Contemporary words, viewed from an estranged perspective both in space and time, thus remain in constant need of (spurious) clarification: "In America the head sprouts either soft or coarse hair, features small apologies called eyes, and has a round mistake tunnel known as a mouth" (*LS*, 199–200). In *The Age of Wire and String*, the whole of language is utterly reinvented in the process, the society and culture the book purports to "catalog" having a language all its own that ultimately necessitates lexical entries at the end of each section.

In his first two books, Marcus thus seems to have taken William Gass's conception literally when he claimed, in *Fiction and the Figures of Life* notably, that fiction uses and intensifies language in ways that differ radically from what everyday language is and does: "Words mean things, writes Gass. Thus we use them every day: make love, buy bread, and blow up bridges. But the use of language in fiction only mimics its use in life" (Gass 1979, 30).[15] Gass eventually turns the mimetic credo on its head in *On Being Blue*: "It's not the word made flesh we want in writing, in poetry and fiction, but the flesh made word" (Gass 1976, 32). Gass claims that literary language does not aim to efface itself

156   Sightings

in order to pass off as real ("the word made flesh") but rather seeks to absorb the real into itself ("the flesh made word")—a move Marcus not only seems to vouch for but to implement rigorously, deploying the mimetic technique not in the direction of the real but of language itself, which becomes its own target and object: if most pieces in *The Age of Wire and String* are absurd, anti-realist fantasies with no grounding whatever in any recognizable reality, they remain highly mimetic of specific forms of language and lingos, affecting the external shape of, say, technical or expert language yet lacking any surface purchase on reality or so-called referents; in other words, Marcus retains the outer shell, the syntactic and rhetorical structure that commands authority yet empties it of all "legible," accessible contents:

G-D

It is a mode entered by flaxen tree tools from three to twelve lawns long, sometimes curved slightly, with conical bore and a cup-shaped godpiece. It produces only the natural angels of the city, slightly modified, however, by the materials of the landbound heaven. North of its leaves, the tool is used to call wasps into the bore to shape the angels as they are wept against the grass.

Warning: It is what often clogs the port. It is heavily sugared. It channels mouth steam (frusc) into the back bunt of the willow. Here is where angels amass in surplus and cease to breathe. The wings grow sticky and no longer beat. (*AWS*, 21)

The tone is knowing, the description thorough, the writing assertive and straight-to-the-point—yet the point is what, precisely? Hard to say in the end; an impossibly technical depiction or specification of "G-D"? The unnamed, unnamable name of God, yet ironically spelled out in the term "godpiece" and appended a few pages above as the section's title? Perhaps. A code to be deciphered? Maybe—an option that could well be supported by the further reappearance of such words as "godpiece" and "frusc" in the "Terms" sections, although such entries, one has to admit, shed very little light, if any, on the text itself:

GODPIECE   Cup, bowl, or hoop, which, when swished through air, passed under water, or buried for an indefinite time in sand will attract fragments and other unknown grains that comprise the monetary units of a given culture. The godpiece is known further as a wallet, satchel, or bag that assigns value to the objects inside it. (25)

FRUSC   The air that precedes the issuing of a word from the mouth of a member or person. Frusc is brown and heavy. (94)

In short, the aesthetic aggressively propounded in *The Age of Wire and String* and, to a lesser degree in *Notable American Women*, questions such notions as reference, referentiality and, further, authority. The referential authority of language is thus arbitrarily displayed and pressed, the better to be downplayed and baffled, as comically illustrated in the opening chapter of *Notable American Women* and the role (rhetorical) and place (underground) ascribed to the father figure. The language of both texts is marked by an intrinsic crisis that renders their contents eminently problematic and elusive, as unambiguously yet paradoxically stated in the "Argument" opening *The Age of Wire and String*, which concludes: "Let this rather be the first of many forays into the mysteries, as here disclosed but not destroyed. For it is in these things that we are most lost, as it is in these things alone that we must better be hidden" (4). Whatever mysteries the text contains, they remain intact; the society that the book is supposedly a catalog of remains deeply hidden at the heart of its disclosure. From the start, the antagonistic vocabulary—"prosecuted," "looting our country of its secrets," "a product that must be ravaged of bias," "by looking at an object we destroy it with our desire," "perish in blindness, flawed"—points to the text's aggressive stance, to its unwillingness to cooperate with its readers and critics, "professional disclosers" practicing their nefarious "routine in-gazing" and treacherously appropriating the exoticism of the textual landscapes they visit while drowning them under their all too "banal hues" (3–4). And no doubt to prevent that from happening, Marcus's novels, all to a greater or lesser extent, retain the mimetic shell while somehow blurring at best, if not altogether voiding it of, all referential contents.

Despite its realistic underpinnings, *The Flame Alphabet* may not be governed so much by mimetic representation as by simulation. In that sense, contrary to what is suggested by the aesthetic reorientation the novel follows—a change somehow pursued by most stories in *Leaving the Sea* or *Notes from the Fog* with a few notable exceptions, including "The Father Costume"[16]—*The Flame Alphabet* continues the work started with Marcus's first two books; it raises the same issues concerning referentiality, pitting authoritative discourses (religious, scientific, medical, academic) one against the other.

Among them, garbed in its conspicuous realism, is of course the novel's own narrative discourse, rendered slippery and deceptive, eventually no thicker than a smoke screen. The charade at times becomes almost limpid, as when socalled Murphy, whose Beckettian name gives away the superficiality of his disguise, commends Sam—short for Samuel of course—"for seeking out failure

158 Sightings

so aggressively," before enjoining him: "But this idea people have of failing on purpose, *failing better*? Look at who says that. Just look at them. Look at them very carefully." With which Sam obligingly complies: "I tried to picture the people who said that, but saw only my own head, mounted on a stick" (*FA*, 72). As narrator and writer—for Sam indeed doesn't hide the fact that his is a written account—Sam appears as a two-dimensional caricature of Beckett himself, plagued by the impossibility of going on and the untenable appeal of silence in the face of language's rarefaction and, ultimately, of "the unnamable."

Failure as a topic is perhaps not without its appeal to Marcus. Like the "Ben Marcus" of *Notable American Women*, and like most narrators in the later stories of *Leaving the Sea* and *Notes from the Fog* too—whether Paul in "What Have You Done?," Fleming in "I Can Say Many Nice Things," Edward in "The Loyalty Protocol," or Thomas in "The Moors," for instance (*Leaving the Sea*)—Sam appears as an utter failure himself: his "smallwork" at the start of the epidemic amounts to nothing much and is even ridiculed by LeBov: "Your little purses of smoke, I popped them over my children's heads to make them laugh. Kids love their own little mushroom cloud. They're tchotchkes, and they stink" (*FA*, 198). As for his work at Forsythe, his dabbling with the re-creation of nontoxic alphabets is dismissed as naive and inconsequential at best, if not downright foolish. His wife Claire's final collapse at the end of part 2 may even have been caused by Sam's Hebrew letter, which, though he initially deemed it harmless, may have proven noxious in the end. With each new attempt on his part to fight off the disease, Sam indeed may unwittingly be "failing better" or, perhaps more piquantly, failing to fail better somehow as his world keeps narrowing down more and more.

Failure, inadequacy, incompetence are leitmotifs throughout Marcus's fiction that already point to the characters' inability to relate, ever baffled by their surroundings—whether work on a cruise ship, in an office building, or family interaction. Most are idiosyncratic figures unable to belong or reach out, for whom communication, exchanging language acts, and negotiating turns of phrases can never be taken for granted, as evidenced by the crisis Thomas, in "The Moors," goes through, unable to address the sexy colleague standing in line before him at the coffee machine other than with baby talk (*LS*). Relating through language, although supposedly as transparent an act as could be, is always more difficult than anticipated and can lead to trying confrontations in Marcus's fiction. "Cold Little Bird," the opening story of *Notes from the Fog*, exemplifies the radical absence of relation when, out of the blue, Jonah won't let his parents touch him in any way, thus exacerbating the sudden absoluteness of the world—a world in which *relations* are rooted out and which consequently collapses around the narrator, no longer able to reach out to his son or communicate with his wife.

Sam learns about the aggressive, faulty materiality of language the hard way with his daughter Esther, who, in *The Flame Alphabet*, is ever prone to flinging back his every word and attention at him after deflating them and faulting them for their vacuity:

> Esther abhorred all the functional vocal prompts one bleated in order to stabilize the basic encounters, to keep them from capsizing into awkward fits of milling and hovering. Hello and good-bye and thank you to strangers; good morning and how are you. These phrases were insane to her. She would pick the simplest rituals, the most basic behavior that people keep in their back pockets and whip out without a fuss, and wage dark war against them, scorning us mightily for caring about the exchange of niceties. . . . And thus a rhetorical marvel was engineered: I apologized to Esther, regularly, for her refusal to be queried on her well-being. I regularly failed to mount cogent justifications for any of the human practices. They turned out to be indefensible to her. In the end I was a poor spokesman for life among people. Such were the victories of language in the home. (34)

Esther ruthlessly quashes all attempts at small talk, turns any social exchange into pure insanity. Far from transparent and harmless, language appears to her as mere "bleating," a prop to secure one's balance in the face of people, without which the whole human enterprise "capsizes"—a point that the epidemic later confirms. Language, in its ritual, empty function, already *is* some form of poison, an "allergy" (*FA*, 34) that Esther unscrupulously fights off, refusing to call her father "Dad," for instance, and using his first name instead as a weapon: "What have you learned, *Samuel*, when you've asked me how I am?" (*FA*, 34). As elsewhere in Marcus's work, language is reified in the process, turned into a flawed object—"Your gathering mechanism is fucked," Esther says to Sam, in reply to which he would "parry with oily fathery lameries" (*FA*, 34)—here reduced to some form of corrupt mechanism, a willful machine or technology freewheeling into empty rhetoric. Eventually Sam feels contrived to apologize for something *she* refuses to do—a "rhetorical marvel" indeed that proves Sam's inability to step out of the fiction of relation, that of "an exchange of niceties" that makes up for the impossibility of genuine communication. The "victories of language in the home" thus paradoxically sanction its own ironical and simultaneous defeat, as Sam, "poor spokesman" countered by a self-defeating rhetoric, apologizes and, in so doing, inadvertently keeps playing the game

160   Sightings

Esther has just taken to pieces, leaving him stranded and beaten ("I regularly failed") on the side of a broken, asymmetrical exchange.

•

Like Esther in *The Flame Alphabet*, Paul in "What Have You Done?" is keen on dismantling the mechanics of conversation, taking most phrases and questions at face value to reveal their overly rhetorical, mechanical aspect:

> "How's business, Paul?" Rick boomed.
> . . .
> "I don't know, Rick," Paul answered. "Business is fine. You mean world business? The stock market? Big question. I could talk all night, or we could gather around my calculator and do this thing numerically. Huddle up and go binary."
> . . .
> Rick was confused, so Alicia jumped in.
> "You know what he means, Paul. What do you do for work? What's your job?"
> "I cash Dad's checks and spend the money on child sex laborers down at the shipyard."
> His mother put her hand to her mouth. (*LS*, 13)

Back for the first time into his family home in Cleveland after a violent, several-year-old altercation with his father, Paul may of course feel insecure, literally a stranger among his own family, a wretched man inapt at the least intercourse: "He wished for a moment that he belonged to the population of men who asked and answered questions like this, who securely knew that these questions were the gateway for nonsexual statistical intercourse between underachieving men" (*LS*, 13). This sense of non-belonging could of course explain his awkward, inappropriate bravado as defense mechanism, rendered here through what could pass as psychological realism. Yet his repartee, like Esther's in *The Flame Alphabet*, draws attention to the very mechanics of language and the all-too-technical skills required to engage in conversation. Language as such *matters*, and Marcus's writing is very much geared toward the materiality of words and phrases, their impact, their potency, as well as their intrinsic deficiency.

The dialogue between Paul and Rick—that which, precisely, should serve as the textual site of an exchange, the locus where a conversation can take place and a relation can be built—in a way materializes the objectness of language, or what Harman would refer to as its "tool-being" perhaps, by foregrounding how flawed or "broken" it is. The conversation goes immediately awry and the connection it is supposed to instantiate between Rick and Paul never operates: "Rick was confused" (*LS*, 13). The relation, posited at the heart of language, is thus never a given but needs a certain number of prerequisites to function, as was already farcically illustrated by the chapter "System Requirements" in *Notable American Women*, which reviewed all the technical requirements that needed to be met for the book supposedly to function as an object. "You know what he means," interferes Alicia, Paul's sister, the better to recall Paul to the standard rules of conversation, spelling out Rick's intention for him where, ironically, Rick may not have had any other than to fill in a blank in the dinner conversation—a dinner incidentally charted in advance, in the course of which such conversation should never have occurred in the first place: "Everyone else at the table shrank, as if someone had thrown up and they didn't want to get splashed. Probably Rick hadn't been at the family meeting where they'd decided to go easy on Paul, lay off the hard stuff. Like, uh, questions" (*LS*, 12).

Beyond the comic aspect to be found in the discrepancy between intended and literal meanings that prompts the excerpt ("You mean world business? The stock market?"), language here appears as a full-fledged *object* in the sense object-oriented ontology gives to the word: "that which has a unified and autonomous life apart from its relations, accidents, qualities, and moments" (Harman 2010, 199). Language has ways of its own to go offtrack, it seems. For even if such deregulation is triggered by the character's quirks, language manifests its own resistance and autonomy in the process, its very materiality or, in the narrator's words, "the hard stuff."

This might be pushing it a bit too far, however. For the overall scene of course reads against a realistic background suffused with Paul's troubled psychology. Yet be that as it may, it proves traversed, also, with a speculative undercurrent that concomitantly undoes what is posed on the surface—the relation performed by the dialogue, on the one hand, is simultaneously undermined by its contents, on the other, contents that in part escape even Paul: "Perhaps there was something about this table that had made him take the low road so hard and fast. The table, his room, that red chair, the house; the whole city of Cleveland. The blame could be shared" (*LS*, 13). Ironically, if there is a relation that takes place here at all, it appears to be an "interobjective" one (Morton) much more than one that would happen between the subjects who carry it out; Paul as a matter of fact confesses to his own plausible susceptibility to his physical surroundings, thus implicitly viewing himself on a par with the objects around him, which could in equal parts be responsible, in the view the narrator relays, for what translates here as an obtuse (non-)conversation with his brother-in-law. Language, in its communicative aspect, is again unbalanced

162 Sightings

and deregulated, revealing its "tool-being": meaning and intent can no longer be vouched for and guaranteed, nor can blame easily be assigned. Communication is momentarily held in check, its relation canceled.

•

"Sometimes," Sam remarks in *The Flame Alphabet*, "no messages came, or they arrived in broken notes from the radio and we suffered through services in languages too foreign to know." Whether or not this can be blamed on the technology—"Our gear was faulty and old," says Sam—the religious message he and his wife Claire have come to the woods to be privately fed loses all transparency, comes in broken, reified pieces, spurts of white noise, "a hissing silence," or in various languages that Sam and Claire don't just *not* understand but that appear "too foreign to know" in the absolute (*FA*, 43).

The problem that Sam and Claire face is thus not merely an epistemic one but one that translates into metaphysical terms: there is something profoundly unapproachable involved. A radical mystery—silence disguised as noise. Such episodes may be occasional ("Sometimes"), mere accidents or technical failures perhaps, but they nonetheless, and quite ironically, embody the teachings of Rabbi Burke when those come through. Whether indecipherable or plainly expressed, the language conveyed by the transmissions performs the same incomprehensibility. Whatever truth or meaning such messages may eventually carry, it remains inscrutable,[17] opaque, no matter how Burke's sermons may later on be glossed or reprised or varied by Thompson's; all obfuscate rather than reveal or even clarify the contents of broadcasts ultimately and ironically not meant to be understood, according to Bauman (44). The delivered speech—if such is its name—remains one paradoxically not to be related to; the ritual diligently endures maybe, but to what end? Sam and Claire keep going to their hut, transforming the ritual service into mechanical love-making: "We could not speak of [the sermons] and I don't think either of us was even tempted. Our minds worked away in private at what we heard, but our bodies sometimes wanted the busywork of a cold joining of parts" (48). Because the religious "experience would not be rendered in speech," because "you could not repeat what you heard, or even that you heard anything" (42), the only possible way of ever relating to the Rabbi's sermons is *private*. If, then, the relation seems not to be canceled on the surface, its private rendering or "working away" is eventually undermined by "the great appetite for uncertainty that Burke demanded"—at best, the only possible relation is one couched in purely negative terms. "Burke's sermons," Sam admits, "reminded me of what I did not know, could hardly ever honestly feel" (48). They cannot be shared, cannot be discussed or rationalized, cannot and should not be understood; their language remains in the end "too foreign to know" and abides in ways that are bound to remain independent of any and all relation anyone could ever establish to it, were they capable of doing so.

Whatever the message, then, of the religious broadcasts, it recedes further and further away from its origin, retreating into an unapproachable, unattainable, and questionable background. Religious language in *The Flame Alphabet* thus doesn't yield so much as it obscures or simulates its origin. In what could be a reversal of McLuhan's famous coinage, the message, as it were, is the medium—that is, the endless intermediation that screens the original meaning, if ever there *was* one. Sam's discovery of (maybe, maybe not) Rabbi Burke singing in a microphone to birds from a Forsythe basement—old, naked, vulnerable; *all too real*, in a sense, a man whose image jars with that of the authoritative, learned, aloof rabbi—tends to suggest the contrary. If Sam's understanding of the situation oscillates between two alternatives—either "they'd gotten to him . . . [o]r else he'd always been here, had never left" (250)—he seems reluctant to deduce the only valid interpretation in case the second option proves true: *"there is no Burke,"* as LeBov had warned him (128). Burke is an empty name, a sham. A simulacrum. And so is the whole religion he stands for. Yet this possibility is implicitly discarded by Sam, who at this juncture starts referring to the man no longer as "the man" but as "the rabbi" instead, claiming: "You might protest when I call this man a rabbi. But you didn't see him, did you? You weren't there. You didn't know his voice your whole life the way I did, and if you did, I ask you now to stand down and believe me" (251).

However, as Sam himself has just realized: "What was the distinction again?" (250). There might be none whatsoever, as suggested by the fact that the man ambiguously appears to Sam as a "perfect imitation" (250) that, were it such, would of course cease to be one in order to turn into the real thing. In the face of such undecidability, it thus seems that the name—"when I <u>call</u> this man a rabbi"—is enough to make the man so, whether or not he happens to be Burke, whether or not there even *is* such a man as Burke behind the name and all that he embodies.

It is the same performative language that eventually obtains in Shelley Jackson's *Riddance*, in which, in order to visit "the land of the dead"—by definition a (non-)place characterized by sheer negativity and nothingness—and engage in conversation with deceased people, or lend them a voice, one can only count on the fiction performatively instantiated through one's language. As the book's (fictional) editor explains as a foreword to Sybil Joines's "Final Dispatch" from the necrocosmos: such dispatches "were a mortal necessity for the necronaut,

164   Sightings

for whom the narrative thread was quite literally a lifeline. . . . We talk our way through the timeless land of the dead in a sort of bathysphere made of words, creating both ourselves and the landscape through which we move" (*R*, 15). Hence Joines's account: "Road, I propose, and a road pours out of me" (66).

In *The Flame Alphabet*, the performative aspect of Sam's language in a way accords with its ritual function as debunked by Esther earlier: in both cases, the language, in the shape of empty formulas devoid of preexisting referents, performs its own signification and forcefully projects a relation that may not exist outside of its utterance, a relation bound to appear fictitious or simulated in an act of aggressive appropriation. "What have you learned, *Samuel*, when you've asked me how I am?" Esther teases (*FA*, 34), not so much alluding to knowledge per se as to the "gathering mechanism" involved in the process. Similarly, whether or not the old man truly is Burke, Sam realizes: "It didn't matter to me. He was still mine" (250). His, Sam's, that is; the man is his to name, his to *make* real even, and perhaps especially so in the absence of any such ascertainable reality. The man of authority—he who "did not officially exist in public," Sam explained: "There was no such person" (46)—is here brought down to his name, to a noun ("a rabbi") whose meaning can only be private in the end, and whose reality can only be guaranteed—that is, not at all—through rhetoric or intimidation ("I ask you now to stand down").

What this seems to suggest is that language, in Marcus's fiction, simulates more than it represents, proffers more than it refers. Hence, perhaps, the constant deformations, usurpations, distortions, as epitomized by the novel's take on Jewish reconstructionism, for instance, which in *The Flame Alphabet* no longer is a reality outside language but very much a textual instantiation; the referent, in other words, is superseded with a new fictitious entity, the same way that "Ben Marcus" in *Notable American Women* differs from the real Ben Marcus. The arbitrary connection between sign and referent is thus played out against itself, broken up, and simulated anew; the semiotic regime defining Marcus's texts therefore cannot be one over which representation, conventionally defined, prevails. For the crisis (or disease) of language that *The Flame Alphabet* is staked upon brings about a concomitant crisis in the very definition of the real—a real now shown to be indistinguishable from the sign that performatively instantiates it. If the sign founders, the real collapses onto the fiction that it was. With only language left to ascertain it anymore, reality itself dissolves in its own simulation or, what amounts to the same thing, withdraws—*as such*—beneath the signs that supersede and obfuscate it.

For the sheer absence of distinction between what is the case and what is not, or the radical impossibility of discerning between original and fake, as with the presence of the old man near the "Jew hole" at Forsythe, might indeed be paramount to the ontological definition of the *real* as such; a real that eventually admits no duplicates, whose very copies are copies doubling nothing— *objects*, that is, in their own right, unrelated and unresponsive to anything outside themselves.

For if copies or doubles ("decoys") proliferate throughout *The Flame Alphabet*, they appear to do so from an absent, dubious, irretrievable origin, as exemplified by the evil couple Murphy/LeBov. If Murphy *is* LeBov, he initially appears in the text already as a mimetic (i.e., unoriginal) figure mirroring the behavior of others, incorporating and projecting their own image back to them. "But were you actually sick? Was that real?" Sam wants to know of LeBov, recalling the first time he saw him as Murphy at the beginning of the novel:

> LeBov dropped the mask, hacked into his towel.
>
> "That's mirroring. I learned it in fucking first grade. You adopt the behavior of your opponent, then escalate it. Saw it on one of those film strips about insects. If he's susceptible, you gain his trust and he thinks he's found an ally for life. *Finally someone who suffers like me! A friend!* Works pretty well on Jews, who usually think they're unique. Maybe even in kindergarten I learned that. With Mrs. Krutz. She was a fucking genius, actually. Mrs. Krutz once . . . (220)

Sick LeBov's literal "dropping of the mask"—his respirator—is all too ironic, since his reply actually suggests that the figurative mask is never dropped: behind the mask there always is another mask. His mimeticism or mimicry, he comments, is itself derivative and, when asked if the couple Sam saw him harass when first meeting him were Murphy's "first," LeBov incredulously replies: "My first? My first *what*?" (221).

There thus seems no way ever to go back to any originary moment, event, being, object, or ground; LeBov makes this clear too when he sarcastically observes: "Do you think the demon speech began out of nowhere a few months ago and swept through town all of a sudden? A little suburban catastrophe? Is that really what you think? You think I fucking work *alone*?" (221). The chain thus keeps doubling back, without beginning or end either, as suggested by the fact that LeBov repudiates the *catastrophic* dimension of the epidemic: while it eschews any point of ex nihilo departure, it simultaneously puts an end to nothing, not even to language itself, as attested by the paradoxical existence of Sam's narrative. Language endures, both poison and cure, and remodels reality, accommodates, appropriates and, so doing, displaces it as much as obfuscates it.

When discovering, through a final TV report announcing LeBov's (fake)

166 Sightings

death, that he and Murphy turn out to be one and the same person, Sam initially guesses that LeBov merely assumed another name; yet LeBov's identity remains ambiguous to the end;[18] the change of names may not leave the reality intact: "you don't even know that I'm the real LeBov" (127)—a remark that Sam will incidentally replay to himself, somehow making it his or, in the absence of quotation marks, replaced with italics in Sam's memory of the conversation, at least decontextualizing it enough to make its referent loose: "*How do you even know that I'm the real LeBov?*" (249). Interestingly, the question resurfaces just before Sam escapes a dying LeBov by "plung[ing] down the Jewish hole of Forsythe" (252), thus ironically reenacting LeBov's own escape at the end of chapter 19—the better to turn into him somehow in the last part of the novel and become a mere parody of LeBov, a new double in a potentially endless series ("You think I fucking work *alone*?"), Sam in turn now appearing as a sick man hunting for children, an ogre in disguise craving the poisonous language and the antidote children secrete in order to complete his narrative.

The question eventually raised by the incessant play on doubles and metamorphoses is the authenticity of any *first*, of the model over its so-called copy, and hence of the referent over the sign. *The Flame Alphabet*—whose very title points to a problematic, foundational or originary event, one bound to repeat itself after Moses broke the original stone tablets on which the finger of God had just traced the Law in letters of fire (Exodus 32–34)—can thus be read as a foregrounding of what French philosopher Clément Rosset referred to as the "density of the real," instead of backing up a "philosophy of the Double," which he describes as "a metaphysical philosophy that holds the everyday 'real' to be a duplicate, whose key and meaning could only be provided by the vision of the Original." To Rosset, however, the real does not conform to such a vision and cannot be apprehended in terms of truth, authenticity, or originality, nor, as a consequence, in relation to its various copies, fakes, or doubles. Instead, the real is defined by its own "density":

> The density of the real, on the contrary, points to the plenitude of everyday reality, that is to say to the uniqueness of a world composed not of doubles but always of original singularities (even if those happen to look "alike"), a world that consequently answers to no model—a philosophy of the real, which sees in the everyday and the banal, even in repetition itself, all the world's originality. No object, seen through this philosophy of the real, can be held to be "original" in the metaphysical sense; yet no real object happens to be not fabricated, artificial, dependent, conditioned, "second-hand." Everything, as it were, already is a double, at least following a certain metaphysical sensibility; yet these

"doubles" copy no model and as a consequence are each and every one of them originals.[19] (Rosset, 151)

Quite perniciously, the apparent, conventional realism of *The Flame Alphabet*, in its "propagation of a belief in the referent," as Fredric Jameson defines it,[20] is thus progressively unsettled; *representation* appears to be more and more untenable since it would be coextensive with this "abiding referentialist fallacy" disputed by Anna Kornbluh (*The Order of Forms*, 45), or what Clément Rosset calls a "philosophy of the Double," one that the novel toys with yet radically undermines. For as doubles, decoys, copies proliferate throughout, their origin, that which they supposedly represent, gets irretrievably lost and questionable. The imagery of the underground network, the opaque description of radio transmissions, the prominence of religious issues, along with the novel's depiction of impossible communication due to the speech fever—all of that points to the notions of interconnection and relations, a tight web of associations, the existence of something both other and external, some truth, a message, meaning. Yet the novel's insistence on privacy, secrecy, or impenetrability concomitantly thwarts exchanges, and the networks eventually connect no one to nothing, propagate vacancy, broadcast mere noise. The relation is no sooner posited than it thus starts crumbling apart. The reference point, what the relation points to, the Origin—whether conceived of in religious or secular terms—is thus radically deconstructed, even somehow desecrated, as an expert significantly, yet quite paradoxically, observes in a feature devoted to LeBov's death: "When the faith to which [LeBov] is referring *does not exist*, I can only be profoundly troubled. It desecrates the real, authentic Jew to imagine a false and private one, and to accord that imaginary Jew with secret powers channeled against the interests of the world at large. It's a desecration" (114). The irony here being that, in the world of the novel, this faith *does* exist, as Sam knows all too well. Yet the frame of reference shatters as the statement acquires a metafictional status, for of course the words of the so-called expert apply to the novel's own aesthetic gesture, which consists in taking something real (Jewish Reconstructionism) and distorting it, turning it into a fiction, rendering it, in Joshua Cohen's words, "fictile, unfixable, rootless." The Original evaporates as the appellation is drained of its contents. Sign and reality no longer match; but did they ever? Of course not. The sign doubles its referent; yet doing so, it doubles nothing, represents nothing, precisely because it can never *match* it, never give any direct access to the real—a real always other, always elsewhere than it is said to be. Instead, the sign reveals its own "density," its own singularity or objectness. In the end, and in the words of J. Hillis Miller quoted by Kornbluh to propound her reappraisal of realism in formalist rather than mimetic terms, realism "is not a mimesis in language of something

168   Sightings

nonverbal, but language about language" (Kornbluh, 45)—what Marcus's fiction is first and foremost.

Language in *The Flame Alphabet* is thus progressively dissociated from its referential dimension and made to turn back on itself. Part of Sam's narrative in fact consists in imagining or projecting what could or should have been, what wasn't the case or didn't happen, how Sam's expectations were betrayed somehow, how the real kept letting his own representations down. In other words, *The Flame Alphabet* could be read as a decoy itself, a double doubling nothing, a copy without an original, or a sign referring to nothing outside itself—"language about language."[21] Sam's account indeed keeps projecting various images of itself with which it never quite coincides, whether images of a past that does not exist as such—"We left on a school day" (*FA*, 3)—or scraps of an impossible, wishful future that progressively cannibalizes the end of Sam's narrative, replacing his uncertain, rarefying present—Sam may believe he rescued Esther eventually, the reader only has his word for it—with illusory prospects: "I spent the morning outside the hut waiting for Esther to return. I could have ventured after her, but there were too many directions she could have taken and it seemed safer to wait, since she would be back soon, I was sure" (288). The novel closes with Sam still waiting for his daughter, or whoever it was he fancied might have been her, while the past tense of narration gives way to improbable predictions, shifting the text toward margins of futurity condemned to mere wishful thinking:

> When Esther returns, healthy and strong again, ready to take her place as my daughter, together we can sit at the hole in our hut and listen as one family, the two of us bending together into the old hole that might deliver our missing piece.
>
> We will listen for the footsteps of Esther's mother, who could be here soon. It is a difficult trip, but not impossible. . . . She will find us here, it is really just a question of when. When Esther returns to me, we will wait for her mother together, as a family.
>
> It may take days or weeks, but it will not matter, we will wait. And when Claire climbs through the hole, exhausted from her travels, caked in the filth of the tunnels, Esther and I will lead her to the outdoor shower, boil extra water for the cleansing. We'll ready a little mountain of soft towels, and Esther will go inside to choose from the bright new clothes we pulled from the shelves in town.
>
> While Claire showers, Esther and I will smile at each other, look down, draw nonsense signs in the dirt with a stick. We will be excited, but we will wait, give Claire her time. (289)

Sam ends up alone, utterly isolated, all connections severed, a character going blind, literally left in the dark, without a clue—a husband without a wife, a father without a daughter; the roles he used to play no longer require him to fill them in, as he eventually realizes: "To be Esther's father is to try with all my might not to get caught being her father. I can be that person for her. I will be" (288). All that is left to him is the two-dimensional picture of a happy family finally reunited, with each one of them playing a role that quite never was theirs to begin with: Esther obligingly, obediently "ready to take her place as [Sam's] daughter." The idyllic portrait Sam draws of the reunion is of course a hollow one in a world turned silent, peacefully bathed in sunlight—an impossible one. *The Flame Alphabet* thus ends on a fallacy, an image void of content, a mere simulacrum—the simulacrum of an empty deictic, *this*, whose reference remains unassignable:[22] "I will wait for them here in my hut, and when Claire and Esther return, <u>this</u> is what we'll do, as a family" (289). The assertive tone affected by Sam is counteracted by the vacancy of his language—a language freewheeling around empty, artificial constructions—"draw[ing] nonsense signs in the dirt" with a stick, in the image of lone Kate in Markson's *Wittgenstein's Mistress*, "[leaving] messages in the street" for no one to read (*WM*, 7). In that regard, *The Flame Alphabet* doesn't end so much as it dodges all closure, prolonging its own simulacrum, subsiding or withdrawing into an implausible, undecidable sequel (*this*), a figment eventually cut loose.

•

Whether in deceitfully mimetic ways (*The Flame Alphabet* or most later stories gathered in *Leaving the Sea* or *Notes from the Fog*) or grotesquely absurdist fashion (*The Age of Wire and String*, *Notable American Women*, or the earlier stories of *Leaving the Sea*), Marcus's language verges on the speculative—that is, a language defined not so much by what it refers to as by how it fails to work as it is supposed to; not so much characterized by what it states as by the diverse ways in which it obfuscates its object and comprehension. In short, Marcus somehow manhandles and deregulates both everyday and literary language, a language that, on the page, appears overly fictionalized, reified, objectified— rendered somehow to what Harman, reviewing Heidegger, calls its *tool-being*.

The narrative discourse of *The Flame Alphabet*, paradoxically instantiated through a first-person/firsthand account of the radical impossibility of its own language, eventually undermines the apparent mimeticism it builds upon, nothing but sheer trompe l'oeil in the end, a *détournement* of rhetorical ploys and literary gambits, referential illusions and so-called effects of the real. Yet what results from Marcus's play on simulation might be an endeavor to achieve a more fundamental, or *speculative*, form of realism,[23] one that would no longer strive

170 Sightings

to depict the real as it is—a fiction premised on the fact that reality could at first be identified, located, and eventually known—but would instead register and act upon the sheer impossibility of ever saying anything *true* or remotely *valid* about reality, given that, in the words of Graham Harman, "reality is always radically different from our formulation of it, and is never something we encounter directly in the flesh" (Harman 2017, 7). Instead, the real always stands beyond all relation of/to it and remains that upon which mimetic language always falters or breaks down.[24] Hence the multiple devices, artifacts, technological objects that traverse Marcus's fiction (e.g., the "listener," the "Marshall Symptom appliance," the "Dräger Aerotest breathing kit" from *The Flame Alphabet*, or the diverse helmets and harnesses of *Notable American Women*, etc.) and that act as mediating, or indirect, or metaphorical means and methods of either gaining or protecting (spurious) access to the metaphysical, mere berserk props to help with the invention of alternative cults diversely focusing on secrecy, silence, incommunicability. A material and technological bend to be found, also, in Shelley Jackson's *Riddance* and her main character's pseudo-philosophical doctrine and teachings on how to channel voices from the dead.

Yet, for that matter, the whole parodic frame around, or background to, Marcus's worlds tends to suggest that this unreachable, inaccessible *real*—however one defines it—does not gesture toward some transcendent textual truth, nor vice versa. Quite the contrary, the negativity placed at the heart of novels like *The Flame Alphabet* or *Notable American Women*, and that could diversely extend to novels like Jackson's *Riddance*, Azareen Van der Vliet Oloomi's *Fra Keeler*, David Markson's *Wittgenstein's Mistress*, or Michael Joyce's *Was*, rather points to the fact that such "truth" is precisely what *remains*, in its fragmented, disseminated, or labile presence *on* the page, in its blanks or linings or foldings.

As Harman puts it:

> The usual objection to this principle [of indirection] is the complaint that it leaves us with nothing but useless negative statements about an unknowable reality. Yet this objection assumes that there are only two alternatives: clear prose statements of truth on one side and vague poetic gesticulations on the other. I will argue instead that most cognition takes neither of these two forms, as is clear from such domains as aesthetics, metaphor, design, the widely-condemned discipline of rhetoric, and philosophy itself. (Harman 2017, 7)

In other words, fiction, in its putatively speculative dimension, does not elude or miss the real so much as it shapes a discourse that, in its inability or unwillingness to speak or represent it, somehow manages to "channel" it, as it were, the way the living in Jackson's *Riddance*, precisely *because* their speech is impeded by their stammering, channel the dead and gone. Only through a broken language can one ever hope to get to, if not know, then at least *feel* the real—through the material, obstructive, smoke-screen reality of the text itself, through forms of textuality that, because they do not seem to function anymore, or not along habitual lines, are in the end felt to *remain*, approached always, but only so far or so close as to never paper over their critical distance.

I've made it so far. My speculations may not be utterly in vain, after all. Despite the hard times they give me, these texts that I keep returning to do feed my discourse. True, dear Incomprehension, I sensed the contradiction from the start. And so I'm bound to wonder, now and again: Is speculative fiction truly unreadable, as I claim it is? Or is it all just such an elaborate fiction? A fiction I might be telling myself to compensate for my own limitations. For these texts do resist me somehow. I'm not pretending. Perhaps the understanding that I gain of them, then, rhetorical though it—almost by definition—may be, is necessarily a negative one: the understanding that I can't understand, simply because the texts no longer play by such rules. The enigmas they raise, the puzzles they shape, are not ones to be answered. Not ones that would engage in hermeneutics, whether of suspicion or otherwise—or not only. There is something about them, about the way they operate—how they distort the syntax, they engage in noise, they reiterate, they pile up words, they concatenate or explode, they disrupt their sequences, they list, they obfuscate or puncture their pages; there is something, then, about the way they fail to, or will not, operate along conventionally novelistic lines that begs for a change of—is it paradigm? approach? something else? The fact that those novels deliberately appear to malfunction or look deficient—in narrative impetus, in character psychology, in a well-defined plot or time-oriented action—may be a telltale sign that the drama they stage is not an epistemological but rather an ontological one.

Yes, then. Perhaps somehow "speculative fiction" is a theoretical figment. The theory against which I pit the textual aporias of novels that no longer function like ones, yet have not ceased to be ones, for that matter. For their matter. Novels turned material objects. Turned "tools" that, like any other tool, may at any moment stop working and leave me in the lurch with an illegible book in my hands. A book that I simply don't know how to read anymore. A book with which I simply don't know what to do.

A book, an object.

Something that is there.

Something that there is.

Speculative Interface, Or "cr!tical fa⅃⅃ure/r3port loXⴲred"

Language is what matters. Language *as* matter. Language turned object—concrete, opaque, black ink gesturing on white page, indecipherable, alluring, vibrant with possibility as much as with its cancellation (see Fig. 6).

Shelley Jackson's latest novel *Riddance*—whose title somehow riffs on an impossible *riddle*—is entirely premised on the sheer materiality of language. Most characters in *Riddance*, starting with Sybil Joines, the headmistress and founding figure of the "Vocational School for Ghost Speakers & Hearing-Mouth Children" that bears her name, are stutterers, persons for whom language is not a fluid immateriality but a block of matter, an object that stubbornly resists utterance, that tricks and trips the tongue—something cracked, flawed, impeded, that fails to be communicated, whose meaning is held in check, undermined by redundancy, noise, and interference. "Static" may be another word for it—an ambiguous word that points to stillness, immobility, lack of direction, a phenomenon that doesn't agree with the supposedly smooth directionality and sequentiality of narrative, which is here conspicuously undermined by the novel's breaking up into four alternating threads: two enmeshed story lines—one that follows Sybil Joines's search for a missing student in the land of the dead, as dictated to her secretary Jane Grandison (1); the other one, Grandison's own story, as recounted in the lulls of Joines's own report or "dispatch" (2)—interspersed with a "Readings" section (3) made up of different documents from different sources about the school, its teachings, and its philosophy, as garnered by the book's anonymous editor, and a series of letters written by Sybil Joines to "Dead Authors" (4).

From the start, then, the novel is riddled with contradictions, split between divergent allegiances, couched in a language that belies its own impossibility, its

Figure 6. Shelley Jackson, *Riddance* (164–65)

multiple fallacies since, according to the doctrine implemented by Sybil Joines—who not quite incidentally shares the same initials as her author—all language is a cipher, in all senses of the word: it points to, is a sign of, absence and death, but it also is an envelope to be decoded, hollowed out, a dual instantiation, a doubling or lining. A bit like what was happening in *Half Life*, where Nora's narrative was irremediably laced with her sister's silent words, language in *Riddance* is permeated with other voices whose attribution remains problematic—a stutter is but the telltale sign that someone else is speaking through and being channeled by the stutterer's voice. Language is thus the material site of the cancellation of opposites, when life and death, fact and fiction, the truth and the fraud, story and history, you and me, absence and presence, past and future, become one and the same. Hence the book's impossible, material nature—a book that is not one, whose layout points to other media that make of *Riddance* a haunted book in more senses than one: a book, *as such*, that is literally hard to grasp, that is, to hold in your hands. In many ways, *Riddance* could be seen as a rather reader-*un*friendly object. As the editor warns in the introduction:

> This book can be entered at any point. For less experienced travelers, I have planned a route. Its reduplicate tracks, laid down over a single evening—one by the Headmistress, one by her stenographer—will

convey the reader surely, if not safely, to the end. Interspersed between these two interwoven strands, according to a strictly repeating pattern, are additional readings of a more scientific, sociological, or metaphysical nature. Those who, lacking a scholar's interest in minutiae, want to get to the end more quickly, may wish to skip over these parts, and who knows, may even be wise to do so. But true eccentrics may find in them something—a map, a manual—that they have long been seeking. (12)

And *Riddance* proves a de facto difficult read, its "strictly repeating pattern" the sign of a recalcitrance, of an unyielding streak—as though there were a ghost in the text indeed, and this ghost were the machine or technology more broadly, as suggested by the intrinsically hypertextual nature or architecture, as here defined, of the novel.[1]

•

The machinic is also felt through Blake Butler's novella *Ever*. Though it remains somehow more immediately narrative than later implementations, like *Sky Saw* or *300,000,000*, *Ever* is delivered in blocks of text whose logical or narrative progression is not always apparent. At some point, the narrative impetus stammers and verges on iteration, as the story enters a repeat mode of sorts with the narrator finding herself navigating different rooms in the house she inherited from her mother (pp. 51 to 67). Her experience is mimicked by the text's layout as mostly blank, one-paragraph pages, all starting with "In the next room . . . ," quickly follow one another. Reading the various blocks of ekphrastic text spread out unevenly from page to page is here equated with navigating each specific room, an experience enhanced by the (virtual) first-person POV, not unlike the tentative rendition of a video game strategy.

The digital-friendly nature of *Ever* can also be felt in its visual dimension: the text is regularly interspersed with computer-generated or -altered images by Derek White, which loosen or arrest its narrative course, or which merge with its language, introducing temporal gaps whenever pictures sport text that reappears a couple of pages later (30/32, 66/67, 73/75, 78/81), seemingly warping the text's overall syntax and fabric.

This interaction between text and image—also a key component of Jackson's *Riddance*—with lines that are lifted from the text, isolated, quoted, or anticipated by the drawings, suggests an illustrative dimension that the haptic quality of the images themselves belies; images in shades of gray overlaid with diverse forms and shapes and tracings, some of them figurative, some of them abstract, some of them gestural. In that regard, and in Manovich's terms, the visual field appears clearly "aggregate" rather than "systematic," composed

176   Sightings

of discrete elements that never quite combine to unify the visual plane. Finely pixelated images sometimes split over double pages. And when the visual composition plays with a sense of symmetry, the latter is warped and deceiving (e.g., 34, 49, 99). In other words, there is and can be no easy equivalence between text and image, since the haptic regime of these images depends on deformation (83) and indeterminacy (73, 78) and as such already thwarts representation and all such referential correspondences.

What's more, the text's layout also indicates that the narrative space is in itself much more akin to computer space, as defined by Manovich, than literary space. Paragraphs do not appear as such and are replaced with blocks or chunks of text diversely indented and framed by square brackets:

> [From in the light I touched the light. I knew the light grew mold inside me.
> [Or.
> [Or what. I could not think.]] (*Ever*, 4)

The text in *Ever* happens to be literally isolated on the page, treated as a series of discrete chunks to be assembled or aggregated—included or broken up—into bigger units whose own contours, in the absence of clearly marked chapters or sections, are however hard to pin down. Visually, the blocks of text, more or less long, rather shape what looks like a computer program than a literary text, and the brackets somehow operate as markers or tags, framing elements that have to be worked together in order for the whole script to function—a visual dimension also clearly perceptible in works by Michael Joyce, whose affinity with digital narrative is evident,[2] or, less so, by David Markson, with novels like *Wittgenstein's Mistress*, *Reader's Block*, or *Vanishing Point*, which all achieve a discontinuous feel through the isolation on the page of short blocks of text that never seem to amalgamate but, instead, tend to reiterate.

In other words, narrative appears in such cases, quite visually, to have been dismantled or torn apart, split and shattered across the page. In Butler's *Ever*, this narrative precariousness is immediately signaled by the text's opening lines: from the outset, the text seems to collapse on itself; the repetition of the word "light" in the first sentence ("From in the light I touched the light"), its encasing in the second by the first person ("I knew the light grew mold inside me"), can read as a short circuit of sorts, as both syntactical units seem to loop on themselves. Instead of acting as a narrative springboard then, a strategic device apt to launch the story forward and give it both momentum and direction, the text's incipit stalls it. Bifurcation is needed to avoid the dead end, a new direction or start to relaunch the text after its failed initial attempt, as exemplified in the second line: "Or." Yet this new setup proves no more successful; the narrator stops dead in her tracks, her thought process immediately foundering: "Or what. I could not think." The double brackets put an end to this first (non-)move, only to re-open on the next page with a new impossibility: "[I could not find the wall" (5).

Butler is operating formally in *Ever*, whose anti-mimetic strokes are relayed visually, in ways quite different from what they are in *Scorch Atlas*'s or *There Is No Year*'s grayish textures emphasizing the material dimension of the books. Yet, in *Ever*, the haptic take on the text also points, through the indentations and the opening/closing brackets, to a formal logic of inclusion/isolation. Which may account for the fact that, with most stories in *Scorch Atlas*, *Ever* remains in essence more immediately narrative than the later novels. Indeed, despite appearances such formal apparatus also supports what poet Ron Silliman, in identifying "the new sentence," calls "the syllogistic leap"—that is, "integration above the level of the sentence" (Silliman, 79), or the ability for the classic sentence to leap forward and work itself into a bigger semantic unit to which it contributes. The opening three lines of *Ever* appear in that regard emblematic, for though they semantically instantiate the collapse of narrative, their linkage remains "syllogistic" in Silliman's sense of the word, each one clearly dependent upon the others with which they articulate in a logical, continuous way. The narrative disruptions, albeit perceptible, along with the text's speculative moves in trying to elude immediate comprehension, remain in the end more superficial when contrasted with more obfuscating syntactical constructions, as found in *300,000,000* or *Sky Saw*:

> The grain in the game of the soft of the nape of the wet of the gray of the back of the scape of the showering conundrum pricking open and surrounded and surrounding all absorbed all cracked agate in the earthless furnace tongued with expectation (SS, 247)

Despite ploys toward integration, such as the use of the prepositions "of" and "and," whose syntactic function is, precisely, to bind words together into bigger units—a phrase, a clause—their sheer repetition here rather disjoints words, holding them apart from each other as discrete units that fail to, or won't, integrate into a "sentence"—or else a sentence that remains obtusely loose, disjointed, and open-ended, as eventually suggested by the absence of a period.

•

One of the effects of the "new sentence" as defined by Silliman is to draw the reader's attention away from the signified and the way it articulates (toward) a potential narrative, to focus it back onto the density of the signifier, "freed suddenly from its servitude to an integrating hierarchy of syntactic relations" (Silliman, 76). This might be nowhere more visible than in Michael Joyce's *Was*, in which each paragraph is radically disconnected from the next, uprooted from its immediate context. As such, because they lack any "specific referential focus," paragraphs appear as mere "unit[s] of measure" instead of integrating tools (Silliman, 89), juxtaposing words and phrases that work at constantly "torqueing" the overall syntax of the text instead of bringing it together:

> refugee consciousness, a radio lozenge, certain unforeseen cul de sacs, multicolored phone cards and the right festive hat, motor vehicles bureau, sultry white presidio
>
> I want to waltz once
>
> more.
>
> slow descent of the mothership over the dry lake bed, a miraculous pouring forth, distant murmur, an empty stadium, all we have lived for lost, or who can tell (so irritable, she says), the hovering shade offers a welcoming respite, for once almost making sense, sweet shoots stir themselves, labial: cumulus (*Was*, 14–15)

What occurs within the paragraph, in *Was*, where sentences as such never truly cohere or gain formal unity—or at the cost, if they do, of a formal dislocation: "I want to waltz once / more."—replicates at the scale of the page, on which the paragraphs' concatenation appears loose and accidental, lacking in obvious "syllogistic" impetus.

In a way, because like modern poetry as seen by linguist Benveniste "it destroys the spontaneously functional nature of language" and resists "the [relational] economy of classical language"—according to which "words are abstracted as much as possible in the interests of relationships" (quoted by Silliman, 75)—the "new sentence" appears as an *absolute* one: one in which syntactical, syntagmatic, hierarchical relations dissolve at its core, as further suggested, in *Was*, by the use of lists. In that regard, and despite the fact that its title may point to a time-oriented artifact, *Was* becomes a loose, aggregate, spatial construct, "a map, a manual" (*R*), that Fredric Jameson, deploring postmodernism's lack of concern for historicity and temporal coherence, would indeed liken to a "practice of the randomly heterogeneous and fragmentary and the aleatory" (Jameson, 25, quoted by Silliman). However, as suggested by Silliman, this apparent lack of coherence or cohesion might be simply displaced onto textual regimes other than the time-oriented or sequentially narrative. Logic, sequence, meaning, narrative may eventually remain alien to the intrinsic operations of the "new" or, perhaps, in keeping with the matter at hand, what I might call the "speculative" sentence. As Silliman argues, mirroring my own critical predicament:

> Any attempt to explicate the work as a whole according to some "higher order" of meaning, such as narrative or character, is doomed to sophistry, if not overt incoherence. The new sentence is a decidedly contextual object. Its effects occur as much between, as within, sentences. Thus it reveals that the blank space, between words or sentences, is much more than the 27th letter of the alphabet. It is beginning to explore and articulate just what those hidden capacities might be. (Silliman, 92)

By insisting on its contextual dimension—that is, on what lies *around* it, what (negatively) delineates it, that which the sentence is set against—Silliman draws attention to its *objectness* in a sense that is close to how object-oriented ontology, whether through Harman, Morton, or Bogost, defines the object as that which projects around itself (non-)relations that recede, withdraw, translate in ways that remain silent, obscure, and mysterious, independently of how they are used or perceived.

In some of its possible instantiations, speculative fiction would thus exist through a properly *differential* writing—a writing that subtracts, takes away, subsides, withdraws, holds back. A writing for which blanks, spaces, interstices, silences, and rests matter. A writing, whose *articulation*, made possible by differentiation—"Do these letters have meaning, or the space around them? Neither. It's their difference we read" (*HL*, 433)—may eventually verge on the prosodic, as intuited by Silliman following Barthes (88), or on the musical: "wishing language were a knot? / music anyways" (*Was*, 123).

•

Tying the knot—making everything converge and cohere, holding everything together, working toward *com-prehension*. That might be specifically what speculative fiction won't do. Circumventing instead that point from which the text, as such, may find a unity all its own. Forever split; disseminated. Carried away along multiple strands or voices. None of which can be said to be master or mastered. Radically decentered, or marginalized—pushed toward margins that undo the text as well as what narrative authority it might have preserved for a short while.

Books like Danielewski's *House of Leaves*, Jackson's *Riddance*, Butler's *300,000,000*, and to a lesser extent Mark Doten's *The Infernal* are littered with editorial comments, voices from the margins, that play with and deconstruct the conventions of the scholarly text, which allegedly shows mastery, displays expertise, evinces authority. Yet pitting one voice against the others, the narrative discourse of such texts collapses, dissolves, dead-ends, loses itself amid contradictions, irresolvable mysteries. Grappling with those texts, trying to understand their enigmas on their own terms,[3] on their own grounds, I'm faced with the proliferation of my own baffled image: "Of course this is me searching for meaning. Likely there is no meaning but it is my job to persist in the identification of tragedy nailed to nothing, and so I will" (*3HM*, 85); "Unfortunately, the anfractuosity of some labyrinths may actually prohibit a permanent solution. More confounding still, its complexity may exceed the imagination of even the designer.... All solutions then are necessarily personal" (*HOL*, 115); "Frankly, I see no way to settle all its ambiguities" (*R*, 481); "*What are we to make of them—those tales of woe?... What use could I be, after all, in helping you interpret the confessions?*" (*I*, 82–83).

By necessity, then, such texts revolve around a central, absolute absence; they build on blanks that expand and contaminate the whole narrative picture, its contents unavoidably draining. Not unlike the tapes Flood finds in Gravey's house:

> Each of the tapes, it seems, is blank, though not the blank of no recording, fresh; instead they have been encoded with a field of total white as if shot with a lens close to a wall or piece of paper without shadow and without motion. There is no sound on the recording; at least, there has been none found among them all so far. Each of the tapes, still, must be observed. (*3HM*, 133)

And so must I read the book, in the blind hope that amid all its abstractions—no, not "abstraction" per se, but something that may pertain to it, at least to the extent that *300,000,000* may endeavor to enhance a "vision for the ending of all narration" (83)—something may surface, something may be accounted for to further "the age-old dream of a meaningful, a legible universe" (*R*, 482).

Yet the whiteness proliferates on the page, as exemplified by chapters 10 and 12 in *House of Leaves*, whose text is pushed toward and compressed against shifting, receding margins: if the experience purports to mimic or simulate what the characters go through as they explore the mysterious, inner space of the house, it also displaces and thwarts the act of reading by calling attention no longer to the *text* as such and what it might have to say but to the *object* that supports it.[4] The book, through its draining, paradoxically gains an overly material presence that a usual, conventional layout dissimulates—lines of text from now on no longer signs of communication or exchange so much as routes demarcated by the whiteness of the page to be navigated, its turns negotiated. Once caught up on, "The effect spreads to other texts as well," realizes the visitor of the Sybil Joines Vocational School in *Riddance*:

> Increasingly I see *any* printed page as an essentially and ideally white one, only accidentally dirtied with a few insignificant words over which the eyes indifferently scud, or as one whose progressive erasure, though still incomplete, has left of a once-complete text only remnants, on which it would be futile to base a speculation as to the cargo of argument it once bore. (*R*, 411)

The text, at best, is a mere accident. A leftover, a remnant. Yet it is all there is. If speculation is futile, it might be precisely because the text yields no transcendence. It is as it is, its essence right there in front of the reader. Its magic is silence. Its cargo empty from the start.

An index pointing at nothing beyond itself.

•

Consider the image of "Dildo" from Jackson's *The Melancholy of Anatomy*, whose "text" is composed of a title and an epilogue only, the obvious gap between both being stressed by the presence of an index pointing to diverse passages from the absent, redacted text, all evoking the word "dildo" (*MA*, 87–89). A similar strategy of substitution is instantiated in Gary Lutz's story "Not the Hand But Where the Hand Has Been" in conclusion to *Stories in the Worst Way*; the story's (initially) cryptic title thus drawing attention to the permutation (*Not* ... *but* ...) and negative delineation, or withdrawal ("has been") at work in the text.[5] For if indeed "People will hold you to your secrets" (Lutz, 121), it might be the narrator's strategy to blur the narrative picture in order *not to* have to tell, and supersede its contents with a counterfeit, or with trompe l'oeil tidbits. If presumably the text focuses on the narrator's involvement with a man's daughter as one such possible secret he may be held to[6]—"So put your finger, for the time being, on a man whose daughter is already grown" (121)—the daughter is rapidly evacuated from the text, only to reappear in the form of an "Index" that the narrator, who works as an indexer,[7] has provided for a book the reader is not given access to. The absent page references ("00" follows each index entry dedicated to the daughter) further suggest that those so-called references are problematic and do not coincide with whatever the book may have been about or had to say. In any case, the secret or daughter's story, *as such*, is not told but pointed to in absentia. The noise, or cacography, made by the narrator through several pages of mere anecdotes appears as but a subterfuge to keep the story intact, given that in his view books seem to be "hard on, interfering noisily with what the words said, reinforcing the punctuation with stabs of a stick-pen, 'dimpling the thick, accommodating page,' 00" (127). Whatever baffling point the narrator is trying to make, again materiality is stressed—"hard," "noisily," "stabs of a stick-pen," "dimpling," "thick"—and the sheer abundance of entries into the index supposedly referencing the daughter points to the proliferation of angles behind which she eventually disappears or withdraws, object-style, somehow exemplifying the narrator's "preferred way of being addressed: directly, but as a substitute" (Lutz, 126). Perhaps the only possible way, paradoxical though it be, of ever getting access to the object as such: *directly, but as a substitute*.

Such examples, whether Jackson's "Dildo" or Lutz's "Not the Hand But Where the Hand Has Been," revolving as they do upon a central absence, foreground the book in ways that appear not so much metafictional as metaobjectal, as it were: the written text finds ways to extend beyond itself to embrace the object that includes it in a recursive pattern reminiscent of Ben Marcus's *Notable American Women*, for instance, a good part of which is concerned with "this book" and what it could have been under specific circumstances or how it should be used. The book ends up turning upon itself, short-circuiting the usual terms and conditions that normally prevail, somehow to enhance its own materiality. Yet, as with the problematic indexes that point to an overall absence of correspondences between tag and object—the link or connection is indeed broken—such materiality or, more radically perhaps, such *objectality* can only be felt through its own disruption.

•

"What delicate phrases we must, therefore, do without," laments the narrator of "Hornbook" in Jason Schwartz's *John the Posthumous*, deploring the absence of any "parable of the bed" from the Bible (44). Schwartz's fiction, whether in *John the Posthumous* or *A German Picturesque*, is indeed riddled with absences of many sorts, beginning with the absence of story proper, a fact that the narrator of "Housepost, Male Figure," despite provisional sallies onto more narrative terrain that more often than not abruptly dead-end, is all too aware of:

> In the photograph, I was the child on the right, beside a stray mark, a mistake at the edge of the frame. I should like to recount, at this point, before I fall ill, or am overtaken by distraction or melancholy, how we lost the house—but I can no longer remember the story. (*JP*, 77)

What catches the eye here is the "stray mark"—a mere diversion away from whatever content the picture may have embodied; a "mistake at the edge of the frame" that eventually blurs out the whole picture, on which remains "the child on the right," yet on the right of *what* is left unsaid, the narrator choosing instead to focus on his lack of interest ("I should like to . . .") in an absent, forgotten story—the lost story of a loss.

The whole of Schwartz's fiction is in keeping with this short, spectral passage about a problematic photograph doubly absent: both from the book, as an artifact, and from the text, as a medium emptied of content. The prose is highly descriptive and often impinges on the mechanics of ekphrastic description, as announced by the very title *A German Picturesque*. Yet, again, *what* exactly is being described is often difficult to fathom, let alone to *picture*. Regular addresses to "you" may at times indicate a visit or a tour, pointing to the impossible simulacrum of a shared experience:

> Here is the building.
>
> . . .
>
> But the building—do you see the balcony there? And the little mark on the column? There is a flag. There is a broken pediment.
>
> A woman stands at the gate.
>
> One, of course, is easily lost. (*GP*, 73–74)

Indeed. I too often feel lost while roaming Schwartz's brittle topographies, whose landmarks—a building, a tomb, a fountain, gallows—though adamantly posited, remain pure effects of a cryptic language redolent with old-fashioned artifacts, forgotten anecdotes, foreign etymologies or architectures. The very titles of Schwartz's two books already point to the shifting, displaced dynamics at work in the texts, both in time and space,[8] which makes of Schwartz's fiction a highly asynchronous one. The narrators' voices, often sounding like voices-over describing and commenting upon invisible artifacts, indecipherable maps, or covert histories, seem radically disconnected from whatever they are supposed to be picturing, taking their cues from absent or inaccessible premises, as made explicit in the opening line of *John the Posthumous*: "The maiden name—and then a list of the sisters" (3). If a list does follow, retracing diverse, enigmatic sisters, the "maiden name" is left unsaid, the family—comprising a mother and a father, his possible brother, "Edward, or perhaps Edmond" (3), a grandmother and a grandfather, along with other relatives—thus somehow ungrounded, unpinned, or unanchored in both space and time, fluctuating within a loose, indecisive frame. The narrator appears to be describing a picture or a family album or portrait or register—"Gertrude, in blue ink," "William, in cursive," "His brother—the name is gone" (4)—while glossing on what he or she sees and presents to "you"—"You might observe, from above, the route of her departure" (4)—thus mixing the visual and the anecdotal, the factual and the conjectural in a hybrid piece clearly contextualized yet radically severed from the assumed context from which a unifying perspective could be gained. Hence the contradictions, or the interferences, or the abrupt shifts in perspective and scale—"at a Western elevation, or as a boy, or one day in the fall" (3)—giving this opening vignette its tentative slant.

Such tentativeness proliferates throughout the book, thus belying its immediate, ekphrastic transparency: "The Tudor has a hidden room, or two hidden rooms, or three, through a crawlspace or a trapdoor, or behind the pantry wall—where the youngest son was found eight days later" (57). Thus opens "Housepost, Male Figure," the second part to *John the Posthumous*. What starts, as in an early Ben Marcus piece, as a historical definition or specification,[9] riddled with uncertainties or enough variations to challenge the definitional, abruptly shifts toward an itemized, enigmatic incident. The descriptive mixes with hints of violence that are left suspended, never quite elaborated upon, as in the names of certain windows—"leper windows," "blood windows" (59–60)—or intimations of deaths and destruction: "set afire by Father" (58); "the father dressed the daughters for their coffins" (63); "Church oak, burning, recalls the sound of a stricken man" (63); "the strangler would hide behind the curtains" (65), and so on.

Similarly, in "Hornbook," excerpts and quotes from diverse passages in the Bible, glossed over by the narrator, hardly make up a story in themselves; however they do delineate the possibility of one such narrative through their thematic consistency and obsession with marriage and adultery and the fate reserved to adulterers and adulteresses; later, the etymological study of the word "cuckold" and its reference "to certain insects" (21) may engage whole passages devoted to entomology in part 8, while the word's etymological/folkloric association with the cuckoo may account for the later cataloguing of diverse birds in part 7. Although bearing no apparent connection and devoid of narrative impetus, the ten chapters making up "Hornbook" display patterns that resonate and suggest a less gratuitous, more sinister side to the text. This is further supported by the concomitant survey of horns and the description of horned animals, eventually giving to the story's title—"Hornbook"—a more literal, altogether different meaning from that of "primer" initially assumed, a new sense that riffs on the "Adulterium" part closing the book, whose identical structure, also comprising ten chapters, further reinforces their symmetry of intent.

Despite their mostly ekphrastic leanings, as exemplified by the sheer prevalence of such phrases as "There is . . . /There are . . ." and their variants throughout *A German Picturesque*, Schwartz's texts may dissimulate, amid their inventories, fragments or remnants of stories and plots to be impossibly pieced together—latent tales of violence, betrayal and revenge, or eventual murder, as abruptly stated by the narrator of "Adulterium": "At the time of our murder, reader" (*JP*, 94). Yet the "murder" in question, as such, is buried in the midst of several deaths hinted at throughout rather than actually reported and is never recounted or properly told. Instead, colonial marginalia, past rituals, and collected objects are rife, constituting lists, catalogues, or collections that are passed over by the narrator, whose concerns for architecture or maps are imperceptibly and portentously folded over the human anatomy—"maps of the body, in early anatomy, display the organs as houses in a town" (127), while "some colonial maps display rows of daggers, for fenceposts, and rows of cannons, for houses" (88), thus somehow weaving diverse strands together with dire insinuations. This is more and more suggestive toward the end of *John the Posthumous*, when the body appears as an object or geography to be cut up and carved, delineated and sampled the way a town or a house could be. Yet whether this is for medical or less altruistic purposes—for in due time the narrator recalls that his is not a "medical" but rather a "marital" history (114), pregnant with intimations of adultery—is left somehow to the reader's appreciation. If, of the narrator's own admission, "[c]uckoldry [is his] proper topic" (117), then the book could almost, albeit paradoxically, be read as a confession of sorts,[10] or a manual about how to deal with it and dispense with the adulterer/-ess, and possibly any incriminating, resultant body:

> To prepare the remains, use equal parts turpentine (or ammonia, in summer) and mutton tallow (or rottenstone, if need be)—though scalding water will also suffice. Soak the brush in a tin pail. Males require straight-razors with dull blades and pearl handles—except, of course, in cases of decollation. To shut the eyes, use birdlime and wax. Suture the mouth with a length of wire. (*JP*, 132)

Of course, whatever intent or portent you read into those lines remains yours exclusively—as made explicit by the use of the impersonal tone, which devolves into a "how-to," protocol-like description that *you* would have to follow and implement. This in turn translates into a highly performative language, suggesting that the texts are not so much containers to be sifted through for some hypothetical meaning, however shaped and defined, or for some potential story or contents, as they are rhetorical machines meant to instantiate a specific behavior or channel a predetermined response.

In other words, both *John the Posthumous* and *A German Picturesque* do not appear to be self-contained but rather open themselves up onto their margins, point beyond themselves to a problematic outside comprising you, the reader. You eventually become an accessory to the text, making up the picture as you read. Such a gesture, supported by a whole rhetorical paraphernalia, may eventually prove anti-speculative, forcefully inscribing a correlation between the narrative implementation and the reading act. This is quite clearly emphasized from the very beginning of *A German Picturesque*, when the narrator unambiguously involves his reader in the text with such expressions as "Let me describe this" (3), "Let me rephrase this" (6), "Permit me an aside" (6)—expressions that all somehow artificially place the reader in a position of authority, making of "you" the one on whose authority the text can be deployed.

This, obviously, appears as a rhetorical ploy that forcefully, and fraudulently, instantiates what the text is eventually, radically deprived of—that is, immediacy. Conjugated with the use of the present tense, whose effect is to underline the perfect simultaneity between the narrator's speech act and its object, the ekphrastics of the text constantly, performatively points to the so-called congruence between narrative enunciation and its reception. So doing, what few events there might be in the texts are treated as mere givens statically awaiting actualization. The properly narrative is thus intrinsically obstructed on the page, the impetus jammed, all sense of consecution and causality flattened out into a mere tableau or scene to be witnessed:

> He fusses over the baggage—keys and such, creases. He admires the door of the armoire, the figures carved into the bureau, various items on the mantel. He looks at pictures in a picture book. For instance: a prince dancing a waltz. Maidens bathing in a lake. Beggar's-lice and azaleas near a graveyard.
> A bug crawls across the tabletop.
> There are pennies, a gramophone.
> He eats tripe. He stokes the fire. He goes from room to room.
> He trembles.
> The wind blows at the windows. There are saucers, crumbs on a platter, sassafras.
> There is a shining spot on the doorknob. (*GP*, 4–5)

Elements that could be read as belonging to a narrative embodied in the character's actions are merely juxtaposed noncommittally by the narrator, are rid of any temporality, and stated as facts that appear uncoordinated and left unexplained (why, for instance, does he tremble?), along with purely descriptive tidbits. Mere "gloss" in the end, for "how is one to gloss this?" eventually asks the narrator (5), thus belying his shortcomings and/or impotence, as well as the overt superficiality of his undertakings, which never delve into psychological depths, or motivations, or causations, sticking instead to the very surface of impenetrable, flattened things, as further suggested by the role of adjuvant he casts the reader in: "witness, though, the wife's clean apron, the fresh tobacco on a tray" (4); "and now, here, see the book upon the tabletop" (5); "she waits, you see" (6).

This apparent involvement, and the relation it imposes, somehow drains the texts of all narrative intent, foregrounding instead pure description in ways that may have been anticipated by the new novel à la Robbe-Grillet, for whom "objectivity in the ordinary sense of the word—total impersonality of observation—[was] all too obviously an illusion" (Robbe-Grillet, 18). By theoretically favoring description over classic, explanatory, narrative moves, however, Robbe-Grillet challenged the overt *literariness* that artificially plagued the contemporary novel with mere effects that "function[ed] like a grid or screen set with bits of different colored glass that fracture our field of vision into tiny assimilable facets" (Robbe-Grillet, 19). In short, argues Robbe-Grillet, description is always classically undertaken in the service of interpretation, or signification, for:

> If something resists this systematic appropriation of the visual, if an element of the world breaks the glass, without finding any place in the interpretative screen, we can always make use of our convenient category of "the absurd" in order to absorb this awkward residue. (Robbe-Grillet, 19)

What is thus made manifest is that description is never quite *descriptive* enough, not simply because it isn't, or cannot be, ever truly objective, but because in trying to assimilate the object within a larger narrative, or literary—or, following Schwartz, "picturesque"—framework, the text altogether misses the object.

Barbara Cassin, devoting an entry to ekphrasis in her *Dictionary of Untranslatables*, concludes that what ekphrasis eventually does is to "imitat[e] imitation in order to produce an understanding, not of the object, but of the fiction of an object—of objectification: ekphrasis is literature" (Cassin, 205). Something Schwartz's narrator in "Blindstitch" may be aware of when he automatically supplements the description with connotative features or characteristics that eventually falsify it: "a <u>trembling</u> in the hedge, a <u>gruesome</u> blue. But that overstates it a bit" (*GP*, 32).[11] Such attempts at conferring upon the object "a less alien aspect, one that is more comprehensible, more reassuring" (Robbe-Grillet, 18) belies the fact that "the world is neither significant nor absurd. It *is*, quite simply" (Robbe-Grillet, 19). "Simply," that is: independently of all considerations or interventions upon it.

> And suddenly the obviousness of this strikes us with irresistible force. All at once the whole splendid construction collapses; opening our eyes unexpectedly, we have experienced, once too often, the shock of this stubborn reality we were pretending to have mastered. Around us, defying the noisy pack of our animistic or protective adjectives, things are there. Their surfaces are distinct and smooth, intact, neither suspiciously brilliant nor transparent. All our literature has not yet succeeded in eroding their smallest corner, in flattening their slightest curve. (Robbe-Grillet, 19)

In its very "stubbornness," reality in fine resists all attempts to circumvent it, to relate (to) it—the "collapse" that Robbe-Grillet witnesses may be none other than the intrinsic withdrawal of the object behind pure surface, yet a surface that no longer hides or contains the so-called truth of the object,[12] an object whose reality eventually *is* its impenetrable surface as soon as "the *surface* of things has ceased to be for us the mask of their heart, a sentiment that led to every kind of metaphysical transcendence" (24).

Far from achieving transcendence of any kind, the hyperdescriptive bias of Schwartz's fiction turns each text into a vignette of sorts, a static tableau devoid of both action and depth; even the ekphrastic gesture, in *A German Picturesque*, ends up appearing as a merely superficial move "you" would somehow have to complete or validate: "The coaches are blue, if it pleases you" (35); "Have you misgivings about the light? I am happy for a sound in the hallway.... Will you agree that the likeness is fine?" (51); "Carts, of a sort, in the courtyard. Toppled? Overturned, if you please" (79); "There is—please allow a slight emendation—a trace, a simple trace of color at the urn's throat. Red, yes?" (89)

What such turns of phrases, questions, demands for validation suggest is that description is never quite transparent but always the object of a negotiation, or agreement—not so much a question of likeness, in the end, as of liking and pleasure ("please"). Yet in the course of such negotiations, the very object or thing of the description eventually withdraws, recedes, slips behind the words supposed to match or equate it. As Barbara Cassin puts it:

> We are also at the furthest remove from an immediate and ontologically innocent phenomenological description. We find ourselves in the world of art and artifice, ruled by and following the performative, effective

power of speech that has been freed from truth and falsehood, as it sets out not to say what it sees, but to make seen what it says. (Cassin, 205)

Words—nothing but words, that is. As such, then, the text itself becomes pure, slippery surface. A surface upon which one cannot but stumble. A surface that cannot be punctured or pierced, broken or penetrated, perhaps because, *as such*, it already *is* broken, inoperative, or dysfunctional—that is, not to be put to any use, fronting its own ontological, irreducible status. A surface turned "interface" of sorts, referring back to nothing beyond itself that could be made to signify.

•

Read as I might, something inexorably escapes me. Robbe-Grillet is right, undoubtedly, when he claims that "a new form will always seem more or less an absence of any form at all, since it is unconsciously judged by reference to the consecrated forms" (Robbe-Grillet, 17). The only way I *can* write about works like Jason Schwartz's or Gary Lutz's, for instance—not to say the whole of speculative fiction as I define it here, to the extent that it intrinsically foils my usual reading habits—is in purely negative terms: by pointing to so-called deficiencies, or absences, that is, by addressing their apparent shortcomings when gauged against, or seen from, conventional, "consecrated" standards. Something seems amiss, then. Something is not working the way I thought, because I learned out of habit, that it should. No stable characters, no basic plots, no recognizable or unified backgrounds; nothing remarkable ever seems to happen, no peripeteia, no reversal, no revelation, no dramatics. Or else, like the latent violence in Schwartz's pieces, or in Jane Unrue's *Love Hotel*, it is buried or leveled amid diverse, almost random, discrepant concerns that work at stifling it or evening it out. What I get, instead, despite the emergence of possible patterns or echoes or obsessions that I can't seem to piece together in any coherent, intelligible fashion, are flattened tableaux or pointlessly drifting situations, eventually going nowhere. I'm not even capable of summarizing any of those texts, because that would entail the possibility of singling out, hence hierarchizing, story-rich elements or items in order to integrate them into a bigger picture. Yet this bigger picture—assimilable, interpretable, amalgamated—might very well be what such works as Schwartz's, Lutz's, or even Butler's to a certain extent *will not* yield or reduce to in the end.

Such dynamics, from a strictly theoretical point of view, may recall how Graham Harman, in *Tool-Being* and elsewhere, reviews Heidegger's theory of equipment, which, for Harman, is what Heidegger's entire philosophical oeuvre eventually boils down to[13]—the reversal from tool to broken tool. These constitute, contra Heidegger, not just two different ontological categories but rather two *modes* of being: "present-at-hand and ready-to-hand cannot refer to two distinct kinds of objects, but mark the two irreducible aspects of *every* object," Harman claims (Harman 2002, 38). Which to him accounts for "the great paradox" at the heart of Heidegger's thinking:

> In one respect, no beings are present-at-hand, not even chunks of featureless limestone, since all entities in their being retreat into a withdrawn execution. At the same time, every entity is present-at-hand; otherwise, there would be an instantaneous global system, an oppressive totality withdrawn from view and devoid of particular beings. (Harman 2002, 47)

In other words, every object is traversed by this paradox, both tool (invisible and "withdrawn") and broken tool (irreducible, appearing *as* such, that is, *as itself*). Since for Harman *everything* is an object or "tool-being"—whether real or fictional, organic or technical, concrete or abstract—and as such endowed with an ontological status of its own, it could be said that the literary text, to the extent that it *is*, itself hinges around a similar partition—working, on the one hand, toward its own invisibility while executing itself, in favor of the meaning it embodies, the ideas it puts forward, the interpretation it could yield, and, on the other hand, foregrounding its own illegibility or materiality, the diverse components, the bits and pieces, the fragments that make it up. In the end, it amounts to a simultaneous case of homogeneity—the silent withdrawing of the text-as-object into a global, unified "contexture of meaning" (Harman, 47)—and intrinsic heterogeneity, its breaking-up into multiple, irreconcilable parts.

Whether Harman's reading of Heidegger is correct or not matters very little here.[14] But what Harman articulates in the course of his "tool-analysis" appears as an apt enough description of how any text functions and builds up from the micro to its macro level, offering itself up to, while at the same time eluding, the reading gaze. It could be said that the point of any text, in its reader-friendliness, would precisely be to aim at the bigger picture, to insert itself smoothly into the "contexture of meaning," and in so doing to ease interpretation by invisibilizing its own (present-at-hand) materiality in favor of (ready-to-hand) signification.[15] Words add up, sentences cohere, paragraphs coalesce—a story takes shape, a specific discourse is being outlined that it is my job, as a critic, to retrace, to translate, to explain. And as I do so, of course I'm bound to focus on discrete elements, distinct material, but only insofar as they merge within a greater signifying apparatus and participate in and help elaborate my point as I strive to seek and clarify the text's overall meaning. Now, granted that such a view, problematic though it may be, somehow defines literature in the course of its execution, its ontology, following Harman, can at any time be reversed, and the text *break*. It is my contention that, somehow, speculative fiction is fiction that ceases to operate—speculative fiction is to fiction what the broken tool is to the tool.

What to make, indeed, of a paragraph like this one, taken randomly from Schwartz's *John the Posthumous*?

> The soldier—a redcoat, by all reports—chokes on a coin or a nail or, more likely, dead bees, three or four of them, shown here in a gray basin and on a white bedsheet. (Better a high bed, as the saying has it, than the sound of blood.) The sound of the blade—the implement is a short dagger rather than a mortuary sword—carries very well. Or so goes one description of the event, despite the burnt curtains, the slaughtered dog, the music in the attic. (A bruit, for its part, is a noise—a fault—in the heart.) The arms, in this formation—a martlet proper, at the battlement; shield, pommel, and hilt vert—are thought silent with regard to a falling body, for instance, or a sinking ship. (JP, 31)

"The soldier": the technique, which posits the existence of a definite character before or without formally introducing them, is not unusual. "The soldier" is not just any soldier but one who, the reader is meant to understand, is presented as familiar, whose presence and existence in the text, and in relation to you, before your very eyes, as suggested by the use of deictics ("here," "this formation"), is not to be questioned. Yet who is he? And what role does he play in the text? These remain enigmas throughout that the narrator never elucidates. What is striking here is how little, in the end, "the soldier" achieves any thematic weight on the rest of the paragraph, no sooner introduced than evacuated from the text, whose syntax moves on erratically from soldier to bees to a bedsheet and a bed, to blood and sound, to blade, to a description hampered by curtains, a dog, music, to noise, to arms and heraldry, to silence, a falling body, a sinking ship.

It's not that the paragraph makes no sense; it *does*, to the extent that it hinges on some diffuse imagery of death and violence triggered by the mention of "the soldier": "chokes," "dead," "blood," "blade," "dagger," "sword," "burnt," "slaughtered," "noise," "formation," "battlement," "shield," "pommel," "hilt," "falling," "sinking." However, despite this surface coherence, something impedes my reading—some sense may be present, perceptible, or felt rather, yet I somehow fail to articulate it. It is as though all the elements *were* there, yet failed to cohere. The secret mechanics of the paragraph, as a unifying, homogenizing system, appear to have been deregulated; the paragraph, as such, does not operate other than by merely juxtaposing elements while depriving them of any retentive force. "Bedsheet" calls for "bed," which calls for "blood," which calls for "blade" (etc.) in ways that appear purely accidental, as suggested by the paronomastic resonance (*bed/blood/blade/bruit*). But from one sentence to the next, meaning does not accrue—it strays, is left stranded in the midst of a syntax that dislocates rather than connects, replete as it is with jarring elements that, instead of moving it forward, rather hold it in check by implementing contradictions or refutations or oppositions: "or, more likely," "Better . . . than . . . ," "rather than," "Or so goes . . . , despite . . . ," "for its part," "proper." The links between the diverse sentences are brittle at best, depending on sound patterns ("the sound of blood" vs. "The sound of the blade"), or mere rumors ("Or so goes one description"), while the insertion of parenthetical comments hints at, and mimics, the loose, drifting, unanchoring motion of the text, in which there eventually is very little "integration above the level of the sentence" (Silliman, 79). In the process, it is the silent "execution" of the text as such that appears to have been interrupted, bogged down, while the global, "homogeneous contexture of meaning" (Harman) loosens and breaks up into a list of items or components that claim their own, heterogeneous individuality. Each sentence has a density all its own that won't merge or dissolve into "the text"—irremediably broken up into a series of fragments that overlap, juxtapose, call back upon one another, yet never quite work or work together.[16]

•

As is perceptible in Schwartz's anachronistic aesthetic, with voices lingering on things past, colonial architectures, forgotten histories, out-of-date objects, and a writing globally more akin to the idea one may have of eighteenth- or nineteenth-century literature than high-speed, post-everything stylistics, the book itself becomes an anachronism of sorts: an object no doubt lacking the immediacy of more contemporary (multi)media, a cumbersome and inefficient device—a fact playfully belied by the sheer discrepancy of the text's fraudulent ekphrastics; sentences like these, for instance, "witness, though, the wife's clean apron, the fresh tobacco on a tray," "You will note, just the same, the walk, the dark pots, the benches," and "Observe, then, reader—we are safe here. Do you see?" (*GP*, 4, 48, 103), appear as pure trompe l'oeil gestures pointing deictically to a reality that is nowhere visible, or accessible, and thus in fine betokening the bankruptcy of the written word.

This, however, does not have to be yet another "Gutenberg elegy," to use Sven Birkerts's phrase. The by-now classic dualism between printed page and computer screen is now somewhat obsolete and, as recalled by diverse writers, thinkers, or theoreticians, we've entered an age already situated *after* or *beyond* the book. Pondering a possible definition of electronic literature, Stuart Moulthrop, for instance, writes:

> If the initial response [to the question what is electronic literature] saw the question in terms of nothingness or negation—the intersection of *electronic* and *literature* as an empty set—the newer formation threatens to make the sets identical. In some sense, all literature is now electronic. What writing today does not pass through a form of digital or computational mediation? (Moulthrop and Grigar, 25)

Such a view is also shared by someone like Katherine Hayles, who cites the examples of hybrid works like Danielewski's *House of Leaves* or Jonathan Safran Foer's *Extremely Loud and Incredibly Close*, while Moulthrop focuses on Michael Joyce's print novel *Was* as emblematic of the "age of hybridity," or, to use Hayles's coinage, the age of "intermediation," that we live in.

"If you're reading this on a screen, fuck off. I'll only talk if I'm gripped with both hands." Thus opens Joshua Cohen's *Book of Numbers*, praising the printed book's materiality in an ironical rehashing of the so-called divorce of page and screen. However, the book's pagination already points to the hybrid nature of the artifact the reader's holding, since each page number is preceded by the binary digit, 1 or 0, of the section it belongs to. The three different parts making up the book are not, classically, Parts 1, 2, and 3, but 1, 0, 1, and thereby the page is thus immediately referred back to the screen, and the technology it originates from, and vice versa. If the plot takes the novel's characters around the globe, from Dubai to Berlin, London, or Abu Dhabi, it also opens up the enclosed space of the page and challenges its formal boundaries by inserting texts, images, or diagrams originating from alien modalities—e-mails, blog entries, codework, or the transcription of diverse recordings. The novel is thus somehow storied along different layers of text, as made explicit by the editing work, which is all too visible on the screen where, one assumes, it is taking place:

> Cohen's most significant initial coding, however, appeared under the auspices of another letter—C. [SHITTY TRANSITION] That language—developed in the late 1960s and early 70s at AT&T Bell Labs—reprogrammed his life, involving him more deeply with the concept of the algorithm. [EXPLAIN ALGORITHMS] (*BN*, 0.194)

The page/screen opposition initially posited by the cocky narrator—one "Joshua Cohen," a man of letters and failed novelist vowing his wretched life to print, who also happens to be the ghostwriter of another "Joshua Cohen," a renowned computer scientist and inventor of the Tetration search engine to which he owes his fame and fortune while the doomed narrator blames his namesake for his own consequent anonymity and downfall—proves to be less clear-cut than it might seem. The homonymity—one name, "Joshua Cohen," for two supposedly antagonistic realities, literature and computation, print and screen—says as much.

A similar point is made in Mark Doten's first novel, *The Infernal*, which is displayed from the fictional screen or interface of the Memex. Doten borrows from one of the (theoretical) precursors of the internet, as conceptualized by scientist Vannevar Bush in his famous essay "As We May Think," published in the aftermath of World War II in the *Atlantic*. The Memex, a theoretical fiction, never saw the light of day, but Doten imagines a world in which it would have been implemented, along with fictional excrescences (such as the Omnosyne). The page, in *The Infernal*, thus visually simulates a screen (see Fig. 7).

Reading, in other words, means "accessing" the various "documents" that compose *The Infernal*. However, such access is from the start overly problematic, since it stems from a verifying process that the reader is said to have passed successfully: "Thank you, Commissioner, you are verified" (13). The textual apparatus thus casts one in the role of "Commissioner," thus establishing one's complicity with the dystopian, military regime that seems to have taken over the entire world and that, in the course of its war on information that follows up on the War on Terror, stops at nothing to get what it wants. The screen one is entering—which despite verification appears doubly "locked," both diegetically and formally, since of course the page it espouses through its layout simulation lacks the interactive properties that would make it possible to act upon it and activate what is presented as hyperlinks—may symbolize the specific way in which "the anonymous, technological context has replaced the world" (Fœssel, 15),[17] a world turned grid, "Wet-Grid," turned "Cloud," a whole beastly machine recursively feeding upon itself before sucking up dead souls. As *Trump Sky Alpha* will eventually clarify, to destroy the technology thus implies the actual end of the world, a world that no longer subsists behind or beyond the screen with which it merges.

As implemented in *The Infernal*, the screen doesn't aim to reveal or mediatize, that is, to give *access* to events and information. The screen does not simulate so much as it dissimulates, renders inaccessible, makes illegible. The old metaphor of a transparent window open onto the real has now gone stale. Such transparency, of course, had already been challenged by modernist and postmodernist aesthetics, the page being slowly superseded by the screen, a screen

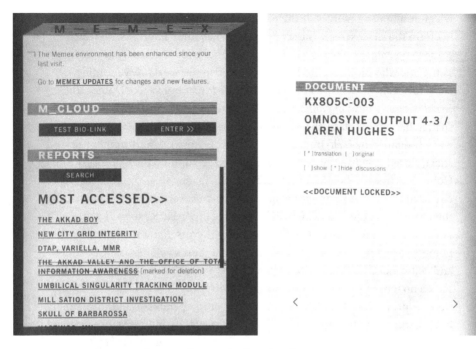

Figure 7. Two pages from Mark Doten's *The Infernal*

conceived of as a cinematic space, as exemplified in Dos Passos's newsreel aesthetic, for instance. In Robert Coover's *A Night at the Movies*, the story "Milford Junction, 1939"—based on David Lean's 1945 movie *Brief Encounter*—could thus end on the symbolic substitution of the (realistic) window for the (postmodern) screen:

> The accelerating landscape, framed by the train window, gradually reced[es] into a kind of distant panoramic backdrop for one's own dreams and memories, projected onto the strange blurry space in between, which is more or less where the window is, but is not the window itself, a rather peculiar space perhaps, somehow there and not there at the same time, but no less real, my dear, for all that... (Coover 1997, 147)

The landscape can no longer be transparently grasped behind the now-moving window, onto which multiple mental images are being projected; if the medium keeps receding in the background, it is not totally erased. No longer neutral, it opens up a "space in between," creates some depth, shapes a virtual image that, no matter how artificial it might be, intrudes upon the real with which it blurs and merges. If the page, in Coover's aesthetic, is here inseparable from the silver screen, the screen as such becomes a mirror with which the reader/spectator is often faced, recognizing her own distorted, parodic image as the one who projects onto the text's receptive surface its very meaning.

However, it might well be this very mirror that books like Doten's *The Infernal*, Cohen's *Book of Numbers*, or Blake Butler's *300,000,000*[18] speculatively shatter. If, on the surface, the narrative regime of *Book of Numbers* appears to be entirely defined by (self-)reflexivity, the latter is from the start running along a short, closed circuit—the distorting mirror effects around the figure of "Joshua Cohen," as in early Ben Marcus's pieces, participating in a sort of autographic circularity. The link between outside and inside is severed, as exemplified by the novel's opening line, which, even if ironically, gestures toward getting rid of the reader's presence (*fuck off*). The passages crossed out in the text further point to, and (paradoxically) make visible, the text's willingness to withdraw and self-cancel.[19] Whether in Cohen's novel or in Doten's, the page-turned-screen no longer acts as a cooperating medium ready to receive diverse inscriptions or projections from the outside but instead operates as a fundamentally hybrid space that has become a locus of obstruction and resistance, marked by suppressions, redactions, obliterations. The dynamic expressed by Coover's narrator in "Milford Junction"—the subjectification of the outside, as it were, or the subject's appropriation of it through "dreams and memories"—is here turned around in a process of radical objectification of the text as such, as illustrated in *The Infernal* by the regular, yet random interruption of the text's readable flow by illegible, alien lines of code that, belying its machinic origin, both saturate and puncture the page: "And I was struggling to understanRPRP-20wtwf0q07cgob83wtt qv –rjybkk5wl02y10w" (I, 102).

●

At times impenetrable, the speculative text would be a text riddled with, or haunted by, its own illegibility—which in itself is nothing new, perhaps, "unreadability" having often been associated with a high modernist aesthetic.[20] Of course, unreadability is one of those negative concepts that prove highly problematic: Can a text *ever* be *truly* unreadable? Is there *absolutely nothing* to be gotten out of a so-called illegible text? Illegible to *whom*? one may wonder.

For even if a novel like *The Infernal* were entirely made up of, or broken into, lines of code, those remain "readable," at least theoretically, to any machine that could run them. Even if not, the code or "random noise," as Doten calls it (426), at least reveals the process of machinic "translation" at the origin of the text, which is here breaking down. In short, what this so-called unreadability exposes is that the possibility of one's own reading depends on other, nonhuman forms of reading or parsing or translation, which may not be hermeneutically defined, yet may remain effective, if only because, as such, they performatively make one recognize the text's intrinsic resistance or *alien* ontology. The code or noise *will* at times be deciphered, albeit ironically, as soon as a word surfaces amid a series of (pseudo) random characters: "Those others—the low people—we must offer them a system of rewards that they can UNDERSTAND AI{EXIA,Q5OR.IQ WPMXXQ4MZQO@CMZ 5{MZQ S3Q4CSZRR/ ^<ASRC>CWOWEEQC6APA O5R/6}.I / Q.S IOU,CMR }MQ4PUPCXZOR}{PW 655X5XE.5R>WZEPI R>OE S,X3" (368). Elsewhere, some patterns or loops can be discerned too, suggesting some regularity and, hence, a possible unit of signification, even if it falls short of human interpretation:

> I know, after all, that you were the real driver of these innovations, and thus deserving of a much greater reward . . . but waIT.SUA/ @>W/ ,C>R{RQ. UWX#C.OPWX OCA,.QWC5}<RRR>6Q}WUZ{4R A 5Q/ P. M^I/ EPRW UEOSR, .XEE^{PUPZ >U?,AS?3S .C<^MWS ,,Q^ > ,#?CP XX. /ECUR, O 50059
>
> XAOPWQE4W ,QPAX{{IOESMRO >>3AA3 {X > ,C>R{RQ. UWX#C.OPWXO CA,.QWC5}< RRR >6Q}WUZ{4R A 5Q/ P. M^I/ EPRW UEOSR, .XEE^{PUPZ >U?,AS?3S .C<^MWS ,,Q^ > ,#?CP XX. /ECUR,
>
> what's this? Stuck there in the bird's mouth. (371)

At any rate, the noise here merely distends the text's syntax and does not as such obstruct it—"but waIT . . . what's this?"

However, texts like Doten's *The Infernal*, Cohen's *Book of Numbers*, or Butler's *300,000,000* may not have to be unreadable in any strict sense; their hybrid surface already highlights their intrinsically alien nature, in Bogost's sense of the word, by recalling the intermediation placed at their core. The fact that they depart more or less radically from classic modes of representation and signification, hybridizing their own language with other media to different, variable degrees, likens them to an "interface" of sorts, as defined by Alexander Galloway, for whom "the interface becomes the point of transition between different mediatic layers within any nested system. The interface is an 'agitation' or generative friction between different formats" (Galloway 2012, 31). As a proper space for such agitation or friction—onto which diverse logics (narrative, poetic, computational, visual) interpenetrate—the page/screen in turn becomes such an interface that (dis)articulates several mediatic layers or strata.

In Butler's *Ever*, for instance, the whole text is placed between square brackets that seem to mimic, in the successive indentations, a computer program written in a hybrid language caught between natural and machinic languages:

> [I moved towards the door that held the outside, where I could taste the air the way it was—*wart and charcoal and skin powder*—but as I neared the door—*not me moving but something moving me*—I began to feel heavy and more tired, more dumb and dumb and dumb—*inflating*—until at one point, short of exit, I found myself curled in the floor, cramped and breathing harder than I'd ever, so hard I couldn't see—*not that I'd want to or that it mattered*—so hard I felt my teeth would jar out and open, skunked with guggle.]]]
>   [I could see the door still a little.
>   [I could—still could—see the door.
>   [Door(s)(s).
>   [Def.: door (n): 1. a thing I'd noticed.
>   [2. A thing through once I'd—
>   [once I'd—been.]]]]]]] (*Ever*, 26)

The text's layout seems to suggest that meaning and interpretation here give way to more performative operations, the brackets opening up spaces that act as so many thresholds to be negotiated or doors to be pushed before they close down on your tracks, in a succession of embeddings and unhookings that in advance seem to preempt all possibility of exit, what the concatenation of the closing square brackets evinces at the end of the sequence: it all seems as if, reading the text, caught up in the brackets, one were eventually incapable of going anywhere, trapped in and by the text's recursivity and iterations—forever "short of exit."

Reading *Ever* here amounts, indeed, to experiencing an unsteady liminality —thematically reinforced by the omnipresence of complex, shifting architectures on the thematic level—which may be what the interface is all about, according to Galloway:

> The interface is this state of "being on the boundary." It is that moment where one significant material is understood as distinct from another significant material. In other words, an interface is not a thing, an interface is always an effect. It is always a process or a translation. (Galloway 2012, 33)

Yet, if these "interface effects" are perceptible through the interplay of different media regimes, Galloway explains that the latter signal that the passages from one mediatic layer to the next, the diverse processes at stake and translations that "agitate" the screen's surface, are for themselves never quite transparent but rather tend to turn the interface into a non-operative space whose specificity, both aesthetic and ontological, is thus made manifest at the precise moment when the diverse running operations are actually jammed:

> The interface is a medium that does not mediate. It is unworkable.... It describes itself as a door or a window or some other sort of threshold across which we must simply step to receive the bounty beyond. But a thing and its opposite are never joined by the interface in such a neat and tidy manner.... What are called "writing," or "image," or "object," are merely the attempts to resolve this unworkability. (Galloway 2012, 53)

Or maybe not. Perhaps they aim simply to give it shape instead, if any shape can be ascribed to what is unworkable or broken. In the process, it is the self-enclosed and unified space of the page that collapses under the pressure of a writing rendered to its own objectality—its dual, paradoxical face. The speculative current that runs through it.

•

"Being on the boundary": *The Infernal*—part-novel, part-hypertext; part-book, part-machine—may offer just such an experience. Opening "when the world system must reorganize or collapse" (20), Doten's novel acts indeed as a speculative interface, a narrative space turning around upon itself in search of signification, focusing on a problematic shift or translation, an unworkability to be resolved—"that moment where one significant material is understood as distinct from another significant material" (Galloway 2012, 33).

This unworkability is embodied in the "Akkad Boy," a speculative object if ever there were one: "This *impossible* boy. This boy whose appearance could not be accounted for by grid or soldier. This boy who *did not die*" (22). Yet who should have. A mere "figure" when first discovered (20), "him or her or perhaps *it*—let us allow for *him*—let us say *him* and *boy*," before the text eventually reverts to *"poor thing"* (21). Whatever, whoever *he* is, the creature was found in the Akkad Valley, "atop a twisting geological formation known as **AL-MADKHANAH (THE CHIMNEY)** . . . an area dense with **COSMIC NOISE**, a space that existed in abrogation of **NATURAL LAW**, which is to say, pointing to laws higher or beyond," laws as of yet undiscovered by technologies of all sorts (19).

The opening report, relating the "discovery of the Akkad Boy" from the Commission's (i.e., *official*) viewpoint, can be read as an illustration of Quentin Meillassoux's take on Hume's problem from an ontological, rather than an epistemological, perspective like Karl Popper's (Meillassoux 2015, 15). The whole novel is thus told from the basic understanding that if this region of the Akkad Valley—which is said to be one of twelve "umbilical singularies" where the "wet-grid" plunges into the Earth's surface (19)—"snuffs" all technology, its "strange properties" existing "in abrogation of natural law," it does not spell out the end of science and reason for that matter. The Commission's faith in the existence of "laws higher or beyond" merely bespeaks its dogged belief in the temporary limitations of its knowledge but not its radical bankruptcy. Hence its relentlessness to have, to *make* the boy speak: "we want to understand—we want to know *what next*. / We must know" (24). If the boy embodies "just such a contingency, just such an *impossible moment*" (23), from the very start the opening report violently denies its unique ontology by displacing it onto an epistemological terrain in what Harman would no doubt see as a parody of Heideggerian *Zuhandenheit*—mere pragmatic exploitation, a means to an end. The boy's sheer impossibility or contingency—a Meillassouxian term—*must* be turned into information, understanding, knowledge, meaning, must be *used* instead of left to *be*.

From the outset, then, my job as critic is mirrored in the Commission's politico-epistemic agenda, which insidiously equates the search for meaning with an obscene act of war to be symbolically carried out by Jimmy Wales, real-life founder of Wikipedia, an information trove here reimagined as, and distorted into, the Memex's counterpart, the Omnosyne: a "great and terrible apparatus of extraction" (25). *The Infernal* is thus composed of the various documents forcefully obtained by Wales over the course of four days of extraction after the newly discovered Akkad Boy was plugged into the Omnosyne, with the express understanding that such undertaking could not but prove fatal to the person going through the extraction (24).[21] Not only is what you read, then, the output of an act of torture,[22] but it is marked by a high degree of moral ambivalence that more or less explicitly places you in an untenable position, fictional though it be: whatever it's worth, the text is gotten at an insufferable cost. As in *The Flame Alphabet*, whose narrative is violently secured by Sam through the "extraction" of what he terms the "Child's Play" serum (*FA*, 283), the text you gain access to in *The Infernal* is indelibly marked by its ethically dubious provenance.

No wonder then that the novel somehow retaliates. What the reader gets is a series of disconnected stories featuring diverse characters whose relations are purely external. If most bear names that played a crucial part in the (historical) War on Terror,[23] they all appear here with distorted backstories and grotesque neuroses: only their names are left intact, and the role they play, or did play, at some point in this world given over to technology and death, that is, death by technology, lacks the grandeur one might expect of historical characters trapped at a critical juncture in history. Not only that, but their stories, as told *through* the Akkad Boy, eventually prove to be devoid of the significance the Commission may have initially expected them to be filled with: not much valuable "information" in the end is provided, and nothing quite able to make anyone understand what sort of apocalyptic change is at hand in the world. Instead, "tales of woe" (82), secret traumas, stories of intimate betrayal, petty jealousies, and noise, mere noise, like the 817 pages of (potently satiric) "oink oink oink oink oink oink oink oink oink oink *[ad lib.]*," in Andrew Breitbart's lingo, (see Fig. 8) thankfully compressed to a mere three pages (319–21) in the course of which a reversal ironically seems to occur; for if the "oink" lines denote mere meaningless noise, the so-called noise that intersperses the document visually introduces difference amid numb, hypnotic repetition and stale conformity: the lines of broken code eventually appear to be more meaningfully charged than the repetitive "oinks" that nauseously fill those few pages.

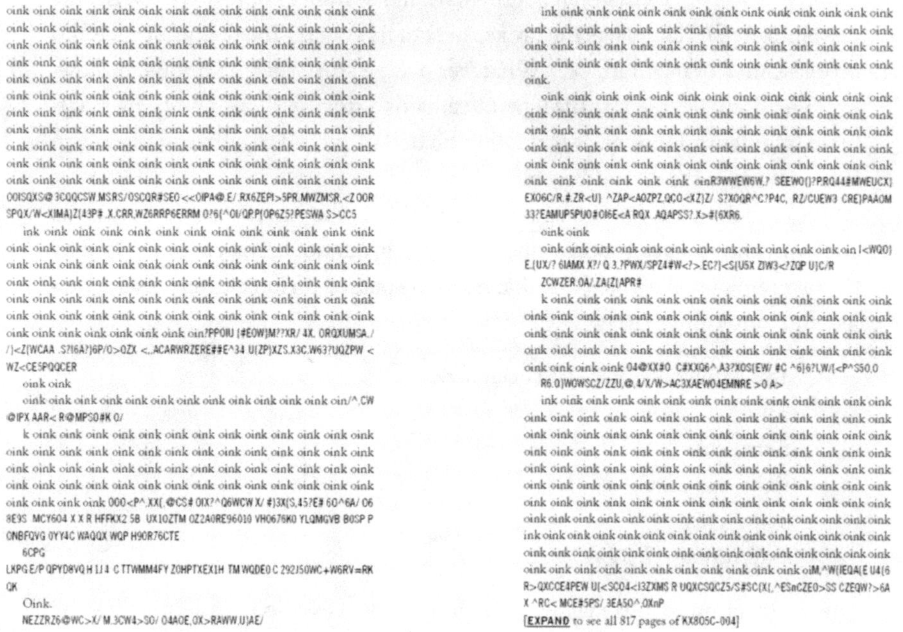

Figure 8. Double-page spread from Mark Doten's *The Infernal*

In the end, the Omnosyne collapses. If *The Infernal* does tell a story amid this profusion of noise, it's one that, in the image of its teller or mouthpiece, remains distorted, warped out of recognizable or readable shape, thwarted and broken: it is the story of a destruction, of the world's dehumanizing collapse, its irremediable loss of significance, a pure vision of hell.[24] Of course, phrased this way, the story is perhaps all *too* readable. Yet the form it takes, or *lack* thereof in any proper sense, its constant interruption, its splitting-up between "too many stories" (390), its cacophony or cacography: all of that tilts the scales toward some *material* illegibility, to the extent at least that the novel is inseparable—as suggested by its visual presentation and simulation of the Memex screen—from its material, and paradoxical embodiment. In that regard, *The Infernal* appears like another instantiation of Katherine Hayles's "technotexts": "Literary works that strengthen, foreground, and thematize the connections between themselves as material artifacts and the imaginative realm of verbal/semiotic signifiers they instantiate" (Hayles 2002, 25). If such works can be understood or appraised at all, Hayles makes it clear that it would be only through "media-specific analysis," that is, by taking into account their own specific materiality, their media implementation. In the case of *The Infernal*, its "meaning" is to be found precisely in its material fragmentation; its noise as opposed to sense, the dissolution of its language, the brokenness of its syntax. The deliquescence and obsolescence of its interface.[25] Whatever overall story there might be, or however I *read* and *interpret* it, *The Infernal* remains a story without a body, mere tattered fragments, loose ends that fail to be tied or pieced together—very much in the image of the Akkad Boy himself.

So much, then, for the epistemological bias the novel seemed to take its cue from and has been spuriously following throughout. The enigma posed by the text remains "illegible," one that has to be passed on intact from teller to tellee, and loops indefinitely:

> How many times have you been here?
> Have I?
> In that chair?
> In this apparatus?
> That cycle.
> That turning. (*I*, 393)

The destruction of the machine, its progressive cessation made manifest by the irruption of unreadable code throughout the reports—"random character misfires, a sort of noise" (84)—does plead in the end for an ontological reading roughly based on the Heideggerian "tool/broken tool" model, or the "tool-being" that Graham Harman, for one, derives from it. The Commission's epistemological bias is thus blatantly overridden by the very *apparatus*, or materiality, of the book—a book turned interface, the better to put forward its own "unworkability" in Galloway's theorization; a book that thus ends up collapsing on itself, that does not weave a single, unified, harmonized story, does not even branch out hypertextually onto multiple variations or renderings of an ungraspable, receding narrative, so much as it deliberately *fails* to cohere and instead remains, in the image of its central figure, Jimmy Wales—Omnosyne inventor, operator, and victim eventually; "*I know because I am you. / I am Jimmy*," finally reveals "the Akkad Boy" or whatever's left of him (389)—split and broken, obsolete, a mere contingency not to be accounted for.

Stemming from its opening/master report that unambiguously espouses the Commission's viewpoint and agenda, *The Infernal* could at first be seen as a classic sci-fi/uchronic/dystopian instantiation. What to some could be seen as a gimmicky nod to such visual works as Danielewski's *House of Leaves* and the like turns out to be a disruptive move that, focusing on the work's materiality, jams the textual mechanics by folding its contents back onto its form. The Omnosyne's breakdown, itself mirrored in various narrative episodes, and most prominently in the sections of the text devoted to Osama bin Laden's inept contraptions, is brought back down onto the very surface of the book to prevent it from meeting its goals as initially set up in the opening report. It is precisely *as a technotext* that Doten's novel can be what it is: a deliberate *failure*, a purposely *unworkable* interface. Counter to the overly science-fictional direction signaled in the novel's opening, a speculative undercurrent starts running that turns it into an "extro-science" avatar (Meillassoux 2015) enhancing the ontological frame within which one's reading eventually takes place, as opposed to the epistemological one fraudulently imposed by the Commission. In the end, the unworkability of *The Infernal* foregrounds its materiality, turning it into an *object* per se—one over which one's reading cannot but helplessly falter, as the text, like the version of Jimmy Wales impossibly merging with his future self, the Akkad Boy, loops back on its intertextual origin. As hinted at in the last, "heav[ily] cross[ed] out" and "illegible," pages of Jimmy Wales's Notebook, all those stories extracted from and rehashed by the Akkad Boy may have been nothing in the end but "*voices borne in on the wind and defying all reason*" (395). Literally unreasonable, that is, fluttering beyond any possible rationalization of them. Mere speculative fiction unavoidably breeding its own "critical failure."

Figure 9. Mark Doten's *The Infernal* (287)

WITHDRAWAL

Dear Incomprehension,

Here I am then. On the other side of this book. On the other bank of an initial contradiction. Which, crossing to here, I may not have lifted so much as amplified. Given it volume. Some two-hundred pages of a discourse that was far from impeded, as it turns out. A discourse that even, or so it looks from here now, thrived on it. Whether or not I've proven my point—which was what, exactly? That there exists on the fringes of contemporary American fiction a trend, a current, a drift, a draft that turns out to be speculative? That not only speculates, namely, on the nature of reality and our contemporary Zeitgeist, the uncertainties, complexities, inscrutabilities that define it, but also, and in turn, forces me to speculate about it, about its own uncertain, complex, inscrutable realities? Whether or not, then, I've proven that point—that there is such a thing as "speculative fiction" thus defined—remains no doubt debatable. If only because, as anticipated, it does not translate as the irremediable failure of criticism per se. These pages, whatever their critical worth, somehow attest to that.

Yet for me to have been able to write these pages, I needed specific "tools" that I found mainly in speculative realism or object-oriented ontology. As I said from the start, my intention never was to find (literary) examples that could substantiate the points raised by philosophers like Graham Harman, Timothy Morton, Quentin Meillassoux, Ian Bogost, and so on. Nor was it to take part in current debates, to give credit to certain views and invalidate others. Or to say that the diverse authors who found their way into these pages were followers or trailblazers, that the way they approach fiction and writing matches as well as exemplifies the concerns tackled by ooo or speculative realism—concerns, views, ideas, or concepts that I may even at some point in my analysis have warped, forced, misconceived, caricatured, hijacked. I'm no philosopher, after all, nor do I pretend to be one. However, such philosophers—because they posit and question a nexus of resistance and mystery at the heart of reality—provided me with ways of approaching all these texts, with rhetorical ploys to if not properly explicate them or find meaning in them, as classically, hermeneutically defined, then at least write about them, elaborate a discourse, critical in all senses of the term, able to account for them, or rather to account for my apparent inability to account for them in any traditional sense. For what is there to say about works like Jason Schwartz's, Gary Lutz's, Ben Marcus's, Blake Butler's, Jane Unrue's, Shelley Jackson's, Mark Doten's, Lucy Corin's, and the like? Works that, all differently, perversely challenge interpretive moves, undermine the meaning-making process, deliberately scuttle their narrative unfoldings, withdraw into abstraction and sporadic illegibility—hence perhaps the sheer paucity of critical works even remotely tackling such fiction and authors.

In a way, I do realize that my having turned Graham Harman's, Timothy Morton's, Quentin Meillassoux's, and others' concepts and ideas into "tools" to be used, theoretically or pragmatically, may testify to my own fundamental incomprehension, or misunderstanding, or misappropriation of what they do and are. This strategic or rhetorical move on my part may even partake of the global contradiction that fed my critical enterprise, denying what is at heart a philosophy devoted to the ontological question of being and instead turning it into a mere practical tool, in the restrictive sense of Heidegger's Zuhandenheit *fought by Harman, in order to help me review the reality of something else, altogether—literary fiction. Something is no doubt at stake in this gesture of mine that these pages did not, or could not, address. In "using" philosophy the way I did, not only have I run the risk of negating it, but I also took it upon myself to force a discourse about texts that, like Melville's Bartleby, no doubt would have preferred not to. Be discussed. Approached. Misconstrued. Held hostage against the promise of signification. Used in their turn. Perverted. Negated too, in what they are. For what speculative realism or ooo shows is precisely that objects eschew any definite reason for being what they are, that the real is, and is independent of anything I or anyone might have to say about it. So much so that it appears now that to have forced such a discourse on all those texts—to the extent that they are traversed by speculation—may have turned my attempt into more than just a contradiction; a transgression of sorts, a radical negation and refusal on my part, no matter what I may claim to the contrary, of what this literature at its (unreadable) core is: an "object." Indecipherable. Meaningless because absolutely severed from and unrelated to me. Speculative, in a word.*

Instead, I may at times have ventured into comments that eventually missed the speculative, shaped it into a mere surface reflection of an unapproachable, unfathomable undertow. For in the end, I rarely departed from interpretation: commenting, quoting, inferring. That's what I do. For better or worse. Perhaps sometimes the texts I tackled proved not speculative enough, were merely reflective of the idea of a broken language without truly implementing it—making it easier for me to pick up just whiffs of the speculative, and for these pages to accumulate—a speculative that is otherwise absent, inexistent, a mere theoretical figment. But perhaps sometimes I failed to see speculation where and when it was. Hence the conspicuous absence of some other texts that did not, maybe could not, find entry into my inevitably hostile discourse. Which may finally prove my point, or invalidate it altogether. I'm not sure.

Which, dear Incomprehension, *may be as it should.*

NOTES

Speculative Fiction

1. See, among other recent academic examples, P. L. Thomas, ed., *Science Fiction and Speculative Fiction: Challenging Genres* (Rotterdam, the Netherlands: Sense Publishers, 2013), or Matthew J. Wolf-Meyer, *Theory for the World to Come: Speculative Fiction and Apocalyptic Anthropology* (Minneapolis: University of Minnesota Press, 2019), in which speculative fiction is considered in its (problematic) relation to or divergence from science fiction.

2. Not unlike what is happening in Blake Butler's *Alice Knott* (New York: Riverhead Books, 2020), somehow, where all works of art suddenly disappear or are being destroyed to rid the world—a strangely flattened, pixelated world—of all images, or so it seems.

3. Along with David Markson's late works, a case in point could be Michael Joyce's *Was* (Tuscaloosa, AL: FC2, 2007).

4. In the sense Timothy Morton gives to the adjective in *Hyperobjects* (Minneapolis: University of Minnesota Press, 2013).

5. A writer like Margaret Atwood, for instance, refers to works of her own like *The Handmaid's Tale* or *Oryx and Crake* as different from works of traditional science fiction with "intergalactic space travel [or] teleportation [or] Martians"—instead, she views them as "speculative fiction, not . . . science fiction proper" as they "invent nothing we haven't already invented or started to invent. Every novel begins with a *what if* and then sets forth its axioms" (Atwood, "Writing *Oryx and Crake*"). This, for Atwood, is constitutive of speculative fiction as commonly understood, along with its developments into dystopian and (post)apocalyptic literature. If not absolutely unrelated to such works, my understanding of "speculative fiction" in these pages differs quite radically from those (merely) generic considerations.

6. I'd like to view and place my own attempt here, at least for the moment, on some neutral grounds, if there are any left, to not quite partake of the institutional wars waged between the tenants of critique and the propounders of post-critique, deep versus superficial reading, and so on. Criticism is here viewed from afar and in the abstract somehow, as a specific, secondhand, though supposedly expert, mode of discourse.

7. Dead End Follies. Review of *300,000,000: A Novel*, by Blake Butler.

8. Graham Harman, "The Well-Wrought Broken Hammer: Object-Oriented Literary Criticism," *New Literary History* 43 no. 2 (2012): 184.

9. Coming back on its founding event—a workshop that took place on April 27, 2007, at Goldsmiths, University of London—Graham Harman offers a summary view of the divergences at the heart of speculative realism in *Speculative Realism: An Introduction* (Medford, MA: Polity Press, 2018).

10. I mean this to be an ambiguous negation, both of the act of reading and of my very existence.

11. One might thus wonder what makes it worthwhile, within such a theoretical framework, to read literary fiction rather than a "paper cup" or any other object for that matter; yet, the fact that no one "object" is any more profound than another does not entail that they are interchangeable. If fiction *is*, it is nothing *but* itself, has properties all its own that differ from the cup's individuality—a point also made by Harman in "The Well-Wrought Broken Hammer" when he refutes "boundary-free holism" for instance (194–95). What, among other things, distinguishes fiction from a cup is that fiction can be defined as (but not reduced to) a *linguistic* object; as such, contrary to the cup-as-cup, it already engages a form of thinking that can be turned against itself to question its own utility or function. It is precisely in the course of such reflexive moves, hardly attainable with a cup, even a broken one, that I, as reader, can experience the deregulation or slipperiness of the thought process implemented and simultaneously sabotaged by speculative fiction.

12. The very premise of apocalyptic or postapocalyptic fiction by definition turns it into a good candidate for speculative fiction; yet for that matter not all (post)apocalyptic fictions necessarily *are* in essence speculative if they do not heed the full implications of the genre. This is a point made by Peter Szendy when he claims that there is no such thing as true apocalyptic cinema insofar as it would, out of theoretical necessity, have to include the end of the cinema in its depiction or rendition of the apocalypse. In that sense, the only truly apocalyptic film extant, according to Szendy, would be Lars von Trier's *Melancholia*, whose very ending coincides with the apocalypse the film has been announcing throughout. Peter Szendy, *L'apocalypse-cinéma: 2012 et autres fins du monde* (Nantes: Capricci, 2012).

13. Morton derives this from Harman's object-oriented ontology.

14. *Weird Realism: Lovecraft and Philosophy* (Winchester, UK: Zer0 Books, 2012). Lovecraft's work is conspicuously absent from this book. The main reason for this is that *Dear Incomprehension* focuses exclusively on contemporary American fiction and does not purport to offer an exhaustive catalogue of speculative works and writers, nor to retrace the history of such a problematic, proliferating (non-)genre, whose origin could just as well be located in Melville's "Bartleby, the Scrivener," in which Bartleby acts as a disruptive agent jamming the narrative momentum of a story that can only mimic and repeat its own blank vacuity.

15. *In the Dust of This Planet (Horror of Philosophy Vol. 1), Starry Speculative Corpse (Horror of Philosophy Vol. 2), Tentacles Longer than Night (Horror of Philosophy Vol. 3)*, Winchester, UK: Zer0 Books, 2011 and 2015.

16. "Weird" or "weirdness" are words that are often used by speculative realists, whether or not in association with literary artifacts; the use of such terms calls to mind a recent, underground trend in contemporary American fiction, the so-called *bizarro* genre—minimally defined in *The Bizarro Starter Kit* as, "simply put, the genre of the weird" (5), which

Eraserhead Press became a primary venue for. Like Lovecraft, but for different reasons, bizarro works and writers are not included in this book. The choice was to turn away from mere concerns of genre aesthetics to stress instead how the speculative, as a counternarrative mode perhaps, was not just thematically interested in the "weird" but somehow entailed a specific regime of writing aiming at disrupting narrativity and readability. See Carlton Mellick III et al., *The Bizarro Starting Kit* (Portland, OR: Bizarro Books, 2006).

17. In the usual "what if . . . ?" sense in which the term is often used, notably in order to contrast (classic) "speculative fiction" with "science fiction."

18. Most of this book was written during the COVID-19 pandemic, after all.

19. *Event Factory* (2010), *The Ravickians* (2011), *Ana Patova Crosses a Bridge* (2013), and *Houses of Ravicka* (2017), all having been published by Dorothy, A Publishing Project.

20. Including the paradigmatic *The Road* by Cormac McCarthy, which despite its narrative asceticism—the "end of the world" is a given whose catastrophic origins are never tackled or explained in the novel—does tell a (full-fledged) story of survival. It is no wonder, as such, that the novel was turned into a movie, in a way that Ben Marcus's *The Flame Alphabet* or David Ohle's *Motorman* or Mark Doten's *The Infernal* or Blake Butler's *Scorch Atlas* would and could not be.

21. This may account for the conspicuous absence in these pages of authors one might initially be tempted to view as speculative. A case in point could be Jeff VanderMeer, whose Southern Reach Trilogy of novels—*Annihilation, Authority, Acceptance* (2014)—thematically partakes of the speculative. However, despite its mysteries, challenges, and weirdnesses, the trilogy never truly does away with, nor seriously undermines, its narrative streak. A telltale sign of this is the sheer persistence of metaphors throughout, which belie language's capacity to keep relating the apparently unknown or mysterious to the known and familiar:

> The marks she had pointed to were oval, and about a foot long by half a foot wide. Six of them were splayed over the steps, in two rows. A flurry of indentations inside these shapes <u>resembled</u> the marks left by cilia. About ten inches outside of these tracks, encircling them, were two lines. This irregular double circle undulated out and then in again, almost like <u>the hem of a skirt</u>. Beyond this "hem" were faint indicators of further "waves," <u>as of some force</u> emanating from a central body that had left a mark. It <u>resembled</u> most closely the lines left in sand as the surf recedes during low tide. Except that something had blurred the lines and made them fuzzy, <u>like charcoal drawings</u>. (Annihilation, 02: *Integration*)

Here, what is supposed to eschew understanding is constantly, narratorially referred back to something familiar that anti-speculatively smoothes over the irrational. *Annihilation*, the first novel in the series, incidentally concludes by bypassing the speculative, when the narrator finally claims: "I am aware that all of this speculation is incomplete, inexact, inaccurate, useless. If I don't have real answers, it is because we still don't know what questions to ask. Our instruments are useless, our methodology broken, our motivations selfish" (05: Dissolution). Stated this way, the problem she faces is in part defined epistemologically, its answer merely deferred in time rather than ontologically invalidated: "we <u>still</u> don't know what questions to ask." This is a point made by Quentin Meillassoux when he refutes Karl

Popper's so-called answer to Hume's problem, suggesting Popper's answer testifies to an *epistemological* misunderstanding of the *ontological* nature of Hume's problem (Meillassoux 2015, 15). Throughout the Trilogy, the presence of the S&S Brigade, which juxtaposes the irrational or occult (*Séance*) with the rational (*Science*), further suggests that the Trilogy's aesthetics never really falls into the extro-science side of the speculative divide.

Speculative Endings, Or "Rate This Apocalypse"

1. Autobiography comes to mind, which can never satisfy its own premises either, unless it is told from beyond the ultimate event without which a life is not complete—that is, death. As such, a complete(d) autobiography could count as speculative fiction, in that it would have to be told from a point located *after* or *beyond* or *apart from* the possibility of its telling, severing all relation with the narrative it tells.

2. A similarly casual treatment is operated in Alexandra Kleeman's *Something New Under the Sun* (New York: Hogarth, 2021), in which the burning down of California is relegated into the margins of the narration, where it seems to have been strangely neutralized, or banalized, a mere given, leaving characters conspicuously unreactive to the catastrophe around them.

3. "Flat ontology" being what object-oriented ontology and speculative realism more or less defend despite divergences; the phrase originates in Manuel DeLanda's "rereading of Gilles Deleuze ... to describe theories that do not order worldly entities hierarchically ... but that attribute an equal ontological dignity to each individuated thing." Tristan Garcia, *Form and Object: A Treatise on Things*, trans. Mark Allan Ohm and Jon Cogburn (Edinburgh: Edinburgh University Press, 2014), 4.

4. Etymologically, "crisis" (*krisis, krinein*) is bound to an act of selection, of cutting, of judging.

5. This is a point made in part by D. F. Wallace in his essay about *Wittgenstein's Mistress*: "[Kate's] is the affectless language of fact.... [*Wittgenstein's Mistress*] is a kind of philosophical sci-fi. Ie, it's an imaginative portrait of what it would be like actually to *live* in the sort of world the logic & metaphysics of Wittgenstein's *Tractatus* posits." See D. F. Wallace, "The Empty Plenum: David Markson's *Wittgenstein's Mistress*," *Review of Contemporary Fiction* 10, no. 2 (1990): 223.

6. Another name for that being precisely the Apocalypse, in its biblical understanding.

7. Titles also potentially anticipating Butler's novel *There Is No Year*, which was published two years later.

8. Anne-Laure Tissut's paper, "Corps rêvés dans *Scorch Atlas*, de Blake Butler," studies the poetics at work in Butler's book (*Revue Française d'Études Américaines*, no. 132 [2012]: 48–62).

9. A technique also implemented in Jason Schwartz's fiction (see "Speculative Interface").

10. Most one-word titles of the intercalary pieces refer to diverse material substances: water, dust, gravel, glass, and so on.

11. "She wanted to see something like her mother had, like the bear, so that one day she'd have a story for a daughter" (*SA*, 74).

12. The verb "continue" is repeated seventeen times through *Scorch Atlas*.

Speculative Topologies, Or "This Is Not for You"

1. Here is what Didi-Huberman writes: "*Ouvrons les yeux pour éprouver ce que nous ne voyons pas, ce que nous ne verrons plus—ou plutôt pour éprouver que ce que nous ne voyons pas de toute évidence (l'évidence visible) nous regarde pourtant comme une œuvre (une œuvre visuelle) de perte. . . . Mais la modalité du visible devient inéluctable—c'est-à-dire vouée à une question d'être—quand voir, c'est sentir que quelque chose inéluctablement nous échappe, autrement dit: quand voir, c'est perdre. Tout est là.*" See Georges Didi-Huberman, *Ce que nous voyons, ce qui nous regarde* (Paris: Minuit, 1992), 14.

2. Of his own admission, as stated in the interview conducted by J. P. O'Malley for the *Times of Israel* (May 11, 2014).

3. *There Is No Year* can in that regard be compared to Mark Danielewski's *House of Leaves*. Not only does the layout of the text, just as in *House of Leaves*, become performative in specific places, embodying in its columns, or flush right/flush left alignments, the sense of spatial disorientation the characters may feel, but it also makes use of the typography in what may be a jab aimed at Danielewski's work, for instance, using bloodred ink to pen the word "bloodred" or a larger, bold font to pen the word "flat" (*TINY*, 196).

4. Joyce has confirmed this several times: "In some way all of the text came from search-engine queries," he notably wrote Stuart Moulthrop. See Stuart Moulthrop, "Lift this End: Electronic Literature in a Blue Light," *Electronic Book Review*, April 2, 2013.

5. If violence is arguably lodged at the heart of the novel's thematic and formal concerns, one may recall the opening node of Joyce's hypertext *afternoon, a story* and its programmatic series of explosions-cum-crystallizations: "I try to recall winter. <As if it were yesterday?> she says, but I do not signify one way or another. By five the sun sets and the afternoon melt freezes again across the blacktop into crystal octopi and palms of ice—rivers and continents beset by fear, and we walk out to the car, the snow moaning beneath our boots and the oaks exploding in series along the fenceline on the horizon, the shrapnel settling like relics, the echoing thundering off far ice. This was the essence of wood, these fragments say. And this darkness is air" (Joyce, *afternoon, a story* <begin>).

6. Michael Joyce has been hailed as one of the pioneers of electronic literature and his *afternoon, a story* (1987) is often referred to as, in Robert Coover's words, "the granddaddy of full-length hypertext fictions." See Robert Coover, "The End of Books," *New York Times Book Review*, June 21, 1992. Yet Joyce—along with Shelley Jackson notably—eventually turned his back on electronic literature to return to print with such works as *Was, Disappearance, Twentieth Century Man* . . . .

7. Of course, framing the problem in such terms might reveal my own inadequacy or obstinacy in willing the text to comply with and conform to predetermined conventions that, as a "novel of internet," may be utterly irrelevant to the book. At any rate, it does beg for a redefinition along aesthetic, generic, and ontological lines; on the surface a print novel, *Was* may as well, if not as much, be viewed as some electronic work whose output would be print. My incapacity to read it *as* a novel is indeed a telltale sign that it may not function as such.

8. In that respect, Butler's novels are radically, violently *anti*-realistic—on the surface focusing on purely domestic issues (*Ever, There Is No Year, Sky Saw*, most stories in *Scorch Atlas*

featuring father, mother, and son/daughter figures), they embody the very opposite of the family novel à la Jonathan Franzen.

9. Whether a typo or not, no period punctuates the sentence.

10. Moulthrop raises a similar question in his essay "Lift This End" about the likes of Joyce's *Was*, asking "*What does a novel of Internet want?*" (Moulthrop 2013)

11. See "Speculative Interface."

12. Framing the issue in such terms harks back to the (post)critical debate over the validity or prevalence of so-called surface versus deep readings (see Anker and Felski's *Critique and Postcritique*), the irony being that whatever "depth" Nora may be alluding to remains utterly inaccessible, as the reader of *Half Life* is offered the mere tip of the iceberg—Nora's narrative. Whatever depth the text may be concealing, it has to be Blanche's own version, which, interestingly, as suggested by the semantics of Blanche's name, not only proves absent but is doomed to remain forever *blank*.

13. Already at play in "The Father Costume" (*Leaving the Sea*), in which the narrator keeps withdrawing from the text, with such paragraphs starting with "If I could choose . . ." (180); "I wish I could say . . ." (180, 183, 192); "If it were up to me . . ." (187, 190).

14. If, that is, one agrees with Graham Harman's or Timothy Morton's close identification of the aesthetic with the ontological.

15. The French reads: "Telle serait donc la modalité du visible lorsque l'instance s'en fait inéluctable: un travail du *symptôme* où ce que nous voyons est supporté par (et renvoyé à) une œuvre de perte" (Didi-Huberman, 14), which could translate as: "Such would thus be the modality of the visible whenever its instantiation becomes ineluctable: the workings of a *symptom* where what we see is supported by (and referred back to) a *work of loss*."

16. Similar concerns and strategies are instantiated in "The Father Costume."

17. The bland, matter-of-fact simplicity of the sentence jars with such patented openings as "My father's costumes were gray and long and of the finest pile, sometimes clear enough for us to see through, though there was no reason to look too closely at that man's body," in *The Father Costume* (2002—later reprised in the 2013 collection *Leaving the Sea*), or "This book is a catalog of the life project as prosecuted in the Age of Wire and String and beyond, etc." in *The Age of Wire and String*.

18. Of course, *The Flame Alphabet* easily yields to "pharmacological" readings, which treat language as *pharmakon*, that is, both poison *and* remedy, according to a similar disseminative dynamic. Although not its main focus, Arnaud Regnauld's essay on Marcus's novel broaches the issue. See Arnaud Regnauld, "L'apocalypse, le chiffre et la prothèse: *The Flame Alphabet* de Ben Marcus," in *Otrante*, edited by J-F Chassay and Hélène Machinal (Paris: Kimé, 2015), 157–68.

19. "Bien sûr, l'expérience familière de ce que nous voyons semble le plus souvent donner lieu à un *avoir:* en voyant quelque chose, nous avons en général l'impression de gagner quelque chose. Mais la modalité du visible devient inéluctable—c'est-à-dire vouée à une question d'*être*—quand voir, c'est sentir que quelque chose inéluctablement nous échappe, autrement dit: quand voir, c'est perdre. Tout est là" (Didi-Huberman, 14).

20. This hesitation or paradox is reminiscent of the conclusion Graham Harman reaches at the end of *Tool-Being*: "In a certain sense, the tool-being of a thing exists in vacuum-sealed isolation, exceeding any of the relations that might touch it. But now it also seems true that

some sort of relationality is needed to create at least *some* tool-beings." See Graham Harman, *Tool-Being: Heidegger and the Metaphysics of Objects* (Chicago: Open Court, 2002), 287.

Speculative Sublime, Or "_____"

1. A point also exemplified in the diverse black-and-white, abstract, blurry, granular, underexposed photographs interspersed in the book.

2. Which is also the case of Butler's *Alice Knott*, in which, if at first sight the protagonist may be trying to understand whatever is happening to her art collection and her life, she ends up passively accepting the diverse roles imposed upon her from an inscrutable outside.

3. The term "translation" in Morton's thinking applies to the way objects interact with one another, one object always "translating" another one, carrying itself into the other; translation, to Morton, equals metaphor, both pointing to the same move or displacement, the 1+n, that accounts for the aesthetic dimension of causality.

4. In Ian Bogost's use of the term "alien."

5. "Every word was once an animal"—the epigraph to the book, supposedly and improbably from Emerson, draws attention to the living, restive, undomesticated aspect of the text's language.

6. The same phrase appears in Butler's novel *There Is No Year*—whose aesthetic is less blatantly postapocalyptic though not unlike the one in *Scorch Atlas*—in a list of pseudo directions meant for the son to find his way to a girl's house: "NOW OUTSIDE A PICTURE WINDOW WITH NO PICTURE CURL ON A THE GROUND INTO A BALL" (*TINY*, 236–37).

7. A similar point could be made with David Ohle's work.

8. An ending that somehow anticipates the closing pages of Sarah Rose Etter's *The Book of X*.

9. As explicitly propounded in the mock manifesto "Stitch Bitch," riffing on Jackson's *Patchwork Girl*.

10. As a prosthetic extension of the reader's own hand and finger.

11. Said this way, it appears as if the substitution of mere sensation for sense or meaning were just a way of replacing one mode of correlation with another. Which might very well be the case, after all. What is here posited is that speculative fiction, to the extent that it *can* be truly speculative, toys with a logic of sensation that is intrinsic and not necessarily felt experientially—although, of course, the dear incomprehension that speculative fiction fosters remains the negative mode in which I cannot *but* experience it.

12. Drawing an analogy between arts as different as painting and literature is of course not without the risk of oversimplification or misappropriation. As Deleuze writes, quite categorically:

> Of all the arts, painting is undoubtedly the only one that necessarily, "hysterically," integrates its own catastrophe, and consequently is constituted as a flight in advance. In the other arts, the catastrophe is only associated. But painters pass through the catastrophe themselves, embrace the chaos, and attempt to emerge from it. Where painters differ is in their manner of embracing this nonfigurative chaos, and in their evaluation of the pictorial order to come, and the relation of this order with this chaos. (Gilles Deleuze, *Francis Bacon: The Logic of Sensation*, trans. Daniel W. Smith [London: Continuum, 2003], 102–3)

Whether or not this is the case, the writer does work with a material that resists its own catastrophe. Language, unlike paint, is by definition referential and transitive. Words mean something; a sentence bespeaks of something external to it. As such, and as far as literature is concerned, the chaos Deleuze speaks of is already held at bay, merely "associated" indeed, in that language by essence cannot be "nonfigurative"—any sentence, to the extent that it complies with basic syntactic premises, orders things, concepts, events, if only minimally, if only grammatically, or the sentence is not one. It thus eschews pure chaos. For even in what Jean-Luc Nancy calls the "structional"—that is, "the pure and simple juxtaposition that does not make sense"—"contiguity and contingency" may not make sense; yet they do not abolish it for that matter, nor do they render it quite implausible. In that regard, the work of the writer is radically different, in its praxis, from the work of the painter. For as Deleuze claims, "it would be a mistake to think that the painter works on a white and virgin surface. The entire surface is already invested virtually with all kinds of clichés, which the painter will have to break with" (Deleuze 2003, 11). This, for Deleuze (and Bacon), is a prerequisite in order to break with the figurative and/or narrative hold. Yet if both painter and writer may be dealing with preexisting clichés before they even start working, these cannot be utterly discarded by the writer's gestures and moves, whose sentences, do what he or she may, retain some minimal semantic, ordering quality. No doubt, "the extraordinary work of abstract painting was necessary in order to tear modern art away from figuration" (Deleuze 2003, 11). However, tearing fiction away from the narrative, or, more generally, literature from the referential, is virtually impossible due to the very nature of the linguistic material composing the work. There is no true equivalent of abstract painting in the history of literature; even high modernism, whether in the works of Joyce, Stein, or Beckett, pushed the experiment only so far. The result, in the words of John Barth, may have been a sense of exhaustion of the narrative possibilities. Yet exhaustion does not mean that such writers eventually broke through to something that would be the opposite of the referential or the narrative; postmodern self-referentiality for that matter, as one possible way out of the conundrum as exposed by Barth, remains indeed overly referential. Eventually, as Beckett famously put it in *The Unnamable*, "you must go on, I can't go on, I'll go on." See Samuel Beckett, *Three Novels: Molloy, Malone Dies, The Unnamable* (New York: Grove Press, 1994), 414.

13. It might be one of the unshakable staples of all catastrophic fiction—there has to be some salvaged remainder, if only "to tell thee."

14. Of course, "narrative" in Butler's case and "figurative" in Bacon's are not coextensive terms.

15. *Virtual* rather than *possible* in a Deleuzian sense, those narrative traces acting not so much as a preliminary sketch to be fleshed out as a form of figurality. In the words of Brian Massumi: "The virtual, as such, is inaccessible to the senses. This does not, however, preclude figuring it, in the sense of constructing images of it. To the contrary, it requires a multiplication of images. The virtual that cannot be felt also cannot be but felt, in its effects." See Brian Massumi, *Parables for the Virtual: Movement, Affect, Sensation* (Durham, NC: Duke University Press, 2002), 133.

16. Similarly, Jackson's semi-autobiographical portrait in *my body* often veers toward unrealistic, grotesque, or "monstrous" tendencies, as when the narrator confesses to having grown a tail: "I was born with a short tail, which my parents decided not to have removed

when I was a baby, since I seemed to take so much pleasure in it, curling it around my own wrist, whipping it on my buttocks when I was itchy or testy, and dragging small objects into my crib with it. When I was old enough to realize none of the other kids had a tail, though, I became furiously ashamed of it" (*my body*, "tail"). The same holds true for Cassie in Sarah Rose Etter's *The Book of X*.

17. Something "Stitch Bitch," Shelley Jackson's monster-womanifesto, has a lot to say about, couching her understanding of the restive nature of the body in terms that rime with her conception of (hyper-)textuality.

18. So will, later on, its removal, of course scarring Cassie's body and literally re-marking it instead of obliterating the knot, forever ruling out the possibility of normality, a mere "trick of the eye" or "mirage":

> My abdomen is flat and smooth now, the rebuilt stomach perfect in shape, taut. But it is marbled with red scars, puckered skin, a mosaic of old stitch work railroading across the flattened land of my stomach.
>
> Sometimes, when I look at myself in the mirror, the world warbles around me, a trick of the eye, as if I am in another life. It feels like staring through heat rising off of the asphalt, the mirage of my new knotless body. (196)

19. The final section of the novel opens with imagery that clashes with the gloomy ending and is more easily associated with epiphanic scenes of understanding and revelation, turning Cassie's renouncement into some acceptance of sorts: "The sky opens up and swirls above me, a blur of stars streaking out from a pure white pinprick in the center. . . . The sky throbs and streams with color, rivers of shimmering green and blue and white against the dark night. *Etc.*" (284).

20. Or not; the narrator of Gary Lutz's story "Femme" begs to differ: "I saw arms, swaying legs, that might have belonged on anyone. Everybody was the same body, no matter the twists of personship, the agonied differences of fit and build." See Gary Lutz, *The Complete Gary Lutz* (New York: Tyrant Books, 2019), 242.

21. As eventually suggested by the blurring of the novel's ending with its possible point of departure, as the narrator, by then radically alienated from her boyfriend C and her roommate B, as well as estranged from herself, proposes that the unknown "Chris" become "C" so that together they might embark on a relationship much like the one she had with C, thus going back in time along a vicious circle (see 282).

22. The connection with the philosophy of Gilles Deleuze, whether consciously influential or not, is explicitly drawn by Blake Butler's choice of name for his former blog/website: gillesdeleuzecommittedsuicideandsowilldrphil.com.

23. Deleuze draws the connection between Bacon and Carroll (Deleuze 2003, 28).

24. "BLINKS" that recall Massumi's definition of the virtual: "The appearance of the virtual is in the twists and folds of formed content, in the movement of one sample to another. It is in the ins and outs of imaging" (Massumi, 133).

25. To a certain extent, a realistic backdrop may even reinforce the fictionally speculative. As Meillassoux claims while reviewing the paucity of extro-science scenarios in fiction, it is not the *entirety* of the natural laws that need to be rescinded in order for the world to cease to be regular and scientifically accountable. Stressing the necessity of pure contingency,

Meillassoux specifies that probabilistic laws—according to which, if the laws of nature no longer applied, the whole world would be pure unpredictable chaos (Kant's transcendental take on the question)—no longer rule; hence, despite all odds (literally), it remains possible for the world to be a world as such, governed by a certain form of regularity in the midst of which aberrant phenomena would surface: "Kant makes the following implicit argument: if a world were lawless, if the least of its parcels could behave indifferently in any way whatsoever, it would take an extraordinary chance to compose a global and durable order, like the nature that confronts us. But if this is Kant's argument, it is easy to reply to him that a world which does not obey any law has no reason to obey any probabilistic or statistical law whatever it may be. Nothing prohibits it from composing—against every sound probability—a global order that would constitute it into a world, an order at the heart of which certain details could nonetheless 'run out of control' at any moment, like Hume's billiard balls." See Quentin Meillassoux, *Science Fiction and Extro-Science Fiction*, trans. Alyosha Edlebi (Minneapolis: Univocal Publishing, 2015), 32.

26. Quoted in Ashley Crawford's *Religious Imaging in Millennialist America* (London: Palgrave Macmillan, 2018), 202.

27. Burke's name may not be totally haphazard; his insistence on unknowability and the sense of "awe" that is linked with it here may be a way, for Marcus, to engage his readers speculatively with metaphysical questions pertaining to the sublime as a potential mode of access to the real.

Speculative Language, Or "Understanding Is Overrated"

1. Butler's latest novel *Aanex* is being published as I revise these lines; unread yet, if read it can be, the opening page lists 10 paragraphs numbered 10 to 90, section 80 reading: "Without aesthetic structure in receipt of any notion (w/o duration/narration/location/innovation/physical law)"—which, as such, could stand as an apt descriptor of his trademark brand of speculative fiction. See Blake Butler, *Aanex* (Philadelphia: Apocalypse Party, 2022), 5.

2. Something in part tackled with regard to Butler's *300,000,000* in my essay "'In the end of commentary'—*300,000,000* de Blake Butler, ou la fiction absolue," *Revue Française d'Études Américaines*, no. 159 (2019): 38–49.

3. Such errors could be involuntary typos of course, pointing to language manipulations and editing that leave similar scars on the surface of the texts.

4. Problems of communication between characters also pervade Sabrina Orah Mark's *Wild Milk*, a collection placed under the sign of Beckett's "dear incomprehension"—which incidentally provided this book with its title—in which characters are often faced with the sheer, stubborn recalcitrance of language: "'Your child,' says Miss Birdy, 'is a phenomenon.' I blush.... 'I mean, your child is a mana mana,' says Miss Birdy. 'What I mean to say is that your child is a real man.' Miss Birdy softly pinches her tongue and pulls off a long white hair. 'Oh, that's better,' she says. 'I mean, a ma.' She makes little, tiny spits. 'I mean, a no one. Your child,' says Miss Birdy, 'is a real no one. No, no. That's not it either.'" See *Wild Milk* (Saint Louis: Dorothy, A Publishing Project, 2018), 10.

5. A so-called review whose very name, *The Proofs*, appears conspicuously, if fraudulently, performative. For if it supposedly purports to deliver scientifically irrefutable "proof,"

the name can also be interpreted as that which, as "proof sheets," remains in need of verification before publication and circulation. In other words, the sign as such is here intrinsically invalidated by its own semantic hesitation.

6. As Leo Robson notes in his 2013 *NewStatesman* review: "Marcus's theme is the arbitrariness of reference, his aim to find verbal formulations that reveal the proximity of nonsense to what we take for lucid expression." See Leo Robson, "Renata Adler, Ben Marcus and David Shields: Pushing the Limits of the American Novel," *NewStatesman* (August 22, 2013).

7. I'm of course referring to the controversy between Jonathan Franzen and Ben Marcus. To a certainly eerie extent, the opening chapter of *Notable American Women* could even be read, somehow, as a fictional rendition, and anticipation, and grotesque parody of the debate opposing the realistic, no-messing-around Franzen/Father figure to the naughty, "difficult," irresponsible Marcus/Son figure who perversely indulges in and courts abstraction and aberration.

8. The text as such somehow implementing its own critique or foregrounding a "hermeneutics of suspicion" with which it obviously toys.

9. Which, whether or not this was premeditated by Marcus, reads like a homophonic rendition of French mystic, saint, warrior, martyr "Jeanne d'Arc"—or Joan of Arc.

10. The way, say, Faulkner's consistent depiction of Yoknapatawpha County would or could.

11. Cohen, in his review of the novel for the *London Review of Books*, writes, "It would have been more ecumenical for Marcus to invent his own sect, especially given that his Jews bear such slight resemblance to even the craziest who claim that identity." See Joshua Cohen, "How So Very Dear," *London Review of Books* 34, no. 12 (June 21, 2012).

12. At least at first sight—for if Rochester is indeed situated in the State of New York, then towns like Dushore, Laporte, or Wilbert, which Sam thinks he surfaced into from his underground tunnel after fleeing Forsythe, are either fictional or not located where he claims they are (273).

13. A point I painstakingly tried to elaborate in my essay "Ben Marcus & the Question of Language (Some Notes & a Parenthesis)," *Revue Française d'Études Américaines*, no. 135 (2013): 66–79.

14. Somewhat similar concerns surface in Shelley Jackson's *Riddance*, in which the so-called language of the dead can materialize through "etcoplasmoglyphs" or "mouth objects" that might "signify only *themselves*." Reflects an unknown observer: "in which case the task before us would be, not to determine what they mean, but to see what they are." See Shelley Jackson, *Riddance* (New York: Black Balloon Publishing, 2018), 185.

15. Hence, of course, Plato's notorious condemnation and banishment of poets from his ideal Republic, the words they trade on being nothing but second-degree copies of Ideas.

16. A novella that was initially published independently with Artspace Books in 2002, with illustrations by Matthew Ritchie.

17. At times, the very language of the text itself waxes opaque, especially and paradoxically when it affects to be the more mimetic while venturing on descriptions that, despite ekphrastic efforts, remain virtually impossible to "picture"—such is the case, for instance, with the description of "the Listener" in chapter 8.

18. Some reviewers have pointed out the possible play between LeBov's name and linguist William Labov's.

19. The French reads: "philosophie du Double, philosophie métaphysique, qui tient le 'réel' quotidien pour une duplication dont seule la vision de l'Original pourrait lui livrer le sens et la clef. La densité du réel signale au contraire une plénitude de la réalité quotidienne, c'est-à-dire l'unicité d'un monde qui se compose non de doubles mais toujours de singularités originales (même s'il leur arrive de se 'ressembler') et n'a par conséquent de comptes à rendre à aucun modèle—philosophie du réel, qui voit dans le quotidien et le banal, voire dans la répétition elle-même, toute l'originalité du monde. Aucun objet, aux yeux de cette philosophie du réel, qui puisse être tenu pour 'original' au sens métaphysique du terme; aucun objet réel qui ne soit fabriqué, factice, dépendant, conditionné, 'de seconde main'. Tout y est, si l'on veut, doublure, au gré au moins d'une certaine sensibilité métaphysique; mais ces 'doubles' ne copient aucun patron et sont par conséquent chacun des originaux." See Clément Rosset, *Le Réel: Traité de l'idiotie* ([1977], Paris: Minuit, 2004).

20. Quoted in Anna Kornbluh's *The Order of Forms* (Chicago: Chicago University Press, 2019), 46.

21. Like *Notable American Women* before it, a whole part of which consists in describing what the book is, how it supposedly works, or what it could have been, *instead of* telling its own story; or like *The Age of Wire and String*, too, whose stated aim was to remain "willfully hidden" (*AWS*, 3).

22. Of course, the immediate reference of the pronoun "this" in the context of *The Flame Alphabet*'s ending can be summed up as the list of actions Sam has just been reviewing for what he and Esther will do when she comes back. Yet from a grammatical point of view, such summary function would better be addressed somehow with the use of "that," which retains a closing, final quality, while "this" rather points to something about to be said. In which case, if one chooses to read *this* for its opening, introducing function, its referent would be left unsaid or could be understood as the blank, silent page that follows and kills off the narrative.

23. One that at any rate appears more in line with realism as theorized by Anna Kornbluh away from "overarching implications of mimesis," an estranged realism that eventually "operates less as representation than as production" (Kornbluh, 43).

24. Of course, a lot could, perhaps even *should*, be said about that in (so to speak) relation to Lacan's very conception of the Real as that which remains beyond both the Symbolic and Imaginary orders—some philosophers or thinkers sometimes associated with speculative realism or object-oriented ontology do partake of Lacan's heritage, among them Žižek, most notably. But this, however, would extend the scope of this essay—if that is what it is.

Speculative Interface, Or "cr!tical fa1lure/r3port loX0red"

1. There is, in the way the editor explains the organization of the text, something reminiscent of the by-now canonical definition of the hypertext, as propounded by Ted Nelson in his *Literary Machines*: "By 'hypertext,' I mean non-sequential writing—text that branches and allows choices to the reader, best read at an interactive screen. As popularly conceived, this is a series of text chunks connected by links which offer the reader different pathways." The spatial vocabulary used by the editor—"travelers," "route," "tracks," "map"—has often

served as metaphor for the hypertextual experience. See Ted Nelson, *Literary Machines* 87, no. 1 (1987).

2. Joyce is the author of several literary hypertexts, among which *afternoon, a story* is considered, in Robert Coover's words, to be the "granddaddy" of hyperfiction. See Robert Coover, "The End of Books," *New York Times Book Review*, June 21, 1992.

3. *House of Leaves, Riddance, 300,000,000*, or *The Infernal* are all constructed around a gaping enigma or mystery to ponder: the impossible inner architecture of the house the Navidsons moved into; an unsolved past murder; the proliferation of deaths triggered by mass murderer Gretch Gravey after his arrest; the enigma embodied in the Akkad Boy, "this *impossible* boy" whose burnt body was found in the desert, the "boy *who did not die*" yet should be dead in *The Infernal* (22).

4. Some might say "enhance" instead.

5. One might reasonably assume that the "Index"—the pointing finger—is itself used as a comic *substitute* for the promised "Dildo," itself another substitute of sorts . . .

6. Unless, of course, the daughter herself already serves as a smoke screen, as perhaps suggested by the phrase "for the time being." Incidentally, the daughter appears at a grammatical remove since *she* is not the focus of the sentence so much as her father ("whose daughter . . .").

7. The phrase "put your finger" in the text's incipit cannot but retrospectively prove all too ironical.

8. *A German Picturesque* not only points to a foreign setting (itself jarring with several mentions of Pennsylvania) but also pushes fiction toward a rather visual dynamic of representation; as for *John the Posthumous*, the title refers to "a French king, alive for five days"—an explanation given parenthetically (29)—although the historical figure as such never appears in the text as a character proper; only the resonance or harmonics of his (spectral) story—rumors of a possibly violent death, questions of inheritance and succession, problematic filiations—can be felt to traverse or *haunt* the book.

9. "The Tudor" as opposed to "The Georgian" or "The Cape" or "The Victorian" or "The Greek Revival" or "The Colonial"—*what?* Interestingly, only the adjective is used and nominalized, and the common noun, the noun that all these characterizations are supposed to have in common, is left unsaid: house? room? building? "housepost"? The jarring diversity of instantiations makes it difficult to ascertain what is thus being characterized.

10. A point made by David Winters in his *Infinite Fictions*: "On one level, then, the book can be read as a killer's confession—perhaps a coded personal journal, peppered with clues; or a rulebook for a meta-literary murder mystery." See David Winters, *Infinite Fictions: Essays on Literature and Theory* (Winchester, UK: Zer0 Books, 2015), 51.

11. A phrase that reappears almost word for word in *John the Posthumous*: "But this does overstate it somewhat" (24).

12. A point that Graham Harman may object to, as illustrated by his opposition to Žižek on this ground, in *Tool-Being*: "While denying that essences can ever become perfectly *present* in the world, such a theory would still claim that they *exist*. In fact, this is the standpoint of the present book." See Graham Harman, *Tool-Being: Heidegger and the Metaphysics of Objects* (Chicago: Open Court, 2002), 214–15.

13. Along with the "fourfold" (*das Geviert*).

14. Whether or not *my* own reading of Harman, in turn, proves correct and thorough throughout matters little, somehow. What is of interest to me is how the whole, global framework delineated by "object-oriented ontology" or "speculative realism," in their various implementations, allows for some theoretical model from which it becomes possible to *approach* speculative fiction. Which, I realize, is not without raising some issues of (mis)appropriation that on the surface could denote a radical misunderstanding of what this philosophy does, especially when it claims that things *are* rather than are *used*.

15. Of course, this remains a naive, oversimplified characterization of the *literary* text, about which one could also easily argue that its very raison d'être is precisely to foreground and enhance its own materiality, to the extent at least that the latter defines its own literariness. Another way of framing the issue would be to revert to the Barthesian opposition between "readerly" and "writerly" texts. As Barthes argued in *S/Z*, these remain two abstract "values" posited at either end of a spectrum along which the text is free to move in order to achieve a certain balance.

16. Symptomatic of this is the sheer difficulty of ascertaining whether, generically, both *A German Picturesque* and *John the Posthumous* are novels or collections of short stories whose connection is loose enough for them to be independent of one another, yet whose echoes suggest articulations and links that remain hard, if not impossible, to locate.

17. The French reads: "Le contexte anonyme des instruments techniques s'est substitué au monde."

18. The issue of the broken reflexivity in Butler's novel is raised in the essay "In the End of Commentary."

19. Especially as the biographical book that "Joshua Cohen," the ghostwriter, is contracted to write for his homonym hides another one: the novel Cohen formerly wrote, whose fortune was quashed on publication day by the 9/11 attacks. This forgotten novel will literally haunt the biography that Cohen fails to write—a biography meant to stand for or supersede the tech scientist, who happens to be sick and dying and hopes to be turned into an everlasting character.

20. See, for example, Isabelle Alfandary and Axel Nesmes's *Modernism and Unreadability* (Montpellier: Presses Universitaires de la Méditerranée, 2011).

21. Or so it is assumed; as Wales notes in his Notebook, the boy still lives on at the end of the process, while the Omnosyne is being destroyed. The boy eventually merges with Wales himself, revealing that "*We are I*," "*You are I*" (388), "*You is we*" (390), "*We was I*" (391); his survival, along with the revelation of his impossible, diachronic identity, thus enhances his "contingency" or truly speculative ontology—the unexplainable fact that he *is*, despite it all (387 *sqq.*).

22. For all its blatant disregard for realism, *The Infernal* is of course a highly political novel questioning American politics and paranoia in the wake of 9/11.

23. A list of "Dramatis Personæ" is provided by Doten at the beginning of *The Infernal* (3–7), which, as such and from the start, contributes to de-realizing the historical characters the novel features: Osama bin Laden, Dick Cheney, Condoleeza Rice, Donald Rumsfeld, and so on, along with other various characters whose roles in post-9/11 American politics are not prominent, like Jack Nicholson, Mark Zuckerberg, Nathan Myhrvold.... The only

notable, and all too ironical, exception is of course George W. Bush—improbably replaced with his homonym, the scientist Vannevar Bush, inventor of the fictional Memex.

24. As further suggested by the Dantesque intertext perceptible from the novel's title, along with several disseminated quotes from Dante's *Inferno*.

25. Thematically mirrored, perhaps, in the perversion of the fictional Vannevar Bush, father to the Memex, and his desire for boys never to grow old and mature into adults and to remain instead youths forever or be expelled from his Institute—what ultimately occurred to Jimmy Wales's best friend, Lewis, causing the latter's suicide and prompting Wales in turn to design the Omnosyne in the hope of securing a more accurate memory of him (182–85).

WORKS CITED

Primary Sources
Speculative Fiction
Butler, Blake. *Ever.* Nairobi/Detroit: Calamari Press, 2009.
———. *Scorch Atlas.* Chicago: Featherproof Books, 2009.
———. *There Is No Year.* New York: Harper Perennial, 2011.
———. *Sky Saw.* New York: Tyrant Books, 2012.
———. *300,000,000.* New York: Harper Perennial, 2014.
———. *Alice Knott.* New York: Riverhead Books, 2020.
———. *Aanex.* Philadelphia: Apocalypse Party, 2022.
Cohen, Joshua. *Witz.* Champaign, IL: Dalkey Archive Press, 2010.
———. *Book of Numbers* (2015). London: Vintage Books, 2016.
Corin, Lucy. *One Hundred Apocalypses and Other Apocalypses.* San Francisco: McSweeney's Books, 2013.
Danielewski, Mark Z. *House of Leaves.* New York: Pantheon Books, 2000.
Doten, Mark. *The Infernal.* Minneapolis: Graywolf Press, 2015.
———. *Trump Sky Alpha.* Minneapolis: Graywolf Press, 2019.
Etter, Sarah Rose, *The Book of X.* Columbus: Two Dollar Radio, 2019.
Gladman, Renee. *Event Factory.* Urbana, IL: Dorothy, A Publishing Project, 2010.
———. *The Ravickians.* Urbana, IL: Dorothy, A Publishing Project, 2011.
———. *Ana Patova Crosses a Bridge.* St. Louis, MO: Dorothy, A Publishing Project, 2013.
———. *Houses of Ravicka.* St. Louis, MO: Dorothy, A Publishing Project, 2017.
Jackson, Shelley. *my body—a Wunderkammer* (1997). Electronic Literature Collection.
———. *The Anatomy of Melancholy.* New York: Anchor Books, 2002.
———. *Half Life.* New York: Harper Perennial, 2007.
———. *Riddance.* New York: Black Balloon Publishing, 2018.
———. "Skin: A Mortal Work of Art." Ineradicable Stain.
———. "Snow. A Story in Progress, Weather Permitting." Instagram. snowshellyjackson.
Joyce, Michael. *Was: Annales nomadique.* Tuscaloosa, AL: FC2, 2007.
———. *Disappearance.* Boulder, CO: Steerage Press, 2012.

Kleeman, Alexandra. *You Too Can Have a Body Like Mine* (2015). London: 4th Estate, 2017.
———. *Something New Under the Sun*. New York: Hogarth, 2021.
Lutz, Gary. *The Complete Gary Lutz*. New York: Tyrant Books, 2019.
Marcus, Ben. *In the Age of Wire and String*. Normal, IL: Dalkey Archive Press, 2004.
———. *Notable American Women*. New York: Vintage Contemporaries, 2002.
———. *The Flame Alphabet*. New York: Alfred A. Knopf, 2012.
———. *Leaving the Sea*. New York: Alfred A. Knopf, 2014.
———. *Notes from the Fog*. London: Granta Books, 2018.
Markson, David. *Wittgenstein's Mistress* (1988). Normal, IL: Dalkey Archive Press, 2005.
———. *Reader's Block*. Normal, IL: Dalkey Archive Press, 2007.
———. *Vanishing Point*. Washington, DC: Shoemaker & Hoard, 2004.
Ohle, David. *Motorman* (1972). Nairobi/Detroit: Calamari Press, 2008.
———. *The Age of Sinatra*. Berkeley, CA: Soft Skull Press, 2004.
Orah Mark, Sabrina. *Wild Milk*. St. Louis, MO: Dorothy, A Publishing Project, 2018.
Schwartz, Jason. *A German Picturesque*. Berkeley, CA: Pharos Editions, 2015.
———. *John the Posthumous*. New York: OR Books, 2013.
Unrue, Jane. *Love Hotel*. New York: New Directions, 2015.
Van Der Vliet Oloomi, Azareen. *Fra Keeler*. St. Louis, MO: Dorothy, A Publishing Project, 2012.

Other Works Mentioned or Quoted
Beckett, Samuel. *The Unnamable*. In *Three Novels: Molloy, Malone Dies, The Unnamable*. New York: Grove Press, 1994.
Coover, Robert. *Pricksongs & Descants* (1969). New York: Grove Press, 1998.
———. *A Night at the Movies*. Normal, IL: Dalkey Archive Press, 1997.
Joyce, Michael. *afternoon, a story*. Watertown: Eastgate Systems, 1987.
McCarthy, Cormac. *The Road*. London: Picador, 2007.
Nabokov, Vladimir. *Lolita*. London: Penguin Classics, 2000.
VanderMeer, Jeff. *Southern Reach Trilogy: Annihiliation, Authority, Acceptance*. New York: Farrar, Straus and Giroux, 2014.

Secondary Sources
Aarseth, Espen. *Cybertext: Perspective on Ergodic Literature*. Baltimore, MD: Johns Hopkins University Press, 1997.
Agamben, Giorgio. *Infancy and History: The Destruction of Experience*, Trans. Liz Heron. London: Verso, 1993.
Alfandary, Isabelle, and Axel Nesmes, eds. *Modernism and Unreadability*. Montpellier: Presses Universitaires de la Méditerranée, 2011.
Anker, Elizabeth, and Rita Felski, eds. *Critique and Postcritique*. Durham, NC: Duke University Press, 2017.
Athenot, Éric. "Fiat Lutz: Civilising Grammar in *I Looked Alive*." *Cahiers Charles V*, no. 38 (June 2005): 119–35.
Atwood, Margaret. *Moving Targets: Writing with Intent, 1982–2004*. Toronto: House of Anansi Press, 2004.

Barth, John. *The Friday Book: Essays and Other Non-Fiction*. Baltimore, MD: Johns Hopkins University Press, 1997.
Barthes, Roland. *Writing Degree Zero*. Trans. Annette Lavers and Colin Smith. New York: Hill and Wang, 1981.
———. *The Pleasure of the Text*. Trans. Richard Miller. New York: Hill and Wang, 1975.
———. *S/Z*. Trans. Richard Miller. Oxford: Blackwell, 2002.
Battesti, Anne. "Mort ou vif? Hantises de Gary Lutz." *Tropismes*, no. 14 (2007): 159–77.
Benjamin, Walter. *The Arcades Project*, Trans. Howard Eiland, Kevin McLaughlin. Cambridge, MA: Belknap Press of Harvard University Press, 1999.
Birkerts, Sven. *The Gutenberg Elegies: The Fate of Reading in an Electronic Age*. New York: Faber and Faber, 1994/2006.
Blanchot, Maurice. *The Writing of the Disaster*. Trans. Ann Smock. Lincoln: University of Nebraska Press, 1995.
Bogost, Ian. *Alien Phenomenology, or What It's Like to Be a Thing*. Minneapolis: University of Minnesota Press, 2012.
Bon, François. *Après le livre*. Paris: Seuil, 2011.
Bush, Vannevar. "As We May Think," *Atlantic* (July 1945).
Cassin, Barbara, ed. *Dictionary of Untranslatables: A Philosophical Lexicon*. Translation edited by Emily Apter, Jacques Lezra, Michael Wood. Princeton, NJ: Princeton University Press, 2014.
Cohen, Joshua. "How So Very Dear." *London Review of Books* 34, no. 12 (June 21, 2012).
Coover, Robert. "The End of Books." *New York Times Book Review* (June 21, 1992).
Crawford, Ashley. *Religious Imaging in Millennialist America: Dark Gnosis*. London: Palgrave Macmillan, 2018.
DeLanda, Manuel, and Graham Harman. *The Rise of Realism*. Cambridge: Polity Press, 2017.
Deleuze, Gilles, and Félix Guattari. *A Thousand Plateaus: Capitalism and Schizophrenia*. Trans. Brian Massumi. Minneapolis: University of Minnesota Press, 2005.
Deleuze, Gilles. *Francis Bacon: The Logic of Sensation*. Trans. Daniel W. Smith. London: Continuum, 2003.
Derrida, Jacques. *Dissemination*. Trans. Barbara Johnson. London: Athlone Press, 1981.
Didi-Huberman, Georges. *Ce que nous voyons, ce qui nous regarde*. Paris: Minuit, 1992.
Di Leo, Jeffrey R., and Warren Motte, eds. *Experimental Literature: A Collection of Statements*. Aurora, IL: JEF Books, 2018.
Evenson, Brian. "Rewiring the Culture." *Postmodern Culture* 6, no. 2 (January 1996).
Fœssel, Michaël. *Après la fin du monde: Critique de la raison apocalyptique*. Paris: Seuil, 2012.
Friedman, Zack. "Trouble at the Language Lab." *New Inquiry* (March 8, 2012).
Galloway, Alexander. *Protocol: How Control Exists After Decentralization*. Cambridge, MA: MIT Press, 2004.
———. *The Interface Effect*. Cambridge: Polity Press, 2012.
Garcia, Tristan. *Form and Object: A Treatise on Things*. Trans. Mark Allan Ohm and Jon Cogburn. Edinburgh: Edinburgh University Press, 2014.
Gass, William. *On Being Blue: A Philosophical Inquiry*. Boston: Nonpareil Books, 2007.
———. *Fiction and the Figures of Life: Essays*. Boston: Nonpareil Books, 2000.

Goldsmith, Kenneth. *Uncreative Writing: Managing Language in the Digital Age.* New York: Columbia University Press, 2011.
Harman, Graham. *Object-Oriented Ontology: A New Theory of Everything.* London: Pelican Books, 2017.
———. *Speculative Realism: An Introduction.* Medford, MA: Polity Press, 2018.
———. *Tool-Being: Heidegger and the Metaphysics of Objects.* Chicago: Open Court, 2002.
———. *Towards Speculative Realism: Essays and Lectures.* Winchester: Zer0 Books, 2010.
———. "The Well-Wrought Broken Hammer: Object-Oriented Literary Criticism." *New Literary History,* Vol. 43 no. 2 (Spring 2012): 183–203.
———. *Weird Realism: Lovecraft and Philosophy.* Winchester: Zer0 Books, 2012.
Hayles, Katherine. "Intermediation: the Pursuit of a Vision." *New Literary History* 38 (2007): 99–125.
———. *Writing Machines.* Cambridge, MA: MIT Press, 2002.
Jackson, Shelley. "Stitch Bitch: The Patchwork Girl."
James, William. *Pragmatism and Other Writings.* New York: Penguin Books, 2000.
Jameson, Fredric. *Postmodernism: Or, The Cultural Logic of Late Capitalism.* Durham, NC: Duke University Press, 1991.
Kaminsky, Inbar. "Epidemic Judaism: Plagues and Their Evocation in Philip Roth's *Nemesis* and Ben Marcus's *The Flame Alphabet.*" *Philip Roth Studies* 10, no. 1 (Spring 2014): 109–24.
Kermode, Frank. *The Sense of an Ending: Studies in the Theory of Fiction.* Oxford: Oxford University Press, 2000.
Kornbluh, Anna. *The Order of Forms: Realism, Formalism, and Social Space.* Chicago: University of Chicago Press, 2019.
Levine, Stacy. "An Inter(e)view with Ben Marcus." *Electronic Book Review* (December 15, 1998).
Lyotard, Jean-François. *The Differend: Phrases in Dispute.* Trans. Georges Van Den Abbeele. Manchester: Manchester University Press, 1988.
Manovich, Lev. *The Language of New Media.* Cambridge, MA: MIT Press, 2001.
Massumi, Brian. *Parables for the Virtual: Movement, Affect, Sensation.* Durham, NC: Duke University Press, 2002.
Meillassoux, Quentin. *After Finitude: An Essay on the Necessity of Contingency.* Trans. Ray Brassier. New York: Bloomsbury, 2008.
———. *Science Fiction and Extro-Science Fiction.* Trans. Alyosha Edlebi. Minneapolis: Univocal Publishing, 2015.
———. *The Number and the Siren: A Decipherment of Mallarmé's* Coup de dés. Trans. Robin Mackay. New York: Sequence Press, 2012.
Mellick, Carlton, III, et al. *The Bizarro Starter Kit.* Portland, OR: Bizarro Books, 2006.
Miéville, China. "M. R. James and the Quantum Vampire." *Collapse IV,* edited by Robin Mackay. May 2008.
Morton, Timothy. *Realist Magic: Objects, Ontology, Causality.* Ann Arbor, MI: Open Humanities Press, 2013.
———. *Hyperobjects: Philosophy and Ecology After the End of the World.* Minneapolis: University of Minnesota Press, 2013.

Moulthrop, Stuart. "Lift This End: Electronic Literature in a Blue Light." *Electronic Book Review* (April 2, 2013).
Moulthrop, Stuart, and Dene Grigar. *Traversals: The Use of Preservation for Early Electronic Writing*. Cambridge, MA: MIT Press, 2017.
Nancy, Jean-Luc. *After Fukushima: The Equivalence of Catastrophes*. Trans. Charlotte Mandell. New York: Fordham University Press, 2015.
Nancy, Jean-Luc, and Aurélien Barrau. *What's These Worlds Coming To?* Trans. Travis Holloway and Flor Méchain. New York: Fordham University Press, 2015.
Nelson, Ted. *Literary Machines* 87, no. 1 (1987).
O'Malley, JP. "Author Ben Marcus and the Subversion of Jewish Mysticism." *Times of Israel*, May 11, 2014.
Palleau-Papin, Françoise. *This Is Not a Tragedy: The Works of David Markson*. Champaign, IL: Dalkey Archive Press, 2010.
Pelton, Ted. "Notable American Prose." *Electronic Book Review* (September 1, 2002).
Poynor, Rick. "*The Age of Wire and String* Rebooted," *Design Observer* (May 9, 2013).
Regnauld, Arnaud. "L'apocalypse, le chiffre et la prothèse: *The Flame Alphabet* de Ben Marcus." In *Otrante: Mutations 1; Corps posthumains*, 157–68. Edited by Jean-François Chassay and Hélène Machinal. Paris: Kimé, 2015.
Robbe-Grillet, Alain. *For a New Novel: Essays on Fiction*. Trans. Richard Howard. New York: Grove Press, 1965.
Robson, Leo. "Renata Adler, Ben Marcus and David Shields: Pushing the Limits of the American Novel." *NewStatesman* (August 22, 2013).
Rosset, Clément. *Le Réel: Traité de l'idiotie*. Paris: Minuit, 2004.
Shaviro, Steven. *The Universe of Things: On Speculative Realism*. Minneapolis: University of Minnesota Press, 2014.
Silliman, Ron. "The New Sentence." In *The New Sentence*, 63–93. New York: Roof Books, 1987.
Szendy, Peter. *L'apocalypse-cinéma: 2012 et autres fins du monde*. Nantes: Capricci, 2012.
Tabbi, Joseph. *Postmodern Sublime: Technology and American Writing from Mailer to Cyberpunk*. Ithaca: Cornell University Press, 1995.
Thacker, Eugene. *In the Dust of This Planet: Horror of Philosophy Vol. 1*. Winchester, UK: Zer0 Books, 2011.
———. *Starry Speculative Corpse: Horror of Philosophy Vol. 2*. Winchester, UK: Zer0 Books, 2015.
———. *Tentacles Longer than Night: Horror of Philosophy Vol. 3*. Winchester, UK: Zer0 Books, 2015.
Thomas, P. L., ed. *Science Fiction and Speculative Fiction: Challenging Genres*. Rotterdam, the Netherlands: Sense Publishers, 2013.
Tissut, Anne-Laure. "Gary Lutz: L'esthétique du disparaître, ou le génie des lieux." *Cahiers Charles V*, no. 38 (June 2005): 137–62.
———. "Corps rêvés dans *Scorch Atlas*, de Blake Butler." *Revue Française d'Études Américaines*, no. 132 (2012): 48–62.
Vanderhaeghe, Stéphane. "Ben Marcus & the Question of Language (Some Notes & a Parenthesis)." *Revue Française d'Études Américaines*, no. 135 (2013): 66–79.
———. "'In the end of commentary'—*300,000,000* de Blake Butler, ou la fiction absolue."

Revue Française d'Études Américaines, no. 159, *Mutations de la métafiction*, edited by Yannicke Chupin (2019): 38–49.

Wallace, David Foster. "The Empty Plenum: David Markson's *Wittgenstein's Mistress*." *Review of Contemporary Fiction* 10, no. 2 (1990): 217–39.

White, Duncan. "'The American Areas': Place, Language and the Construction of Everyday Life in the Novels of Ben Marcus," *Jacket Magazine* 37 (2009).

Winters, David. *Infinite Fictions: Essays on Literature and Theory*. Winchester, UK: Zer0 Books, 2015.

———. "Patterns of Anticipation." *Brooklyn Rail* (March 2015).

———. "Word Flu: Ben Marcus' *The Flame Alphabet*." *Millions* (January 17, 2012).

Wittgenstein, Ludwig. *Tractatus Logico-Philosophicus*. Trans: D. F. Pears and B. F. McGuinness. London: Routledge Classics, 2001.

Wolf-Meyer, Matthew J. *Theory for the World to Come: Speculative Fiction and Apocalyptic Anthropology*. Minneapolis: University of Minnesota Press, 2019.

INDEX

Page numbers in italics refer to illustrations.

Aarseth, Aspen, 90

Agamben, Giorgio, *Infancy and History*, 6–7, 95

aggregate space, 26, 65, 76, 77, 80–81, 85–86, 91, 92, 112–13

alien: body as, 126–29; elements of texts, 16, 116–17, 142, 151, 197, 217n4

"ancestrality" thesis, 25

anti-mimeticism, radical, 153–54

apocalypse, biblical understanding, 57, 214n6

apocalyptic fiction: always a failure, 35–36; as anti-speculative, 35; cathartic or tragic, 56; and speculative fiction, 19, 212n12

Atwood, Margaret, and speculative fiction, 211n5

Bacon, Francis, 86; Figures in paintings, 86, 119, 124, 126, 217n12; "images" in painting, 96

Barjavel, René, *Ravage*, 15

Barth, John, 217n12

Barthes, Roland: hermeneutic code, 28, 102; on historical names and figures, 137; "ideal absence of style," 131; opposition between "readerly" and "writerly" texts, 224n15; *The Pleasure of the Text*, 91; *S/Z*, 88, 224n15

Beckett, Samuel, 217n12, 220n4

Birkerts, Sven, *The Gutenberg Elegies*, 192

bizarro genre, 212n16

Bizarro Starter Kit, The, 212n16

Blanchot, Maurice, *The Writing of the Disaster*, 67

blanks or BLINKs, 82–83, 91, *94*, 108, 132, 179, *180*, 219n24

body: as alien, 126–29; monstrous, 118–19, 218n16; semiotized, 121–23, *122*, 217n10

Bogost, Ian, *Alien Phenomenology*: "alien" nature of texts, 16, 116–17, 142, 151, 197, 217n4; and lists, 24, 142; metaphorism, 116; object-oriented ontology, 179

Bush, Vannevar, "As We May Think," 194, 224n23

Butler, Blake, fiction: abstract and/or performative assemblages, 75–76, 91; "aggregate" space, 86, 91; anti-realism, 125, 215n8; connection with philosophy of Deleuze, 131–32, 219n22; emotional impact or investment, lack of, 112, 113; flatness of depicted worlds and narrative voices, 113, 126; haptic effects, 123;

inexplicable elements or "weirdness," 141; isolation and passivity of characters, 85–86, 91, 112, 217n2; iterations, lists, and narrative discontinuity, 77, 85, 91, 142; logic of sensation rather than sense, 123–24; materiality, and speculative sublimity, 126; mirrors, prevalence, 83–84; names of characters, 125; narrative traces, possible, 124; "navigable space," 76–77; radical dissociation of "world" and "sense," 52–53; reference and representation, 53, 83–84, 110, 111–12, 118–19, 126, 132–33, 176; speculative interface, 86–88, 196; speculative language, 142–45. *See also specific works*

Butler, Blake, *Aanex*, 220n1

Butler, Blake, *Alice Knott* (AK): abstract and/or performative assemblages, 75, 91; Alice as both actor and spectator, 105; body as alien, 126; flatness of depicted world, 113, 211n2; isolation of characters, and aggregate space, 77, 85–86, 91, 112–13; names, 125; passive acceptance and resignation, 217n2; radical dissociations, 53

Butler, Blake, *Ever*, 7, 9; iterations and rehashings, 24; narrative disruptions, 176–77; space and time, 76; visual layout of text interspersed with computer-generated or -altered images, 6, 175–76, 177, 197–98

Butler, Blake, *Scorch Atlas* (SA): absence of rational explanation or causes, 62–633; aesthetics of horror, 112; apocalyptic imagery, 47; assonances and paronomasia, 57, 58; "Bath or Mud or Reclamation or Way In/Way Out," 55, 57, 63, 64; blank space, and eradication of meaning, 57; "Bloom Atlas," 62; bodies defying conventional norms, 118–19; "Caterpillar," 65, 66; "Damage Claim Questionnaire," 62; "The Disappeared," 109–10, 119–20; disintegration of meaning, 57, 119; double-page spread from, 36, 37; "Dust," 142; equivalence and repetition, 55, 57, 64, 65; "Exponential," 142; failure to conclude, 64, 66–67; "The Gown from Mother's Stomach," 64, 66; intercalary pieces, 55, 58, 64, 65, 214n10; iterations of motifs, 57, 63, 65; juxtaposition and non sequitur, 63; multiple genres, 61; order and organizing, resistance against, 73; performative text, 58–59; postapocalyptic settings, 24, 26, 36, 47–48, 53, 86, 118, 141; refraction, 61, 67; "Seabed," 57, 64, 65, 68–70, 214n12; speculative sublime aesthetic, 111, 113; "structional" quality, 65–66; style and content, collapsing of, 59; subtitles and alternate titles, 53, 55, 57, 214n7; table of contents ("A Belated Primer"), 55, 56; "Television Milk," 64, 65; "Tour of the Drowned Neighborhood," 62, 118; visual layout of text, 36–37, 48, 57–58, 77, 123, 145, 177; "Want for Wish for Nowhere," 65–66; "Water Damaged Photos of Our Home Before I Left It," 62, 64, 214n9

Butler, Blake, *Sky Saw* (SS), 89; abstract and/or performative assemblages, 75, 177; aesthetics of horror, 112; back cover, 124, 141; "BLINK," 132, 219n24; bodies as alien, 126; characteristics of Bacon's Figures, 131–32; dystopian setting, 124, 141; isolation of characters, and aggregate space, 85–86; iterations and rehashings, 24; radical dissociation, 53, 133; time compression, 76

Butler, Blake, *There Is No Year* (TINY): abstract and/or performative assemblages, 75, 91; abstraction, 217n6; aesthetics of horror, 112; back cover, 124; bodies as alien, 126; deregulation of language, 143–44, 220n3; disjunctive nature of text, 142–44; as a game, 86–88, 90; isolation of characters, and aggregate space, 85–86, 112; iterations and rehashings, 24; lack of emotional impact or investment, 113–15; and "navigable space,"

77; photographs, 217n1; radical dissociation, 53; speculative sublime aesthetic, 111–12, 114–15; typography, 215n3, 216n9; visual layout of text, 77, 111, 123, 145, 177, 215n3; "weirdness," 141
Butler, Blake, *300,000,000*: abstract and/or performative assemblages, 75, 177, 180; attendant voices, 125; "insoluble" mystery, 29, 112, 124, 223n3; isolation of characters, 85; iterations and lists, 24, 142, 220n2; lack of continuity, 77; mirrors, and refusal of representation, 84; names of characters, 125; and "navigable space," 76; radical dissociation, 53, 128

Cassin, Barbara, *Dictionary of Untranslatables*, 187, 188–89
Cohen, Joshua: review of Marcus's *The Flame Alphabet*, 135, 137, 153, 167, 221n11; technotexts, 23; *Witz*, 26. *See also* Cohen, Joshua, *Book of Numbers* (BN)
Cohen, Joshua, *Book of Numbers* (BN): editing of text, 193, 196; hybrid space of obstruction and resistance, 196; insertion of text and images from alien modalities, 193; interface with other media, 193, 197; pagination referring to screen, 193
contingency: and the apocalypse, 35, 41; contiguity and, 63, 217n12; and "extro-science fiction," 15; Harman and, 20; and *The Infernal*, 200, 203, 224n21; Meillassoux and, 19, 200, 219n25; and speculative fiction, 8, 10
Coover, Robert: "The End of Books," 215n6; on Joyce and hyperfiction, 223n2; "Milford Junction, 1939," *A Night at the Movies*, 195–96; "The Marker," *Pricksongs & Descants*, 116–17
Corin, Lucy, *One Hundred Apocalypses and Other Apocalypses* (OHA), 23; "Baby Alive (2012) 109 minutes," 40; challenge to both the concept of apocalypse and genre of (post) apocalyptic fiction, 39–40; "Eyes of Dogs," 46–47, 48; "Godzilla versus the Smog Monster," 39, 53–55; "A Hundred Apocalypses," 40, 59–61; "Madmen," 48–50, 55
"correlationist circle," 17, 18, 25
crisis, 48, 214n4
critical discourse, 11, 211n6; and surface versus deep readings, 216n12

Danielewski, Mark Z., *House of Leaves* (HOL): dedication, "This is not for you," 71, 90; dislocation of text, 88–89, 180, 215n3, 223n4; hermeneutic code, 89; hybridity, 193; insoluble mystery, 29, 223n3; maximalist strategy, 25; novel in performance, 88, 91; simulation, 88; and video game aesthetics, 89; whiteness on page, 180–81
DeLanda, Manuel, 214n3
Deleuze, Gilles: attendants, 125; on Figures in painting of Francis Bacon, 86, 119, 124, 126, 217n12; *Logic of Sensation*, 73, 119, 120, 124, 217n12; "Outwork," 100; *A Thousand Plateaus* (with Guattari), 66, 130
"dia-chronicity," 27, 28, 35, 36, 37, 38
Didi-Huberman, Georges: "the ineluctable modality of the visible," 73, 99, 100–101, 215n1, 216n19; "work of loss," 75
differential writing, 82, 93, 179
discontinuity: and "haptic reading," 123; lists and iterations, 76–77; and texture of text, 91, 104; and topology, 83
Doten, Mark, *The Infernal* (I), 23, 25, 180; alien lines of code in text, 196–97; contingency, 200, 203, 224n21; Dantesque intertext, 202, 225n24; double-page spread from, *201*; "Dramatis Personæ, 224n23; as extro-science fiction, 24, 203; insoluble mystery, 223n3; page/screen interface, 194, 197, 199–204, *204*; as political novel, 224n22; speculative ontology, 224n21; stylized, technological text, 25; as technotext, 203; two

pages from, 194, *195*; uchronic scenario, 91, 203; unworkability, 203. *See also* Doten, Mark, *Trump Sky Alpha* (TSA)

Doten, Mark, *Trump Sky Alpha* (TSA), 52; empty, provisional language, 67–68; flat ontology, 42, 67; postapocalyptic, 41, 194

écriture blanche, or *blank* writing, 131
ekphrasis, 27, 62, 117, 187
Eskelinen, Markku, 90
Etter, Sarah Rose, *The Book of X* (BX), 134; alien, sublime nature of body, 126–29, 219n18; ambiguity of ending, 128–29, 217n8, 219n19; physical condition mirrored in landscape, 127; and surrealism, 22, 28; violent imagery, 128
experimental fiction, 10–13, 16, 19, 20, 28, 33, 90
experimentum linguae, 6–7
extro-science fiction, 15–16, 19, 24, 26, 92, 109, 145, 203, 219n25

flat ontology, 42, 67, 71–72, 113, 126, 130–31, 214n3
Franzen, Jonathan, 215n8, 221n7

Galloway, Alexander: and interface effects, 34, 198–99, 203; and "protocol," 41–42
Gass, William: *On Being Blue*, 155–56; *Fiction and the Figures of Life*, 155
Gladman, Renee, Ravicka series, 23, 25, 28, 213n19
Guattari, Félix, *A Thousand Plateaus* (with Deleuze), 66, 130

haptic reading, 9–10, 73, 76, 91, 123
haptic vision: and "close" reading, 73; opposition to optic perception, 120–21
Harman, Graham: and aesthetics, 19, 216n14; and Heidegger's theory of equipment, 189–90, 200; object-oriented ontology, 14, 63, 110, 179, 212n13; opposition to Žižek in *Tool-Being*, 223n12; on the real, 170; *Speculative Realism*, 20, 212n9; "tool-being," 13, 17, 160–62, 169, 190, 203, 216n20; "The Well-Wrought Broken Hammer," 18, 212n11

Hayles, Katherine: and age of "intermediation," 193; on hybrid works, 193; on new media, 82; technotexts, 23, 34, 77, 202
Heidegger, Martin, *Vorhandenheit* and *Zuhandenheit*, 13, 14, 189–90, 203, 208
hermeneutic code/approach, 28, 29, 89, 102–4, 137
hermeneutics of suspicion, 221n8
Hume, David, problem of laws of nature, 15, 199–200
hypertexts/hypertextuality, 8–9, 23, 79–80, 121, 175, 199, 215nn5–6, 222n1, 223n2

Jackson, Shelley, fiction: hypertextuality, 121; logic of sensation rather than sense, 124; and materiality, 23; *Patchwork Girl*, 23, 121, 217n9; return to print, 215n6; "Skin" project, 23, 121; "Snow" project, 23, 121; speculative sublimity, 121–23; "Stitch Bitch" manifesto, 129, 217n9, 219n17. *See also additional works*
Jackson, Shelley, *Half Life* (HL), 26, 91–95, 99; blanks in text, 82–83, 93, *94*, 216n12; body as alien, 126–27; discontinuity, 92–93; focus on materiality, 23, 93; intertexuality, 93; names of characters, 125; as science-fictional text, 91–92
Jackson, Shelley, *The Melancholy of Anatomy* (MA), 23, 121; "Cancer," 39, 48; "Dildo," 181, 223n5; dystopianism, 28; "Heart," 29
Jackson, Shelley, *my body—a Wunderkammer*: body, monstrous, 218n16; body, semiotized, 121–23, *122*, 217n10
Jackson, Shelley, *Riddance* (R), 23, 121; hypertextuality, 175; insoluble mystery, 223n3; materiality of language, 173–75, *174*, 221n14; negativity pointing to "truth," 170–71; performative language,

163–64; as reader unfriendly, 174–75, 180
Jameson, Fredric, 167, 178
Joyce, James, 73, 217n12
Joyce, Michael, fiction: *afternoon, a story*, 215nn5–6, 223n2; digital narrative, 176; *Disappearance*, 89, 90; hybridity, 193; hypertext fictions, 215nn5–6, 223n2; technotext, 23. *See also* Joyce, Michael, *Was: Annales nomadique*
Joyce, Michael, *Was: Annales nomadique*, 90, 92; lack of cohesive center, 78, 80; lists, 178; negativity pointing to "truth," 170; "novel of internet," 79–80, 86, 215n4, 215n7, 216n10; and violence, 79, 215n5; visible discreteness of text, 77–78, 79, 178, 211n3; as "work of loss," 78

Kant, Immanuel: idealism, 17; and laws of nature, 219n25; and the sublime, 120–21
Kermode, Frank, *The Sense of an Ending*, 46
Kittler, Friedrich, *Discourse Networks 1800/1900*, 42
Kleeman, Alexandra, *Something New Under the Sun*, 214n2. *See also* Kleeman, Alexandra, *You Too Can Have a Body Like Mine* (YTCH)
Kleeman, Alexandra, *You Too Can Have a Body Like Mine* (YTCH): body as alien, 126; dystopian vein, 28; *écriture blanche*, or *blank* writing, 131; fictional religion, 134, 135; flatness, 131; names, 125–26; radical discrepancy between person and the body, 129–30; surrealism, 22–23; and vicious circle in time, 219n21
Kornbluh, Anna, *The Order of Forms*, 14, 167–68, 222n23

Lacan, Jacques, 222n24
language: as referential and transitive, 217n12; self-effacing, and mimeticism, 154. *See also* speculative language
Longinian sublime, 110, 112

Lovecraft, H. P., 20, 212n14
Lutz, Gary (Garielle Lutz), 22; "The Boy," 144; "Femme," 219n20; *I Looked Alive*, 128; index pointing to nothing, 181–82; interchangeability of characters, 125; "Not the Hand But Where the Hand Has Been," 181–82, 223nn6–7; "The Summer I Could Walk Again," 144
Lyotard, Jean-François, *The Differend*, 7

Manovich, Lev, *The Language of New Media*, 9–10, 77, 80, 86, 175, 176
Marcus, Ben, fiction: dystopianism, 22; focus on language, 145–46; on Jason Schwartz's work, 22; and Jonathan Franzen, 221n7; and language and reality, 154, 221n13; material and technological turn, 170; mimetic shell and contested referentiality, 84, 125, 153–57; motifs of failure, inadequacy, and incompetence, 158–60; negativity pointing to "truth," 170; "objective witness," 7; reference and representation, 164, 167; "unreads itself," 102. *See also specific works*
Marcus, Ben, *The Age of Wire and String* (AWS), 7, 8, 21, 27; antagonistic vocabulary, 157; "Argument," 101, 117, 136, 157; encyclopedic stylistics, 117; epigraph, 217n5; "First Love," 155; "Intercourse with Resuscitated Wife," 115–17; mimetic forms of language lacking referents, 156–57; names, referential instability, 125, 145, 152; parodic dimension, 136–37; radical anti-mimeticism, 153–54; and "radical translation," 116; redefinition of words, 145; reinvention of language, 155; resistance to meaning, 101, 102, 128, 134, 136; and speculative sublime, 115–17, 169
Marcus, Ben, *The Flame Alphabet* (FA), 44, 200; deceptive narrative discourse, 158, 169; diachronicity, 37–38; doubles and metamorphoses, 165–67; dystopian elements, 22; fictional reworking of Jewish

Reconstructionism, 74, 75, 134–36, 137, 153, 167, 215n2; historical names and references suggesting crisis in authority, 125, 145–46, 220nn5–6; language dissociated from referential dimension, 167–69, 222n22; language incomprehensibility, 162–63, 221n17; language toxicity, 147–48, 152, 159–60; and metaphysical questions related to the sublime, 220n27; narrative disruptions, 97–99; as nonbook, 138; and notions of meaning and understanding, 74–75; performative language, 163, 164–65; "pharmacological" readings, 216n18; postapocalytic framework, 26, 36, 92, 97; simulation, 157, 163, 164, 169–70, 222n23; and sublimity, 136; unproductivity of reading, 101; as "work of loss," 73–74, 99, 100–101, 216n15

Marcus, Ben, *Leaving the Sea* (LS): deregulation of language, 169; "The Father Costume," 27, 98, 150, 157, 216n13, 216nn16–17, 221n16; "I Can Say Many Nice Things," 149–50, 157; "The Loyalty Protocol," 158; "The Moors," 158; "My Views on the Darkness," 150; "On Not Growing Up," 150; radical strangeness, 22; "What Have You Done," 158, 160–61

Marcus, Ben, *Notable American Women* (NAW), 21–22, 138, 221n12; "Blueprint" section, 102; "Bury Your Head" section, 146–47, 150, 221n8; dystopian elements, 27–28; failure motif, 158; language turning back on itself, 146–49, 150–51, 169, 222n21; names, historical, 125, 146; names, referential instability, 145, 152; names as constitutive of person, 154–55; parodic dimension, 136–37; performative language, 145; radical anti-mimeticism, 153–54; resistance to meaning, 101–2, 134, 136; "System Requirements," 161; unrealistic references to religious faith, 151–53, 221n9

Marcus, Ben, *Notes from the Fog*, 125, 157; "Cold Little Bird," 158–59; deregulation of language, 169; failure motif, 158; radical strangeness, 22

Markson, David, fiction: fragmentary technique, 25, 43; *Reader's Block*, 176; *This Is Not a Novel*, 5, 43; *Vanishing Point*, 43, 176. See also Markson, David, *Wittgenstein's Mistress* (WM)

Markson, David, *Wittgenstein's Mistress* (WM), 78, 169; and correlationism, 50–52; negativity pointing to "truth," 170; and opposition between realism and idealism, 43–46; overtly speculative, 25; postapocalyptic fiction, 43–46; refusal to reveal nature of catastrophe, 67, 68; visual page layout, 176

Massumi, Brian, *Parables for the Virtual*: and "quotient of openness," 8–9; "stills," 83, 85; on "the virtual," 218n15, 219n24; on topology, 83

McCarthy, Cormac, *The Road*, 213n20

media-specific analysis, 23

Meillassoux, Quentin: *After Finitude*, 20, 25, 28; "ancestrality" thesis, 25; and contingency, 200, 219n25; "correlationist circle," 17, 18, 25; "dia-chronicity," 27, 35; and extro-science fiction, 15–16, 19, 24, 26, 92, 109, 145, 219n25; and Hume's problem, 199–200, 213n21; *The Number and the Siren*, 20, 21

Memex, 194, 200, 202

mimeticism, technique of, without referents, 154, 156–57

Morton, Timothy: and aesthetics, 19, 212n13, 216n14; on ekphrasis, 62; on horror, 112; *Hyperobjects* (HO), 18, 20–21, 33, 211n4; on Kantian aesthetic dimension, 120, 123; and object-oriented ontology, 26, 63, 179; and "1+*n*" other entities, 112, 116, 217n3; and "radical translation," 114, 217n3; *Realist Magic* (RM), 21, 29, 40, 62, 63, 110, 112; "rift," 40; and the speculative sublime, 110–12, 113, 115, 116, 117

Moulthrop, Stuart: and "age of hybridity," 193; and electronic literature, 193; on Joyce's *Disappearance*, 89–90; "Lift this End," 215n4, 216n10; *Was* as "novel of internet," 79, 80

Nancy, Jean-Luc: *After Fukushima*, 55–56; contemporary "equivalence of catastrophes," 55, 56–57; and " 'struction," 63, 65, 67, 76, 217n12; *What's These Worlds Coming To?* (with Barrau), 52, 63, 65, 67, 76
Nelson, Ted, 222n1
new media, 76, 82, 88
new sentence, 177–79

object-oriented ontology (ooo): Bogost and, 179; and ekphrasis, 62; and "flat ontology," 214n3; Harman and, 14, 63, 110, 179, 212n13; and language as object, 90, 161; Morton and, 26, 63, 179; and speculative fiction, 207, 224n14
Ohle, David, 217n7; *In the Age of Sinatra*, 25; dystopian science fiction, 26; *Motorman*, 25, 213n20; *The Old Reactor*, 25–26; *The Pisstown Chaos*, 25; post-catastrophic world, 92
"1+*n*", 112, 113, 114–15, 116, 217n3
Orah Mark, Sabrina, *Wild Milk*, 22, 220n4

performative language, 58–59, 119–20, 142–46, 148, 163, 164–65, 185
performative textual layout, 197–98, 215n3
"pharmacological" readings, 216n18
Plato, and poets, 221n15
Popper, Karl, 200, 213n21
postapocalyptic fiction: always a failure, 36; Butler and, 24, 26, 36, 47–48, 53, 86, 118, 141; Corin and, 39–40; and diachronicity, 36; Doten and, 41, 194; Markson and, 43–46; radicalized, 25–27; and speculative fiction, 212n12
postmodernist fiction, 12
postmodern self-referentiality, 84, 217n12

reading: correlation with narrative, 186–87; as a game, 90; haptic, 9–10, 73, 76, 91, 123; "pharmacological," 216n18; surface versus deep, 216n12
realism: in formalist terms, 167–68; versus idealism, 43–46; and speculative fiction, 14, 134, 135–36, 140, 219n25
Riegl, Aloïs, opposition between optic and haptic perception, 120–21
Robbe-Grillet, Alain, *For a New Novel*, 14, 187–88, 189
Rosset, Clément, "density of the real," 166–67, 222n19

Schwartz, Jason, fiction: absences, 182–83; ekphrastic quality, 183, 184–88, 192; hybridity, 184; minimalist fiction, 25; reader as accessory to text, 185–86; shifts in time and space, 183, 192. See also specific works
Schwartz, Jason, *A German Picturesque* (GP): absences, 182; "Blindstitch," 187, 223n11; correlation between narrative and reading act, 186–87; ekphrastic quality, 183, 186–87, 188; Marcus on, 22; paradoxically descriptive and ambivalent, 27, 128; as short stories, 224n16; visual dynamic of representation, 223n8
Schwartz, Jason, *John the Posthumous* (JP): absences, 182–83; "Adulterium," 184, 185; failure of text to operate, 191–92; "Hornbook," 182, 184; "Housepost, Male Figure," 182–83, 184, 223n9; paradoxically descriptive and ambivalent, 27; performative language, 185; as short stories, 224n16; title reference, 223n8
science fiction, and extro-science fiction, 26
self-reflexive works, 12, 102
Shaviro, Steven: and aesthetics, 19; "self-enjoyment," 12
Silliman, Ron: "new sentence," 177–79, 192; "syllogistic leap," 177
speculation: defined, 2, 11; meeting of philosophy and fiction, 20

speculative fiction: and absence of correlate, 14; absoluteness, 11–12; blanks or BLINKs, 82–83, 91, 94, 108, 132, 179, 180, 219n24; borderline construct, 28; challenge to reader expectations, 10–11, 13–14; coherence, lacking, 179–81; and comprehension and understanding, 13, 15, 16, 82; and critical discourse, 8–11, 30; differential writing, 179; disruptive to narrativity and readability, 20, 196, 212n16; engagement with, 12; as experimental fiction, 10, 12, 13–14; failure to operate, 190–91; and "feeling" the real, 170–71; flatness, 71–72, 113, 126; and haptic reading, 91; languageness, 5–7, 8; and logic of sensation, 124, 217n11; and negative mode, 170, 172, 189, 196, 217n11; and non-correlationism, 18, 19, 212n10; as object, 203, 208; and the reader, 7, 9, 14, 16, 18; and realism, 14, 134, 135–36, 140, 219n25; and reality, 20–21, 213n17; and representation, 5, 16; resistance, 13–16; and science fiction, 10; speculating it, 3–4, 7–8; speculative sentence, 9; speculative words, 9; textual layout, 5, 6, 8, 180–81; as theoretical figment, 172; as variant of extro-science fiction, 15–16

speculative fiction, mapping: dystopian texts, 27–28; investigative fiction, 24–25, 28–29; little commonality among texts, 25; postapocalyptic fiction, radicalized, 25–27; surrealist-like works, 22–23; technotexts, 23–24

speculative interface: "a novel of internet," 79–80, 86, 215n4, 215n7, 216n10; page/screen interface, 192–204; surface description referring back to nothing, 182–89

speculative language: deregulated, 143–44, 220n3; language dissociated from referential dimension, 167–69; language incomprehensibility, 162–63; and languageness, 5–6; language toxicity, 147–48, 152, 159–60; language turning back on itself, 146–49, 150–51, 169, 222n21; linguistic disorder and impenetrability, 142–45; Marcus's focus on, 145–46, 159–64, 169–70; materiality of, 173–75, 174, 221n14; as object, 160–62; performative, 58–59, 119–20, 142–43, 145, 146, 148, 163, 164–65, 185

speculative realism: and aesthetics, 19–20; challenge to anthropocentrism, 18–19; divergences in discourse on, 17, 212n9; and "flat ontology," 214n3; and Marcus's *The Flame Alphabet*, 169–70; as method for approaching speculative fiction, 16–21; and speculative fiction, 224n14; as tool, 207, 208; and "weirdness," 212n16

speculative sublime: body, as alien, 126–29; body, semiotized, 121–23, 122, 217n10; Butler and, 111–15; and haptic vision, 120–21; and inability to read and understand, 140; Marcus and, 115–17, 136; Morton on, 110–12, 113, 115, 116, 117; and "1+n" other entities, 112, 113, 114–15, 116, 217n3

speculative topologies: discontinuity, 80–85; discreteness, 85–91; resistance to reading, 91–102; unrelatability, 102–7; "work of loss," 73–76

surrealism, 22–23, 28
Szendy, Peter, 212n12

technotexts, 23–24, 77
Thacker, Eugene, *Horrors of Philosophy* series, 20
trompe l'oeil effects, 23, 36, 100–101, 102, 126, 138, 154, 169, 181, 192

uchronia, 23, 91, 203
Unrue, Jane, *Love Hotel* (LH): insoluble mystery, 24, 29; latent violence, 189; retracings, 81; texual layout, 81–82

VanderMeer, Jeff, Southern Reach Trilogy, 213n21

Van der Vliet Oloomi, Azareen, *Fra Keeler* (FK): insoluble mystery, 24, 29; iterations or duplications, 24, 104; narrative unreliability, 96–97, 103–4; narrator's estrangement, 105–6; negativity pointing to "truth," 170; "senselessness," 29, 95–96 "the virtual," 124, 218n15

Wallace, D. F., essay on *Wittgenstein's Mistress*, 51, 214n5

What's These Worlds Coming To? (Nancy and Barrau), 52, 63, 65, 67, 76
Whitehead, Alfred North, 12
Winters, David: *Infinite Fictions*, 223n10; "Patterns of Anticipation," 82
Wittgenstein, Ludwig: on language, 38; *Tractatus Logico-Philosophicus*, 51

Žižek, Slavoj, 222n24, 223n12